IMAGES of America

GILMER

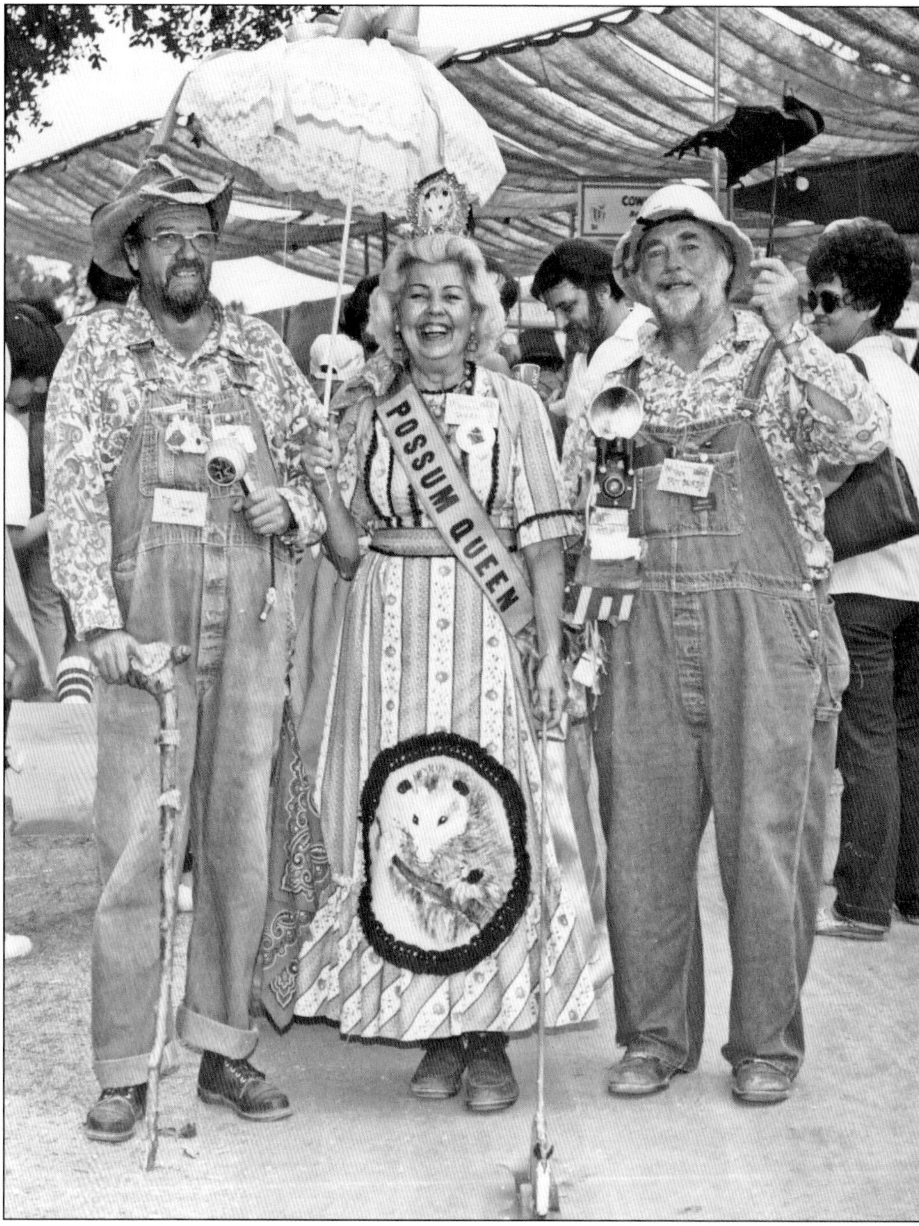

In the 1970s, three Gilmer civic volunteers created new characters after the East Texas Yamboree Association entered the first Texas Folklife Festival in San Antonio. From left to right, Dr. Richard Potter, International Possum Queen Daisy Potter, and Prof. Jack F. "Spot" Baird walk the grounds of the festival, regaling visitors with tales of "possumology" and drumming up business for the people who were serving slices of sweet potato pie. (Institute of Texan Cultures.)

On the Cover: Preparing for the 14th annual celebration of the East Texas Yamboree are these dancers, who would perform during the coronation of Joyce Isbell as Queen Yam XIV by Robert E. Parsons, the president in 1951. Martha King is being chased by Matt "Butch" Davis Jr. In the back row, from left to right, Manion Mathis, unidentified, Bobby Osborne, Cal Bishop, Wayne Arnold, Darrell Nix, Bonnie Williams, and Richard Stolle dance. (*Progressive Farmer.*)

IMAGES
of America

GILMER

Mary Laschinger Kirby

ARCADIA
PUBLISHING

ISBN 978-0-7385-7124-9

Published by Arcadia Publishing
Charleston, South Carolina

Printed in the United States of America

Library of Congress Control Number: 2009923822

For all general information contact Arcadia Publishing at:
Telephone 843-853-2070
Fax 843-853-0044
E-mail sales@arcadiapublishing.com
For customer service and orders:
Toll-Free 1-888-313-2665

Visit us on the Internet at www.arcadiapublishing.com

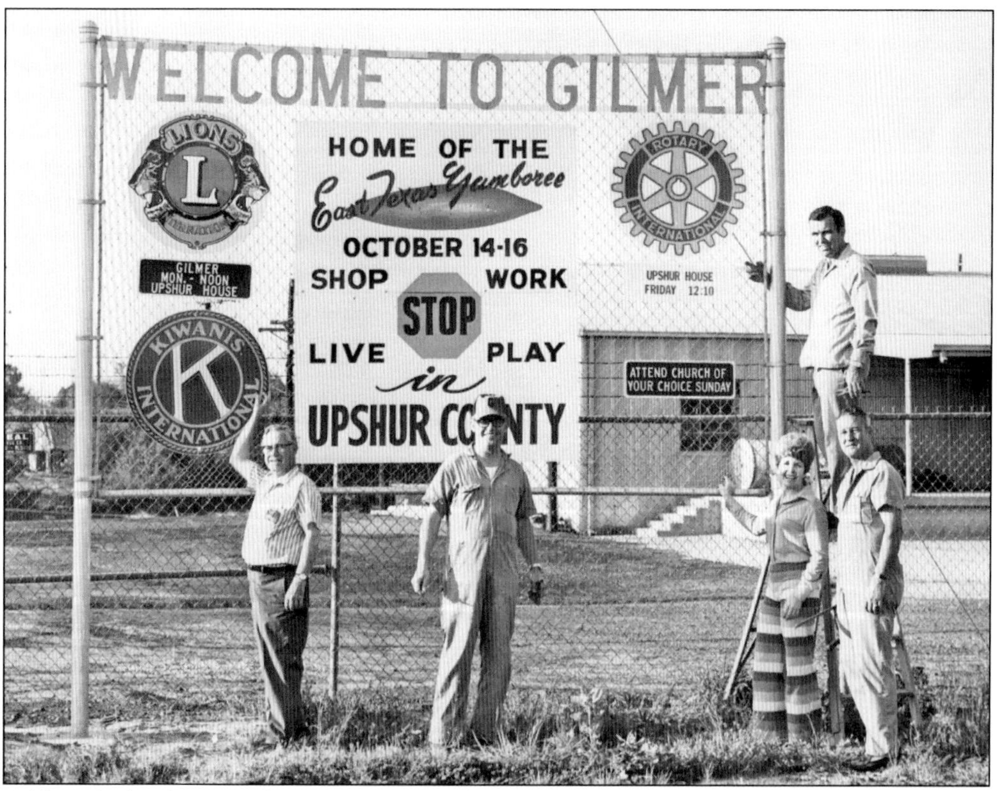

Adding the finishing touches to a new sign informing travelers on U.S. Highway 271 of the service clubs and attractions found in Gilmer in 1971 are, from left to right, John Hill, Tom Davis, Mary Lee Baird, Dee Alexander, and Bill Patterson. (*Gilmer Mirror*/Ray Greene.)

Contents

ACKNOWLEDGMENTS

This pictorial history of Gilmer leans heavily upon the collection of photographs found at the Historic Upshur Museum, especially those found in the J. M. Hays Collection. Most are available as glass negatives with the more recent images on gelatin-acetate negatives; these images give a glimpse into the personal lives and activities of the people of Gilmer, Upshur County, and their neighbors. The years spent by the author cataloging the negatives and the prints at the museum and interviewing relatives and friends about the images discovered laid the groundwork for the original research reflected in these pages.

After 1930, the resources of the *Gilmer Mirror* with its collection of images by Russell H. Laschinger, Ray H. Greene, John Hill, and the author furnished most of the materials contained herein. Personal collections of the publisher emerita, Sarah Laschinger Greene, and the author complemented the collections at the *Mirror*.

The assistance of Upshur Rural Electric Cooperative and RobRoy Industries were invaluable for their most pertinent images.

The board of the Historic Upshur Museum under the leadership of H. M. "Butch" Ragland, and in particular Connie Duke and Joy Valenti, were most helpful in my getting the images from the J. M. Hays Collection in the correct format for this book.

Among the images used in this book, the most common sources will be noted in abbreviated format as follows: the Historic Upshur Museum (HUM), Russell H. Laschinger (RHL), the *Gilmer Mirror* (GM), and the author's personal collection (MLK).

A Brief History of Upshur County by G. H. Baird, *A History of Upshur County, Texas* by D. T. Loyd, *Reflections of Upshur County, Texas* by Sarah Laschinger Greene and the author, and the special edition of the *Gilmer Mirror* published on August 15, 1968, and the author's booklet, *Early Days in Upshur County, 1800–1860*, and various issues of the *Gilmer Mirror* have been the primary sources used.

Finally, the author can never fully express her debt of gratitude to her father for sharing his love of photography and to her sister for the wealth of knowledge she has from her fourscore years of experience spent mostly in Gilmer and Upshur County. Without his training and her support, this work would not be possible.

INTRODUCTION

Gilmer was carved out of a dense virgin forest, which the pioneers saw as being so abundant that it would last forever.

Before the arrival of the Europeans to the area, Native Americans hunted and farmed in these woods. Several sites have been explored and excavated, yielding a fascinating glimpse into the archaic Indian culture as well as the later Caddoan culture.

The archeology done before the construction of Lake Gilmer even included an unexpected burial or two in one of the buildings studied.

It is known that the Caddoes enjoyed clearing an area so the women could plant two types of corn to harvest while the men would occupy themselves hunting and fishing. After the land was worn out, they would abandon their beehive-shaped dwellings and move to another section of forest, where they would start again.

In the autumn, they traveled toward the prairies around modern Sulphur Springs to hunt the buffalo herds, which were migrating south toward San Antonio. After the kill, the meat and the robes would be cured to help with the coming winter cold.

Despite their elaborate rituals and their skill at developing pottery, the Caddoes could not protect themselves from the silent killers that entered these woods with the arrival of Hernando DeSoto, Cabeza de Vaca, and other explorers. By the time the Spanish established missions 80 miles away at Nacogdoches, the population of the native peoples had already been decimated by smallpox, measles, and other European diseases for which the Native Americans had no defense.

After the Republic of Texas was created, the Texans decided that the Native Americans in Texas could not remain. In 1839, under the orders of Mirabeau Lamar, the Militia of the Republic of Texas killed Chief Bowles and drove the Cherokee out of Texas. (The Caddoes had been driven nearer to Dallas County by the arrival of the Cherokee.)

While these events were horrific for the Native Americans, the expulsion of the natives from the areas surrounding Cherokee Trace opened northeast Texas for development from the Red River to Cherokee County. The trace itself served almost like a super highway to draw settlers into the areas flanking the trail.

By 1850, forty percent of the settlers in Upshur County came from the mid-South states of Tennessee, North Carolina, and Arkansas, while another 40 percent came from the Deep South states of Louisiana, Mississippi, and Georgia. Even in the late 20th century, those accents abounded in Gilmer and the surrounding rural communities.

The first pioneers from the United States settled in what they believed to be either Nacogdoches or Harrison County and began to cut down the trees so they, and if they had them, their slaves, could plant a crop of cotton for income, of corn for food (primarily for livestock), and other crops for human consumption. Their hogs, cattle, and chicken roamed freely.

After the creation of Harrison County, the pioneering trail Cherokee Trace served both as a boundary between Harrison and Nacogdoches Counties and as a route to bring new settlers to the productive land.

William Hart and his brother-in-law David Lee came to the county in 1843, developing an east-west route into the area as they came. Hart was a land surveyor who was carving a route from Marshall to what would become Gilmer.

After the Panic of 1838, with the war in Texas over and with the Texans promising cheap land to people who settled the area, people began to flood into the county on both of the pioneering trails.

John Cotton to the south living near the Sabine River, Noah Lilly to the north on Lilly Creek just inside today's Camp County, and Isaac Moody in the West Mountain vicinity were already here when Hart carved his way west.

After Anson Jones proclaimed the Republic of Texas was dead, the Texas Legislature proclaimed on April 26, 1846, that the settlers between Big Cypress Creek and the northern side of the Sabine should organize a county and a county seat.

The legislators wanted to remember two supporters of the Texas annexation who had not lived to see the day: Abel Packer Upshur and Thomas Walker Gilmer. The county would be named Upshur and the county seat Gilmer.

As Secretary of State, Upshur had initiated negotiations with Pres. Sam Houston concerning statehood. Gilmer had left his post in the legislature of Virginia and traveled to join the fight for Texas freedom but arrived in 1838 after the issue with Mexico had been settled.

Gilmer became Secretary of the Navy on February 18, 1844, and was with Upshur 10 days later when a cannon called the "Peacemaker" was test fired from the U.S. steam frigate *Princeton*. On the third test, the gun exploded, killing Gilmer and Upshur, and leading to the creation of the Naval Academy in Annapolis in the aftermath.

The newcomers in the county were too busy clearing the land and getting a crop in to begin a new government on the first demand by the legislature. Finally, after the crop was harvested, local citizens gathered at the home of William Hart when District Judge O. M. Roberts came on December 15, 1846, to hold court.

While Judge Roberts was present, the men selected Hart to be the county clerk and Elias Bishop the district clerk, Gillington C. Patillo sheriff, and J. W. Richardson tax assessor/collector. Both Hart and Bishop have descendants living in the county to this day.

Temporarily Hart's home was designated as Gilmer. In an election in May 1848, the permanent location of Gilmer was selected. After crops were laid by, citizens of Upshur County gathered for an auction to sell the lots and blocks of the new town.

On Tuesday, August 22, 1848, not less than 33 men gathered to bid on the lots being sold by the county commissioners Benjamin Fuller, T. C. Hagen, Holly Page, and Benjamin Gage. Chief Justice Thomas D. Brookes, a veteran of the Battle of San Jacinto, presided.

While there is no record of anyone present other than the buyers, the commissioners, the witnesses, and county clerk R. G. Warren, an occasion such as the establishment of a new town offered the women and children a chance to leave the farm and to meet their neighbors. Especially those with small children may have brought along a slave or two to help with the livestock and the other chores. As many as 250 or more could have attended the establishment of Gilmer.

For the next several years, most of the people flowing into the county would concentrate on clearing the land, establishing a home, and making a living on the frontier.

One

Beginnings
1850–1879

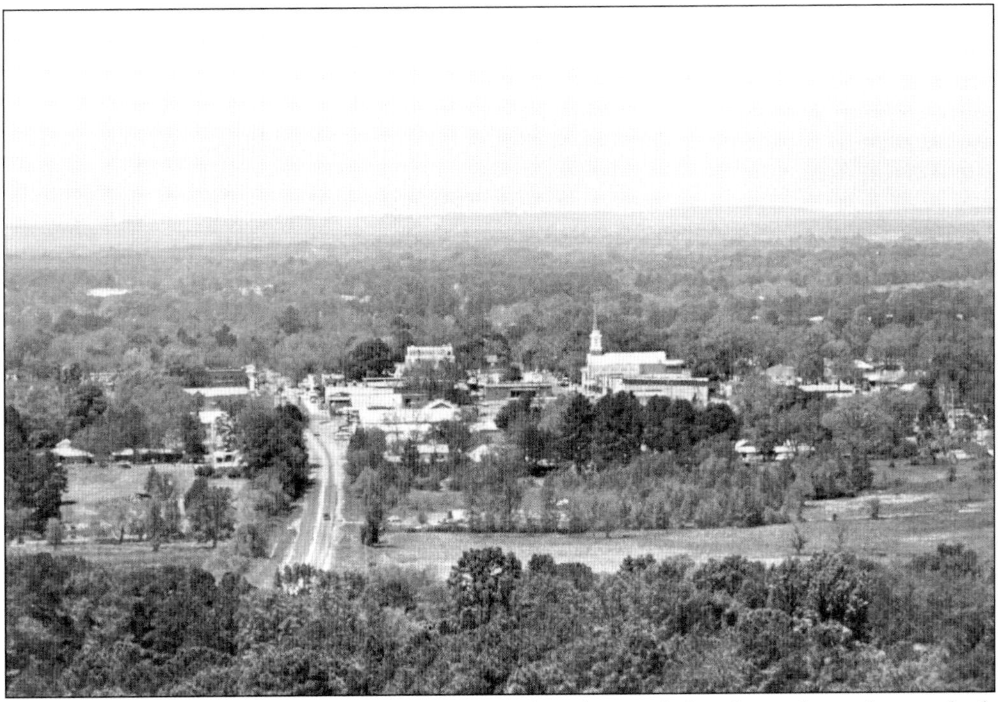

While it is no longer surrounded by virgin forest, Gilmer lies nestled in the piedmont forest, which reaches from the foothills of Virginia to northeastern Texas. Today the spires of the First United Methodist Church, the First Baptist Church, the Upshur County Courthouse, and, on the west side of town, the spire of the Church of Jesus Christ of Latter-day Saints tower over the second-, third-, and fourth-growth trees, which filled in the vast openness the pioneers created. The view is from the east, looking down Texas Highway 154 toward the west. (MLK.)

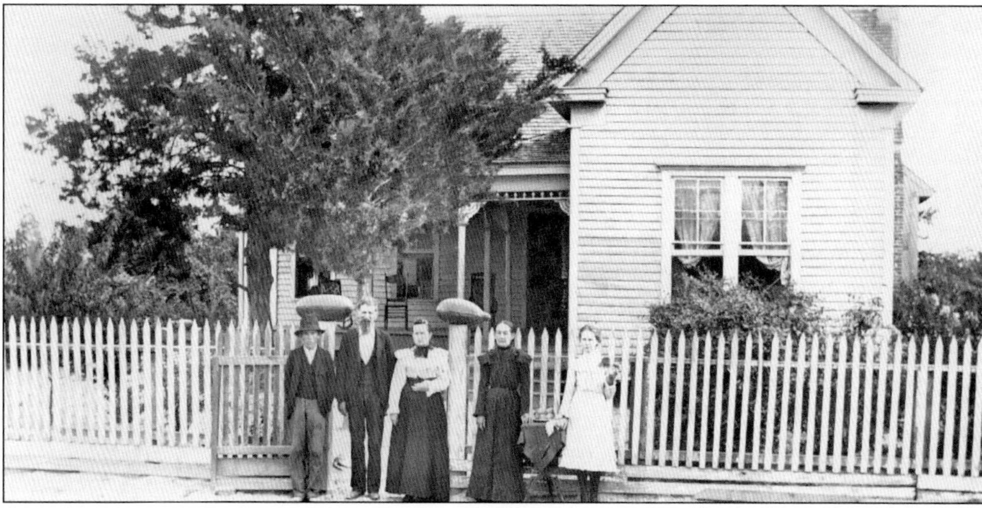

After going to the Civil War, fighting in the Battle of Chickamauga, becoming a prisoner of war, and surviving his wounds thanks to a lady in Chicago nursing him to health, William A. Hart returned home to Texas and became a teacher. After marrying and reading the law, Hart came back to Gilmer to practice law. He built this house in the 1870s northeast of Gilmer on the Old Coffeeville Road and left it at his death to his son, Cassius H. "Cash" Hart. Cash and Vannie Hart are the central figures of this photograph. (HUM.)

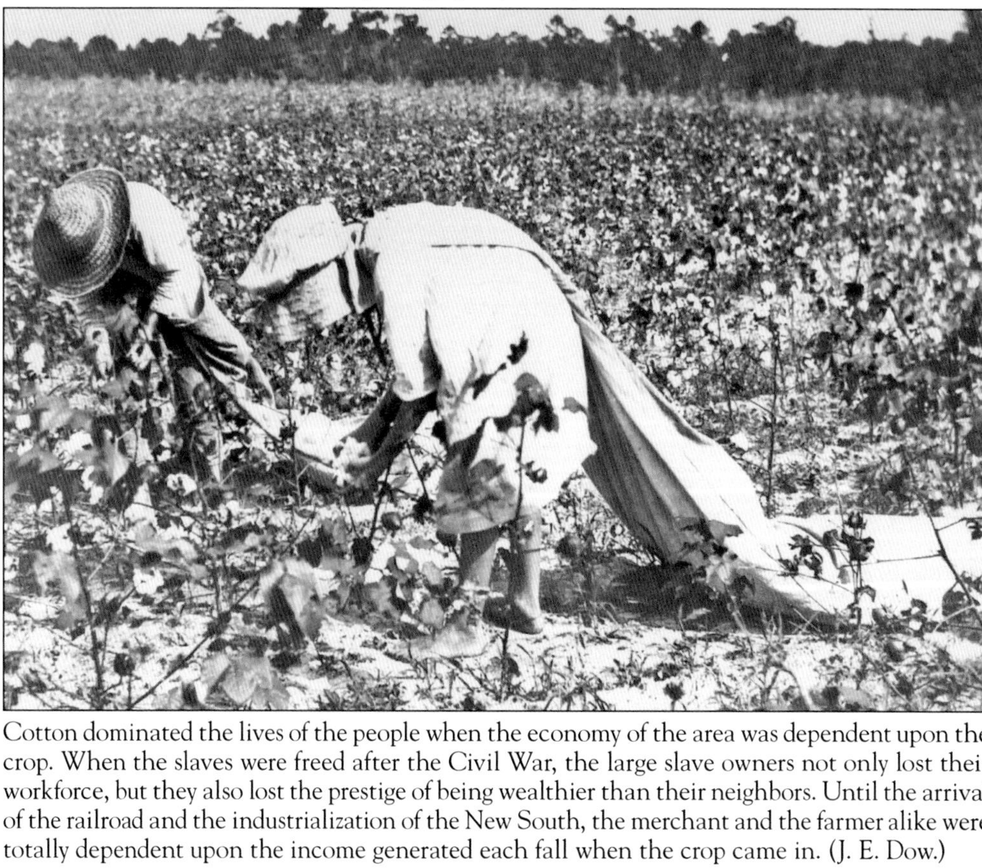

Cotton dominated the lives of the people when the economy of the area was dependent upon the crop. When the slaves were freed after the Civil War, the large slave owners not only lost their workforce, but they also lost the prestige of being wealthier than their neighbors. Until the arrival of the railroad and the industrialization of the New South, the merchant and the farmer alike were totally dependent upon the income generated each fall when the crop came in. (J. E. Dow.)

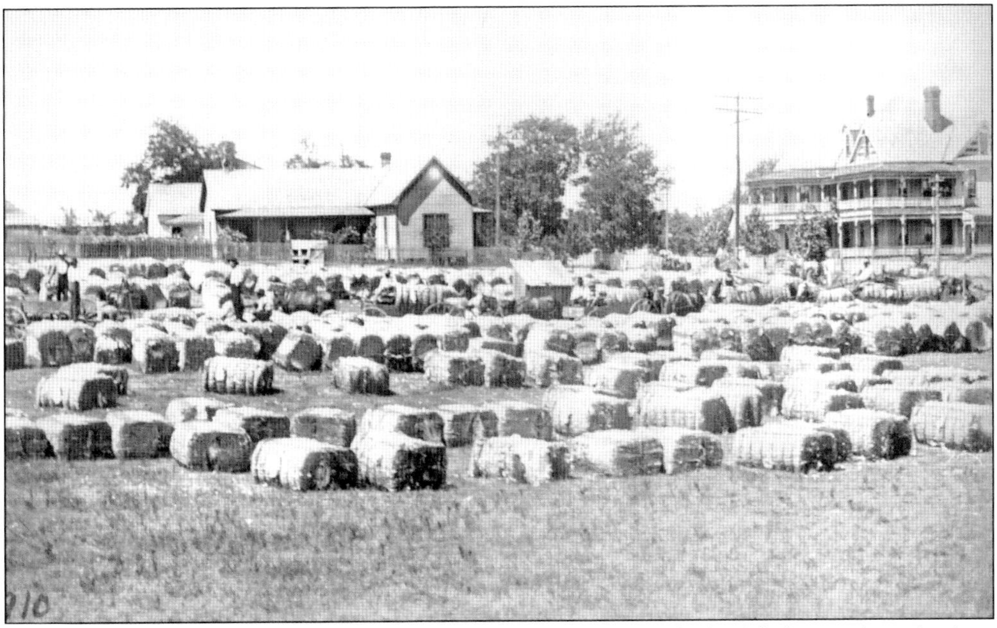

When the crop came in, starting in August and continuing through the fall, farmers brought their wagonloads of cotton first to the gin, where the seed and the cotton were separated, and then to the compress, where as much as 1,500 pounds of raw cotton was converted into a bale of 500 or more pounds of cotton and 100 or more pounds of seed. Once baled, the cotton was stacked in empty lots all around the town for later shipment. In the earliest days, the cotton was pulled by oxen to Jefferson for shipping to New Orleans and points beyond. In this image, the 1910 cotton is stacked where the Dodd Motor Company is currently located. In the background is the stately home of Judge R. W. Simpson, which burned on Easter in 1917. (MLK.)

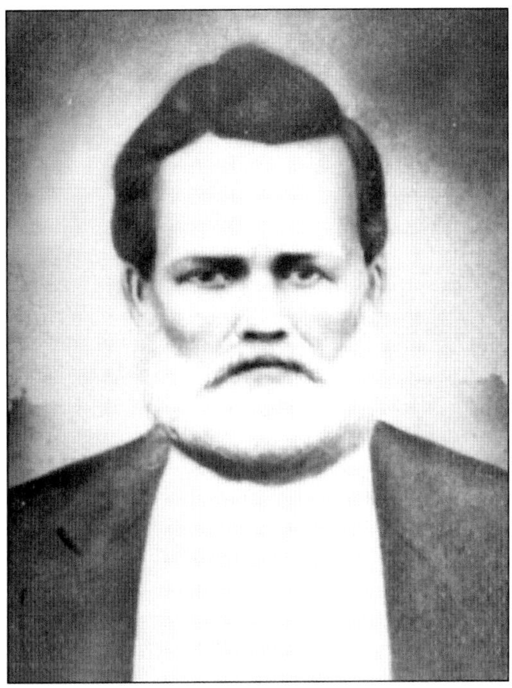

Jesse Glasco was newly arrived when he witnessed the sale of lots of Gilmer in 1848. He served as a deputy surveyor, reported conditions to the Smithsonian, participated in the Mexican War and the Civil War, and served as worshipful master of the Bethesda Lodge of Texas, No. 142, more often than any other man. He even trained the Union officer Capt. Charles Rand in Free Masonry when the New York Yankee lived in Gilmer during Reconstruction. Glasco reported to the *Texas Almanac* in 1861 that labor in the county was equally divided between slaves and white persons and that the greatest portion of cotton was raised by slave labor. (MLK.)

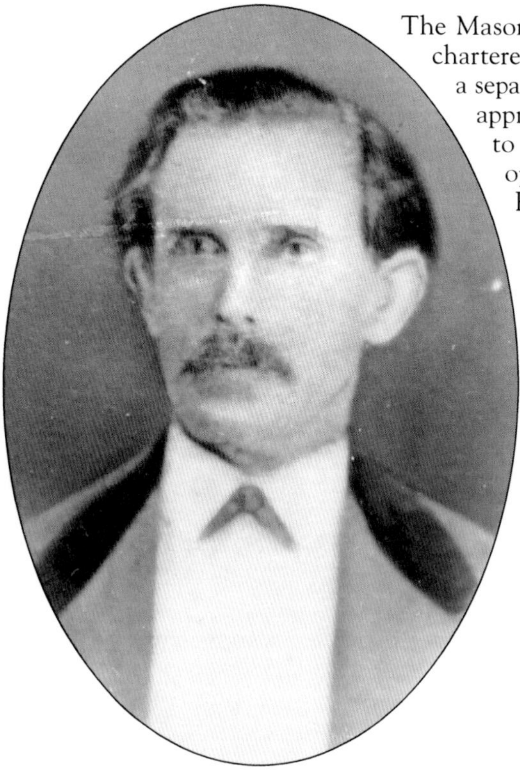

The Masons created Gilmer's first school when they chartered the Gilmer Masonic Institute in 1854 and a separate school for girls. As the potential for war approached, the educational leadership shifted to a native Georgian, Morgan Looney, who operated the Looney Institute for 10 years. Refugees from Louisiana came to Gilmer so their children could attend the school. After Looney left Texas, he established the school that ultimately became the University of Arkansas in Fayetteville. (MLK.)

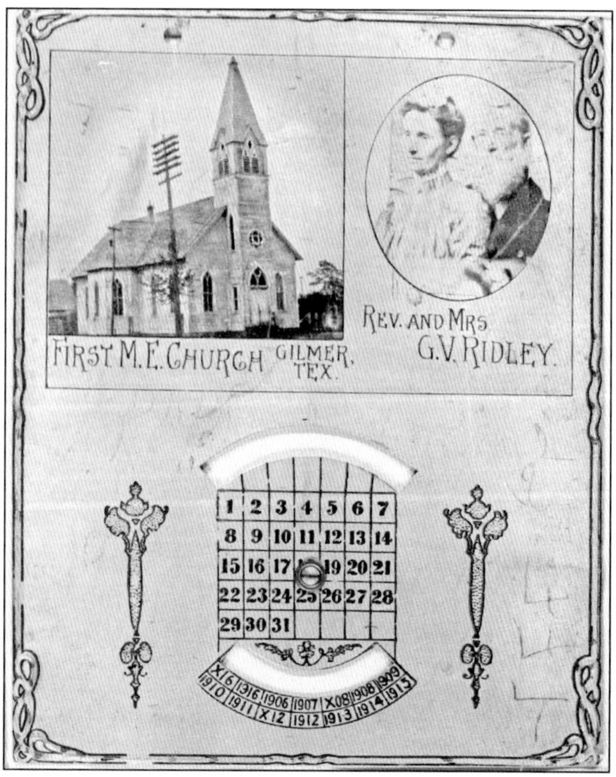

This universal calendar shows the oldest known image of the Methodist Episcopal Church South and its pastor and his wife, Mr. and Mrs. G. V. Ridley. It cannot be determined if the utility pole was for telegraph wires along the railroad beside the church or for electricity. Methodists were among the earliest settlers, and the 1871 building was the first constructed by the congregation for their sole use. Initially they shared the courthouse on alternating Sundays with the Baptists. (HUM.)

Two

Railroads and Lumberjacks 1880–1899

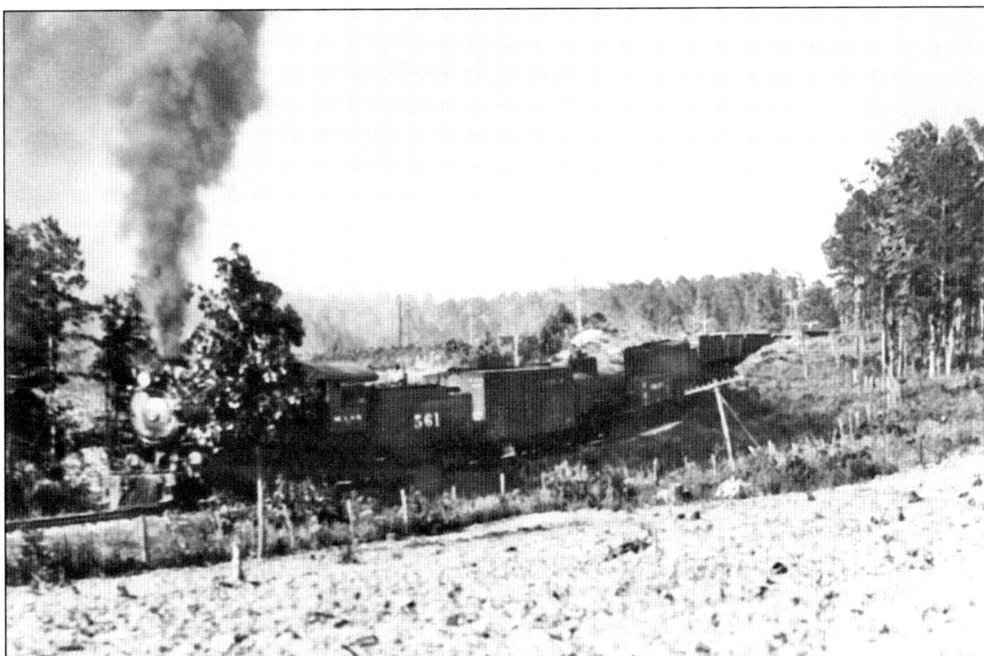

The railroad arrived in Upshur County with the Tyler Tap, a narrow-gauge line extending from Tyler to points north. In 1880, the line was taken over by the Texas and St. Louis Railway. By 1882, the Cotton Belt was advertising passenger fares for "three cents a mile, the only direct route to Waco, Corsicana, Athens, Tyler, Mt. Pleasant and Texarkana." Seen here traveling near Center Point south of Gilmer, this pre–World War II engine steams away at the grade it is climbing. In the 1950s, passenger service was discontinued, but as the Union Pacific Railroad, freight still travels through Gilmer daily. (J. E. Dow.)

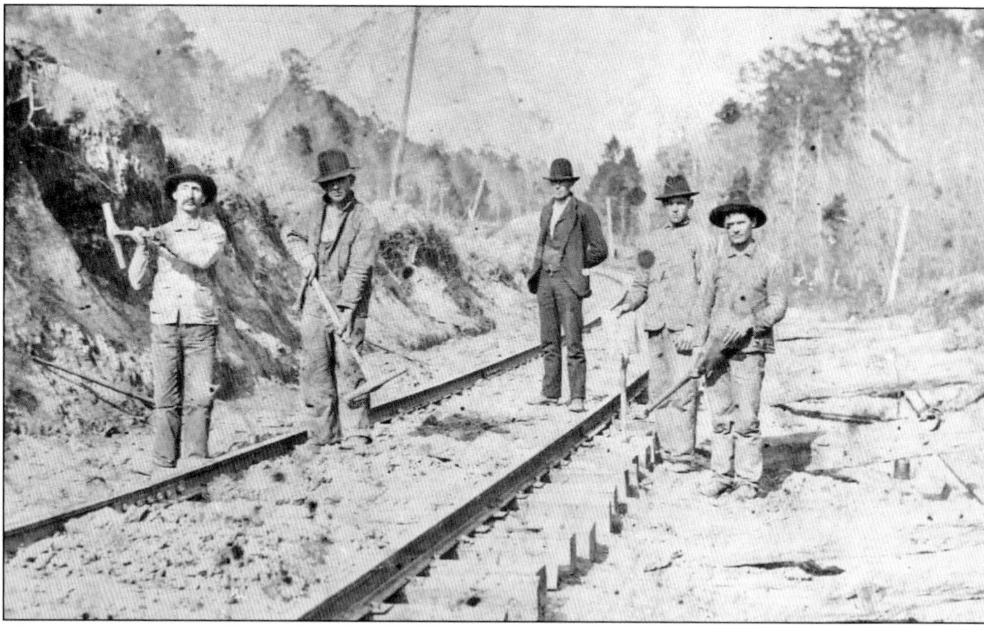

Working on the railroad brought many new people to Upshur County and led to the creation of many communities along the lines, including Bettie, Pritchett, and Big Sandy along the Cotton Belt and Graceton, Rosewood, and Rhonesboro on the Marshall and East Texas. These men are working near Big Sandy in 1905. At right are Robert Randolph Mathis and Lon Williamson. (HUM.)

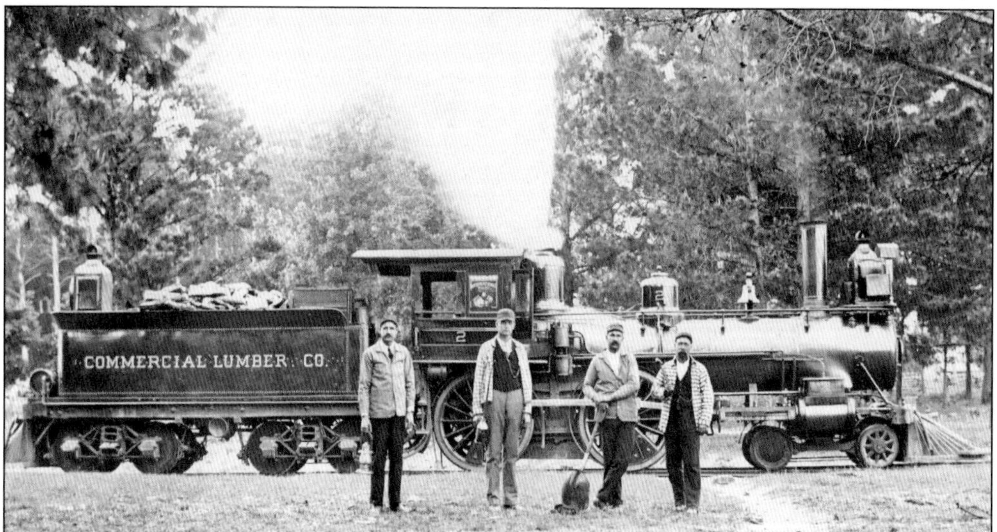

With the arrival of the railroad, the virgin forests of East Texas were open for major exploitation. In 1882, there were 18 sawmills in the county, but with the addition of rail, by 1907, there were 90. In 1895, the Commercial Lumber Company was buying rights-of-way to establish a tramline railway to its numerous country mills. In one deed, the company refers to the "wild and uncultivated land we might own in eastern Upshur County." A big mill for the company was located on the northern edge of Gilmer, out on Titus Street, where a company town was established with houses for black and white workers, along with a company store and a mill pond known today as Crawford's Pond at Smith Avenue and Titus Street. (MLK.)

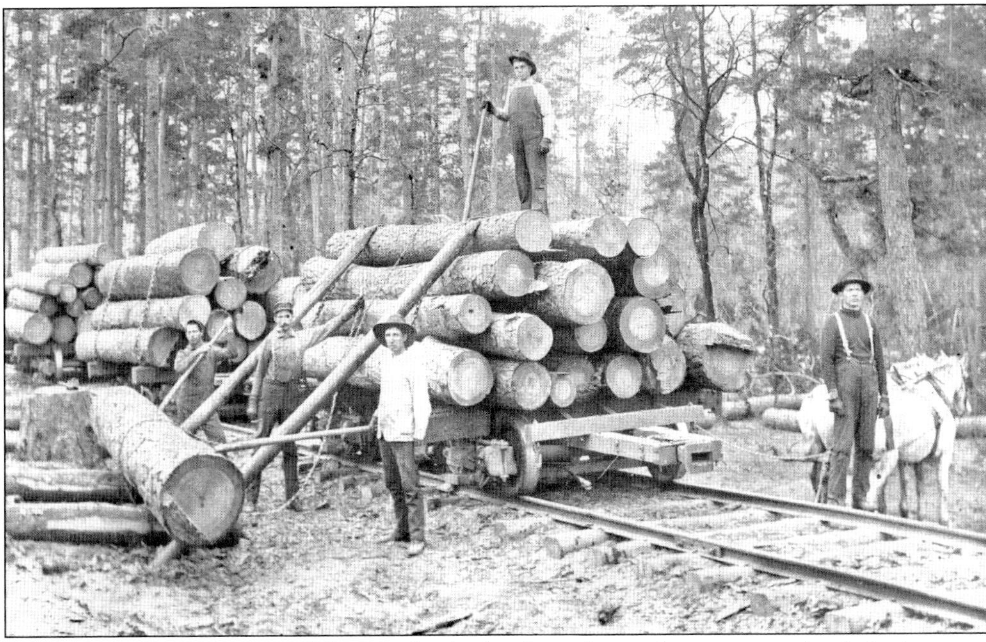

As the tram lines penetrated the woods, the lumberjacks used ox teams to haul the logs near the tram. Workers then used a team of mules and cant hooks to raise the logs onto the flat beds to carry the wood to the mills. Major accidents could cost a worker an arm, a leg, or even a life in an era when there was no worker's compensation or disability. Even so, men flocked to the companies to work where the income was year-round. (HUM.)

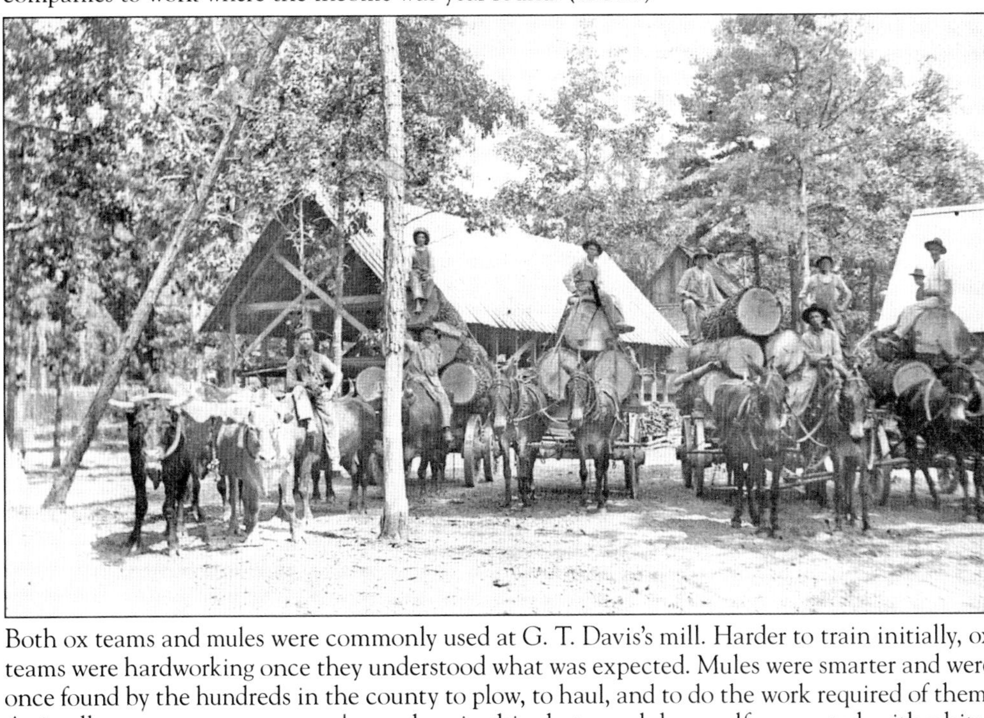

Both ox teams and mules were commonly used at G. T. Davis's mill. Harder to train initially, ox teams were hardworking once they understood what was expected. Mules were smarter and were once found by the hundreds in the county to plow, to haul, and to do the work required of them. As in all matters a century ago, the workers in this photograph have self segregated, with whites to the left and the blacks to the right. (HUM.)

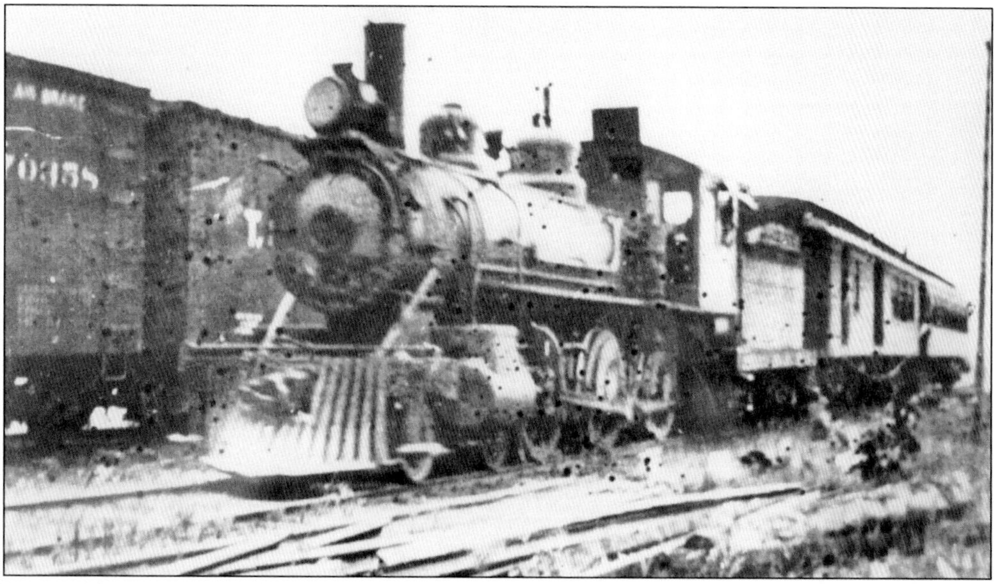

Two rail lines intersected in Gilmer when the Marshall and East Texas (M&ET) entered from the east approximately where the Gilmer National Bank stands today. Two sidings allowed cars to be released from a passing train until the goods contained could be unloaded at the warehouses that lined the rails. After the acquisition by Union Pacific of the Cotton Belt, the sidings were removed since container distribution by truck has replaced the uncoupling of rail cars. (MLK.)

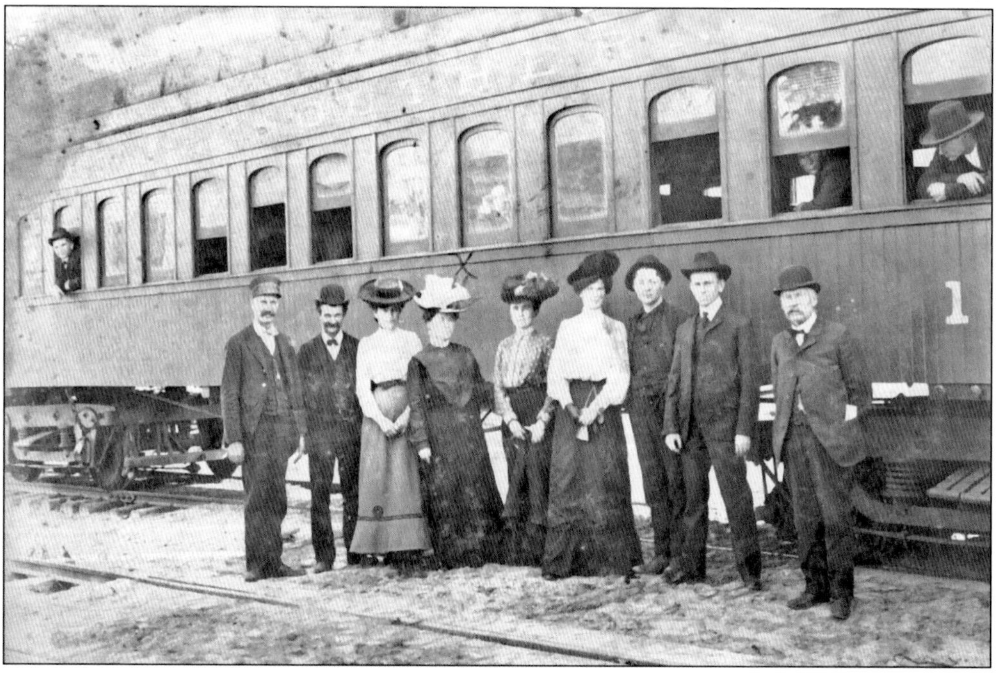

The M&ET earned the nickname "Misery and Eternal Torment" because of its unpredictable travels between Marshall and Winnsboro. Among the group on the first passenger train to Rhonesboro in 1908, Vinnie Barton is standing at left. Sometimes passengers had to collect wood for the boiler, while other times, when the fruit was in season, they might get out and pick peaches, blackberries, or strawberries. (MLK.)

The logging town in the eastern portion of the county developed by Judge R. W. Simpson was named Graceton in honor of his daughter, Grace, seen here in costume and with a new litter of puppies. She married Joe Roberts and moved to Tyler. (HUM.)

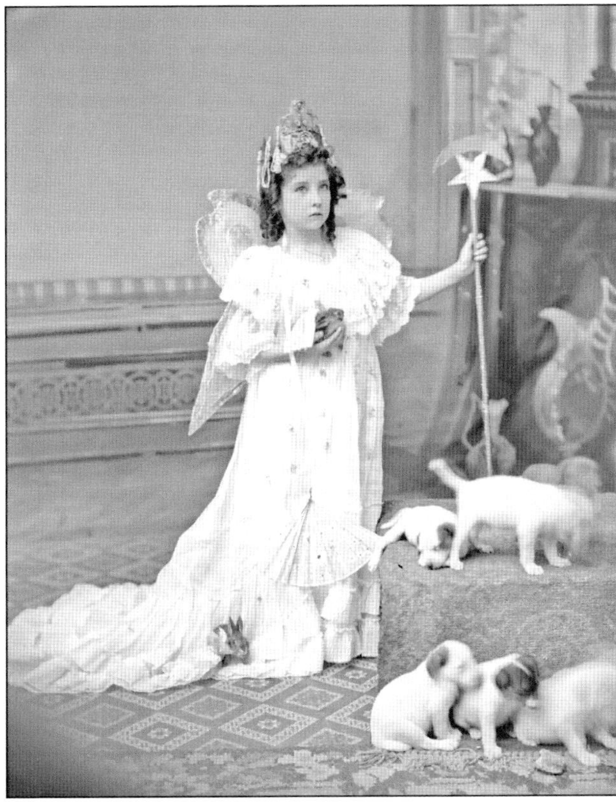

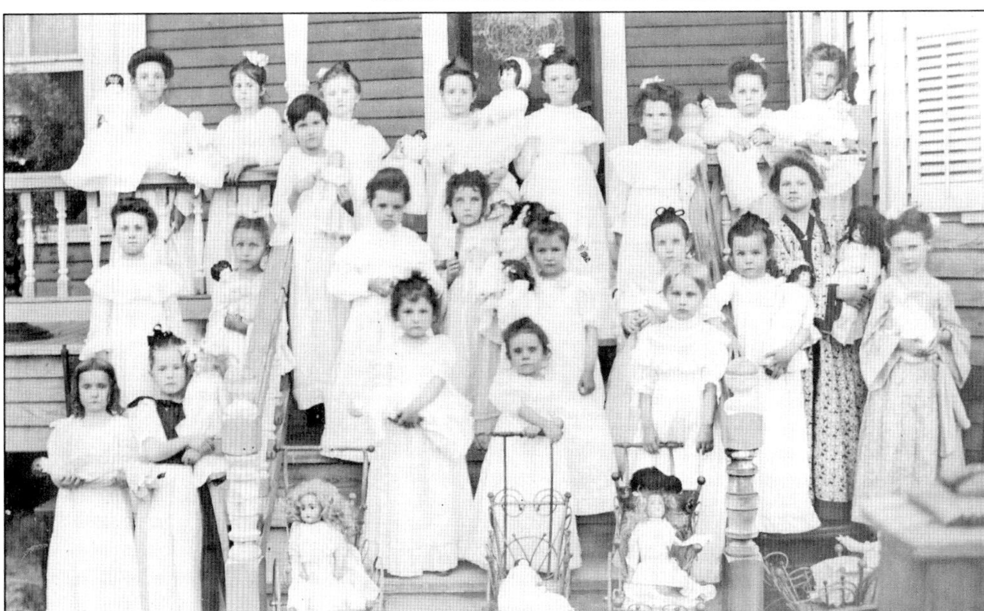

The respectable young ladies of the dawn of the 20th century brought their dolls with them to the party at Judge R. W. Simpson's home. The occasion was possibly a birthday party for Grace Simpson, the judge's only daughter. Her mother, Mrs. Georgia Walton Simpson, became one of the charter members of the Twentieth Century Club. She came to Gilmer as a child in 1853. (HUM.)

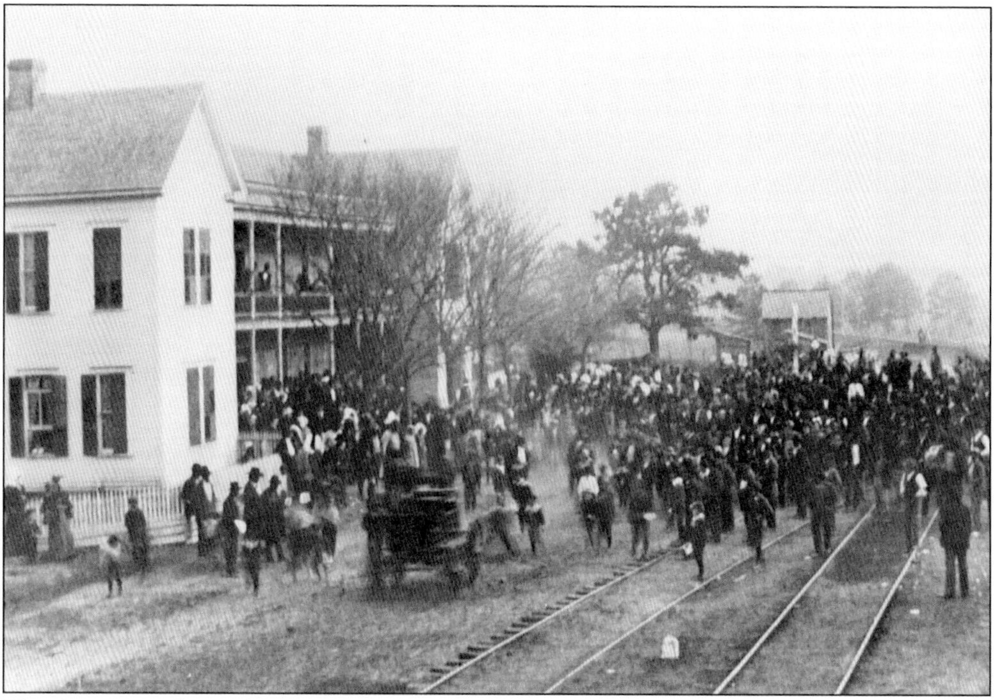

The Commercial Hotel was a major gathering place in the late 1890s for travelers and locals alike. In this view, the crowd has gathered to see the volunteers off for the Spanish-American War in 1898. (MLK.)

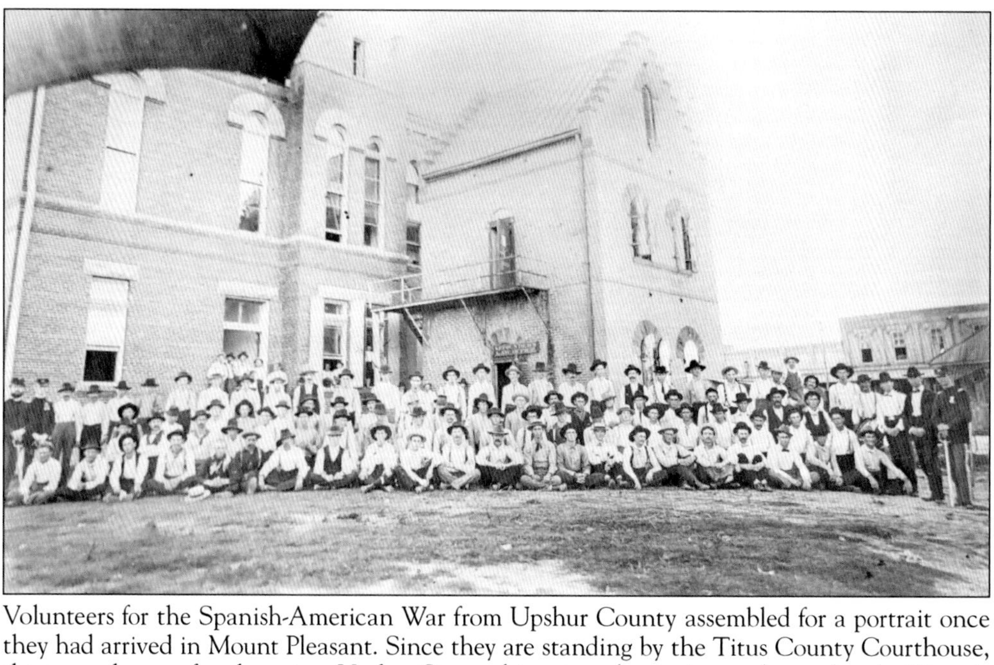

Volunteers for the Spanish-American War from Upshur County assembled for a portrait once they had arrived in Mount Pleasant. Since they are standing by the Titus County Courthouse, this image has confused previous Upshur County historians, but an image donated to the Historic Upshur Museum was correctly labeled as to where it had been composed. Most of the Upshur County men returned without having fired a shot in the brief war. (MLK.)

Three

ENTERING THE 20TH CENTURY 1900–1929

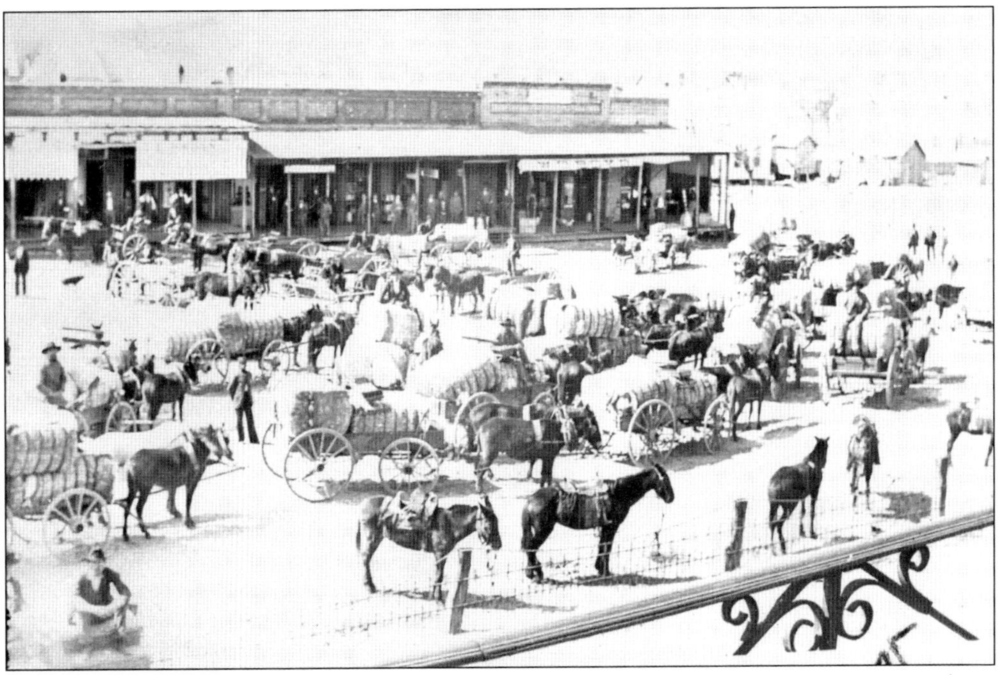

Two men in the lower left sit on the sty, which allowed people to reach the courthouse without letting in what Eva Dodson (Mrs. J. M.) Hays called "Mr. Goat, Mr. Dog, and Mr. Hog," who frequently in the summer sought to enter the cool of the building. When the square was covered in nothing but deep sand, it was said that one could be covered in sand fleas before reaching the courthouse. W. O. Boyd's store is at the right end of the block on the north side of the square about 1895. Boyd had some 2,000 acres of forest land and 200 acres under cultivation in addition to owning a store with his son-in-law, J. W. Marshall. (HUM.)

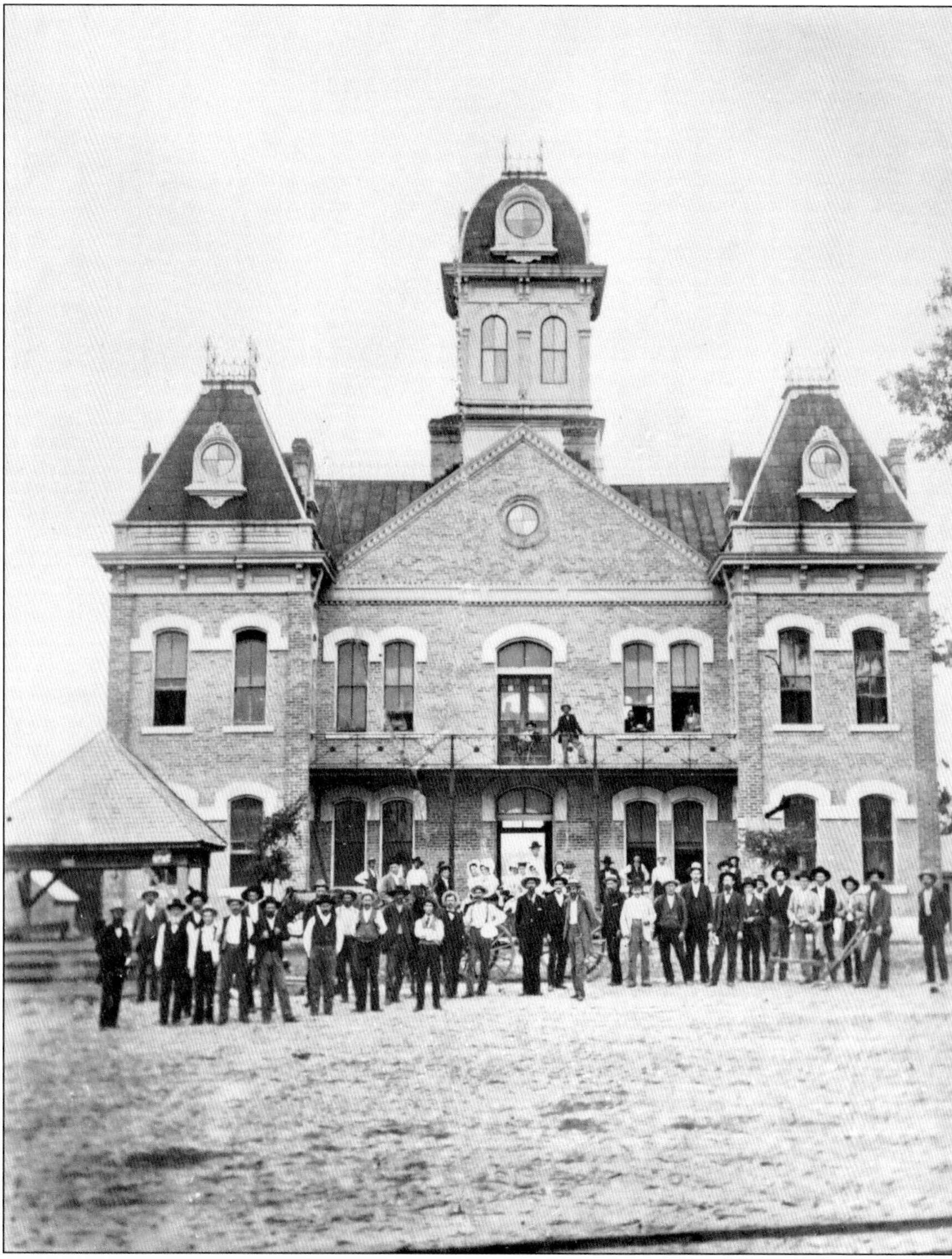

The first brick, fireproof courthouse was built in 1889 for $30,000 after the frame building with a cupola was destroyed in a fire on November 25, 1888. The mixture of Italianate and Second Empire architectural modes, with a tall central tower and four lower corner pavilions joined by cast-iron balconies, blended to form a suitable temple of justice. It was heated by four fireplaces and had no indoor plumbing. Gilmer would not have a city water supply for another 20 years. Part of the contract went for the digging of a well, which not only served the watering troughs at the courthouse, but was also used by the neighboring businesses. (MLK.)

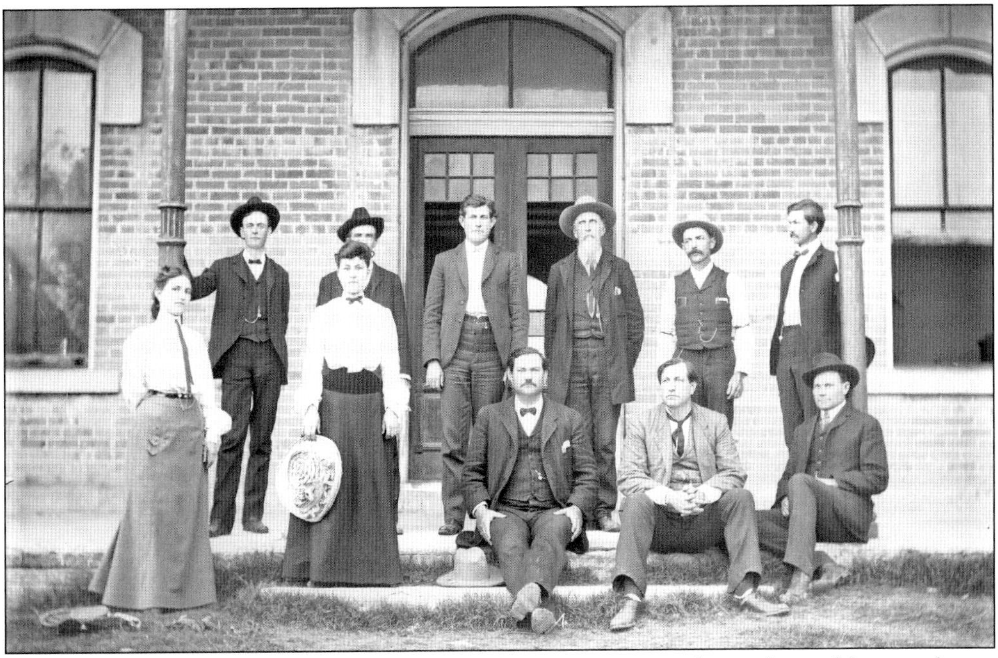

Employees of the county government and elected representatives gather in front of the courthouse for a group portrait. On the left is Ella Briggs, who as Mrs. V. E. Todd became one of the first women elected to the school board, and seated second from the right is Tom Briggs, who was responsible for gravel being applied to the sandy roads in Gilmer. Standing by the pole on the far right is R. W. Simpson, who was the county judge from 1905 to 1909. (HUM.)

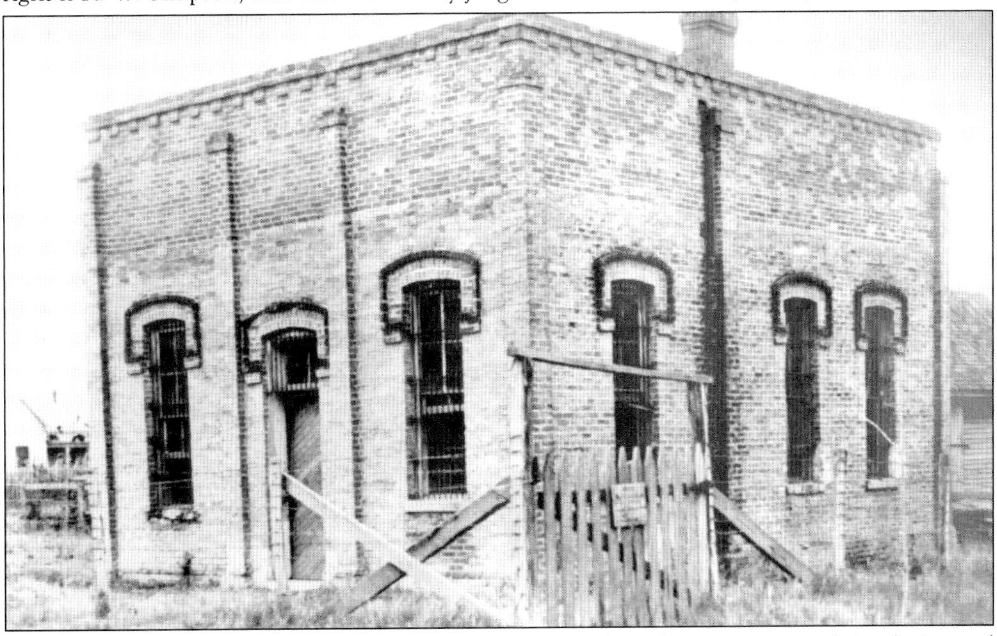

From 1870 to 1882, the county spent money on repairing the jail or putting people in chains and later removing the irons. Even with a high fence around it, they could not keep prisoners from escaping the old jail. Finally, in 1882, the county authorized the building of a jail at the southeast corner of Silver Alley and Harrison Street, which lasted until 1915. (MLK.)

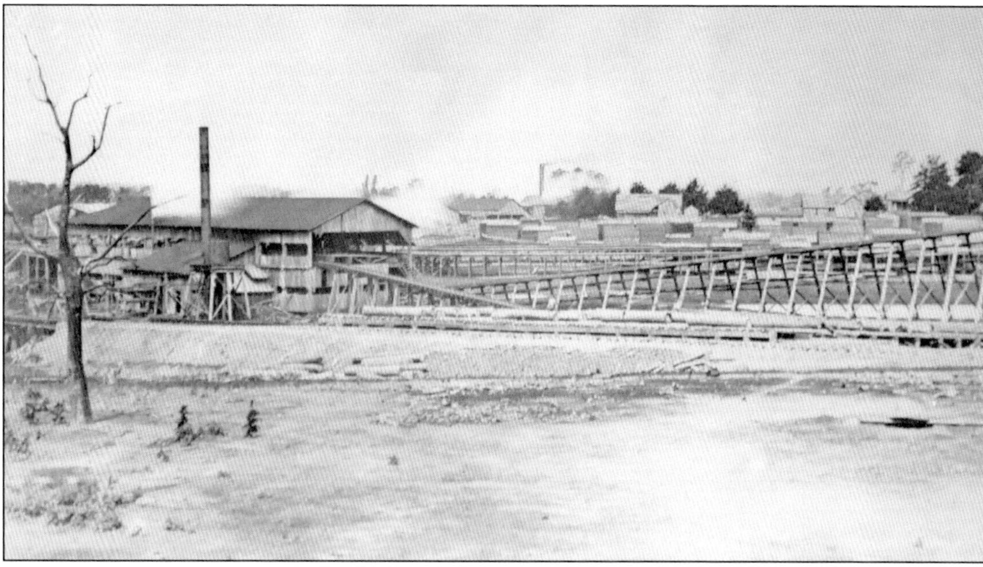

The Commercial Lumber Company on north Titus Street had a commissary, which used wooden coinage with the value pressed in the middle, housing for black and white workers, and a mill pond filled with floating logs. For more than a decade, they worked the logs accumulated from across the county until a devastating fire erupted in 1907. By 1909, it had moved operations to Arkansas, taking many of the workers with it. The loss of the company and its year-round incomes had an immediate effect on the local economy. (MLK.)

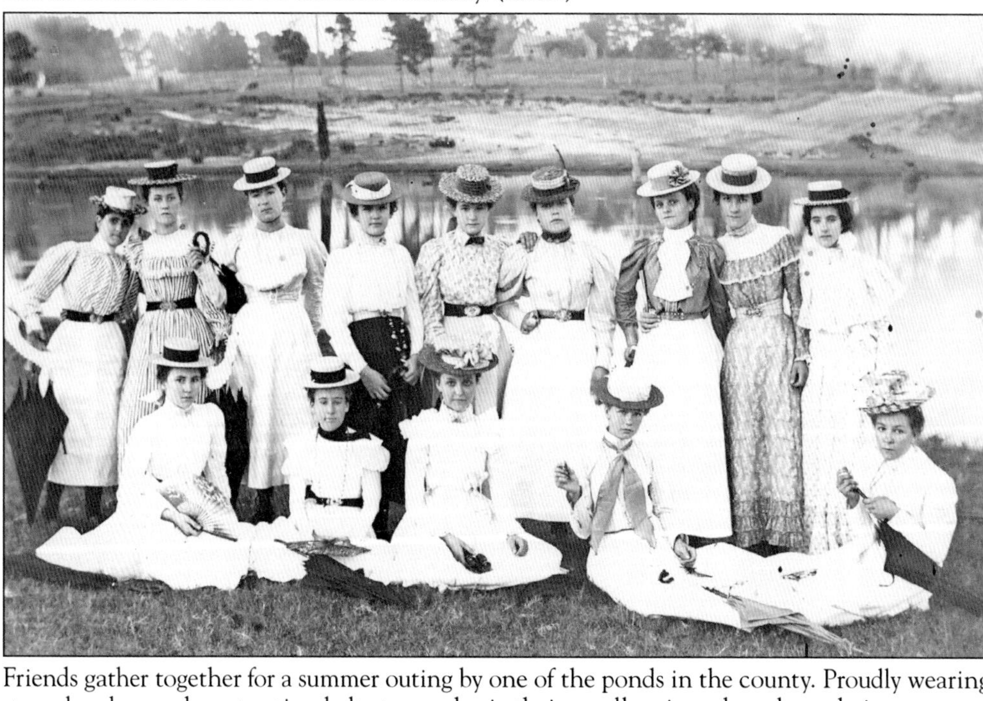

Friends gather together for a summer outing by one of the ponds in the county. Proudly wearing straw bowlers and contrasting belts to emphasis their small waists, they show their awareness of the fashions of the day. What stands out to a viewer a century later is the erosion around the shores of the pond and the great expanse of treeless landscape in what was once verdant forestland. (HUM.)

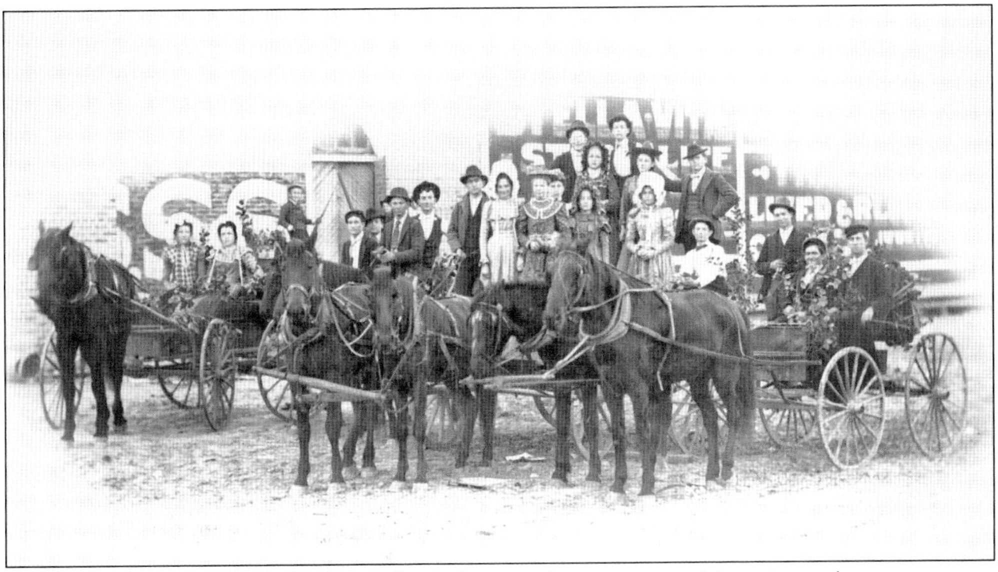

On special occasions, all the family loaded up in the wagons and buggies and came to town together. On this occasion, one young man proudly displays his rifle (or shotgun), probably a prized new possession. While in D. T. Loyd's book this image is shown as advertising patent medicines and a saloon, in this copy of the visit at the Historic Upshur Museum, J. M. Hays has carefully dodged out the reference to the saloon. Both Mr. and Mrs. Hays were passionate members of the Prohibition forces who won the day when Gilmer was voted dry in 1909. (HUM.)

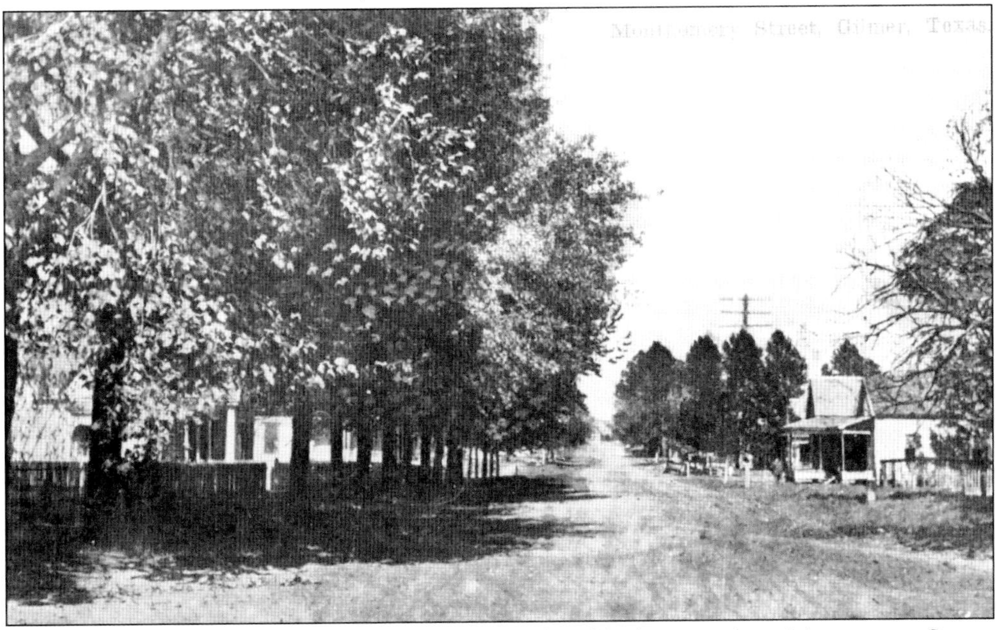

In this earliest known view of a residential neighborhood looking north on Montgomery Street, the predominance of fast-growing sycamore trees is obvious. After cutting down the trees of all types, the homeowners of a century ago put a fence around the yard to keep animals out and then planted sycamores for quick shade. At the end of the road, where early Gilmer ended, T. C. Mitchell's house stands blocking the way. When he sold property to Dr. T. S. Ragland, Mitchell moved his house to the right and opened up the Mitchell addition from Walnut to Pecan Streets. (HUM.)

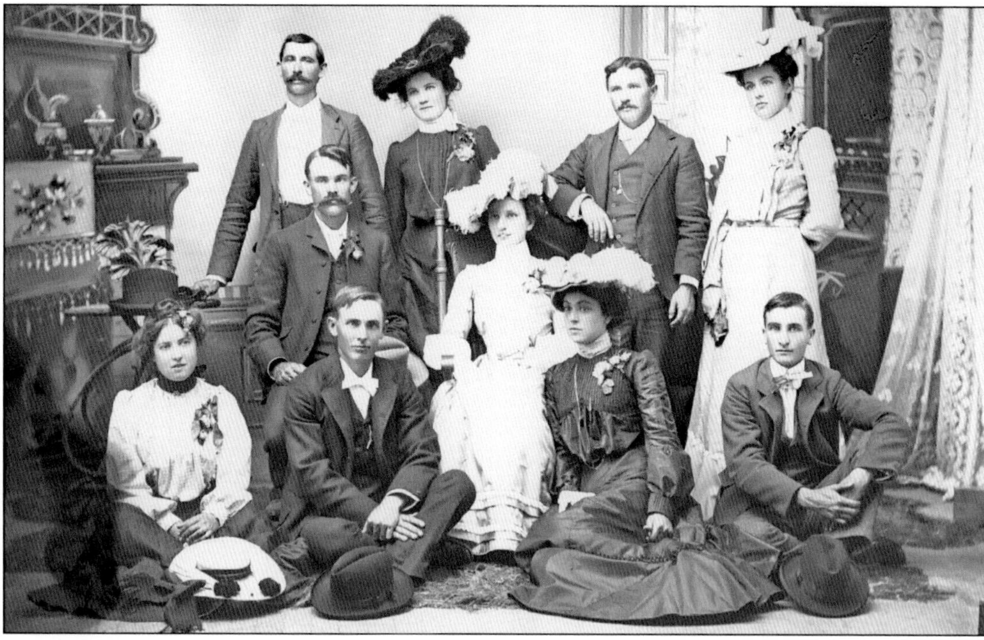

After getting married, John Hiram Pickitt (second row, left) and Mary Dailey (second row, right) gather with their wedding party at the Hays Studio for a wedding portrait in October 1902. Seated in front of the groom is his brother, Joe Pickitt (first row, second from left), and Lillie Mae Dailey Pickitt (first row, third from left). The couple are the future parents of Leonard Pickitt, a Gilmer football star, coach, and principal, and grandparents of Lt. Gen. John Leonard Pickitt, a West Point graduate. (HUM.)

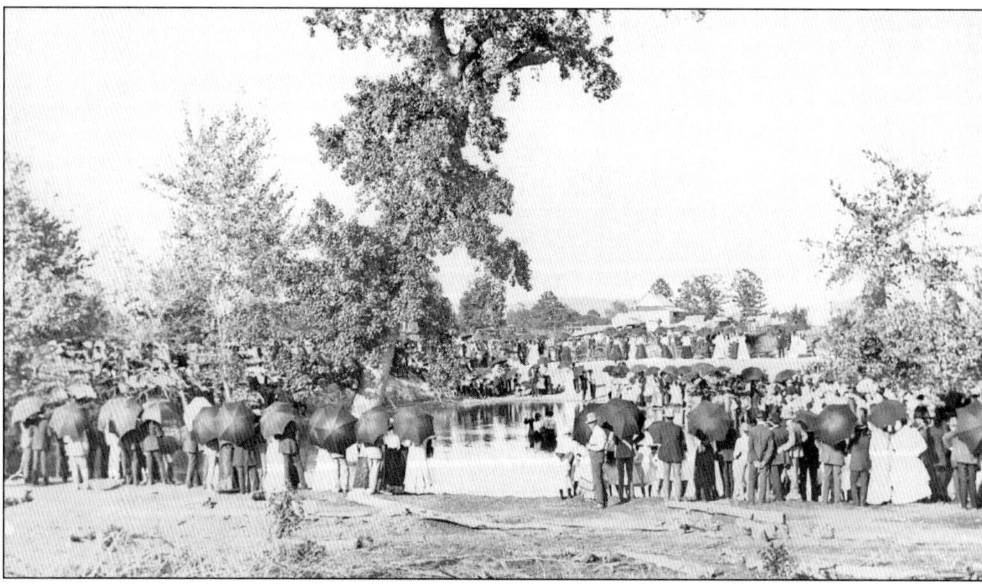

In the summer, when the crops were laid by, it was time first for camp meetings before the churches were established and then, for the first half of the 20th century, for revivals. At the climax of the revival, the members all gathered at a lake or pond, Davis Pond in this case, to watch the baptisms that resulted from the conversions of the sinners. For a community dominated by Christians who did not dance or drink, the revival was a leading source of entertainment. (HUM.)

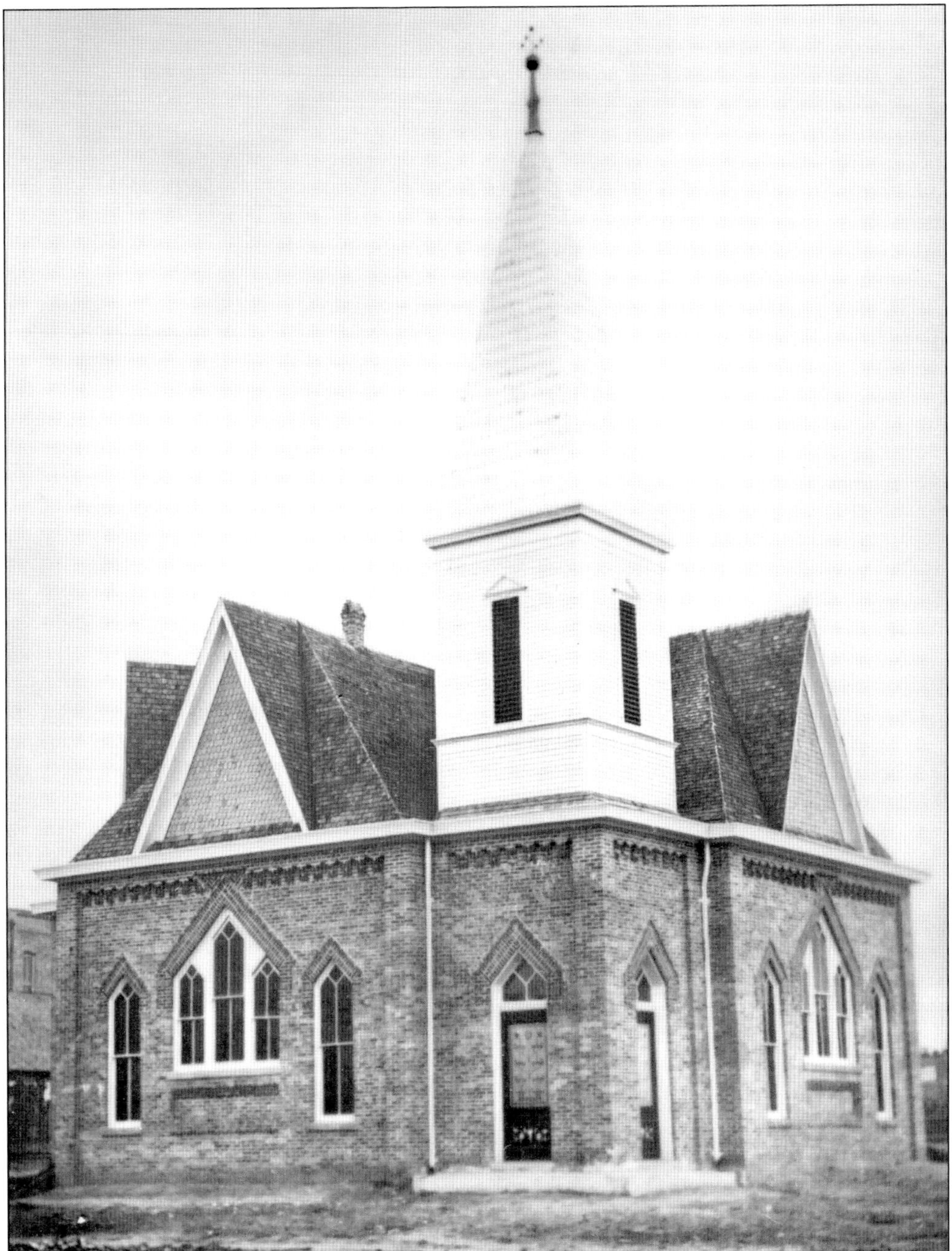

"Since the membership of the church had grown from approximately 90 in the 1870s to 200 in the 1890s, the need for a new church house was felt. In the fall of 1896 a lot on the southeast corner of Buffalo and Trinity Streets was purchased," wrote Dr. David and Melba Jenkins in the history of the First Baptist Church. For $3,000, an elaborate building of red brick with a front entrance on the corner and the pulpit on the south end of the auditorium was built. (HUM.)

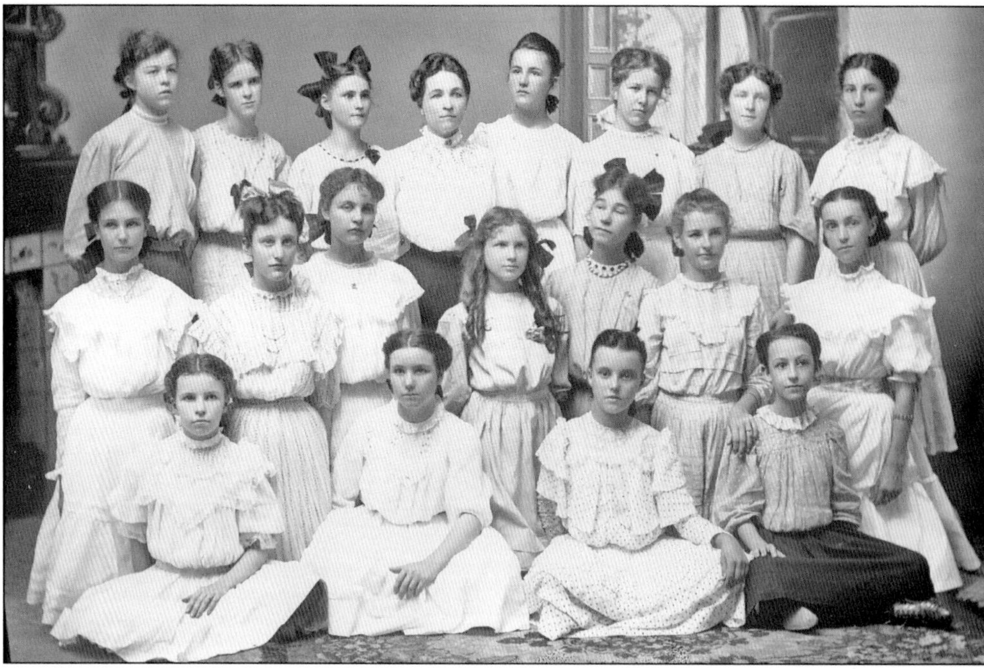

Beulah Crosby's Sunday school class had a group photograph made at the Hays Studio about 1905. From left to right are (first row) Sybil McClelland, Pope Daniels, Daisy Petty, and Maggie Hill; (second row) Ina Dudley, Lula Boyd, Florence Allen, Kathleen McGee, Dee Stephens, Lela Crosby, and Effie Porter; (third row) Ollie Connell, Frankie Schrum, Lillie Stephens, Crosby, Emma Pyle, Gladys Connell, Vera Warren, and Nell Mitchell. Dee Stephens would become a popular clerk at Marshall's store. (HUM.)

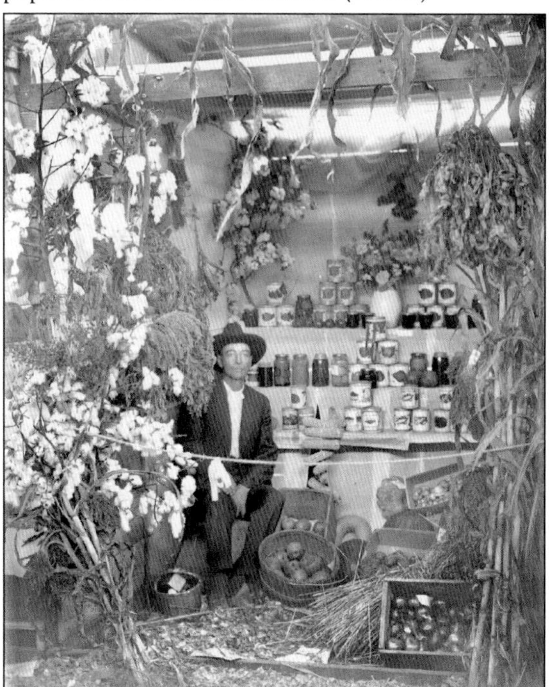

Lionel McKinney had a booth at the Upshur County Fair early in the new 20th century in which he promoted the diversification of agriculture. On the left is cotton and on the right are shocks of sorghum and sugar cane, while leaves of corn hang from the stems draped across the top of his booth. Canned goods in both glass and steel proclaim the proper storage of a bumper crop, while red potatoes, onions, wheat, and barley sheaves fill the space around the progressive farmer. (HUM.)

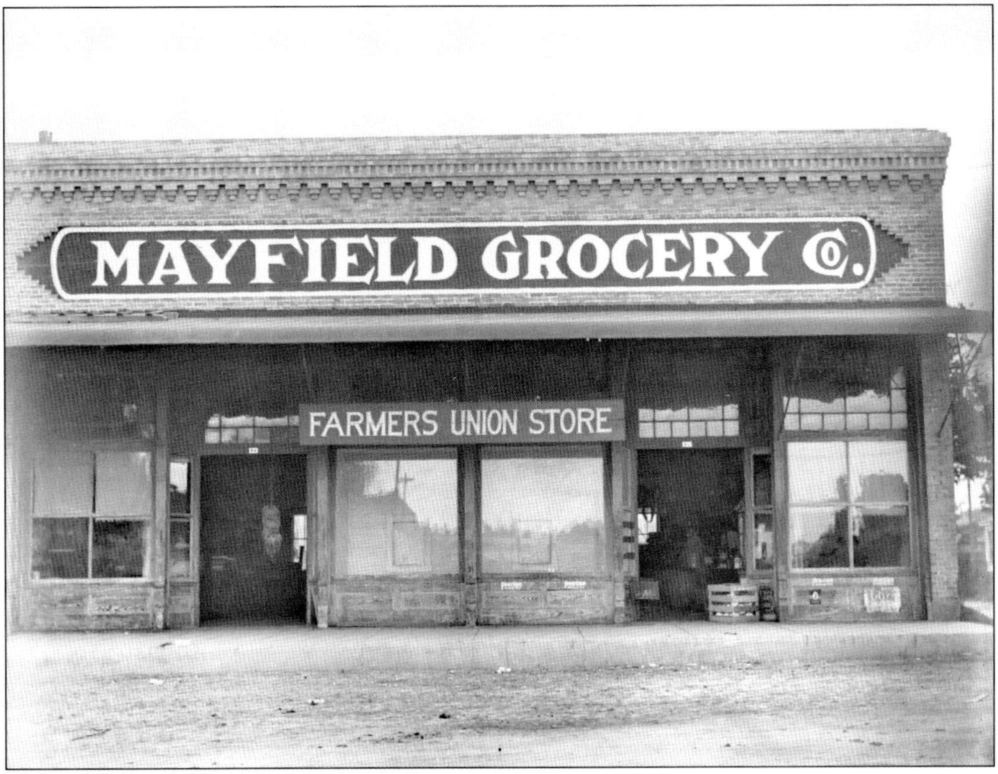

The Mayfield Grocery on the southeast corner of the square facing west sold both produce and canned goods to the housewife while the store bought from the local farmer. In the shadows of the left-hand doorway, a stalk of banana is seen hanging for the selection of the ripening fruit. (HUM.)

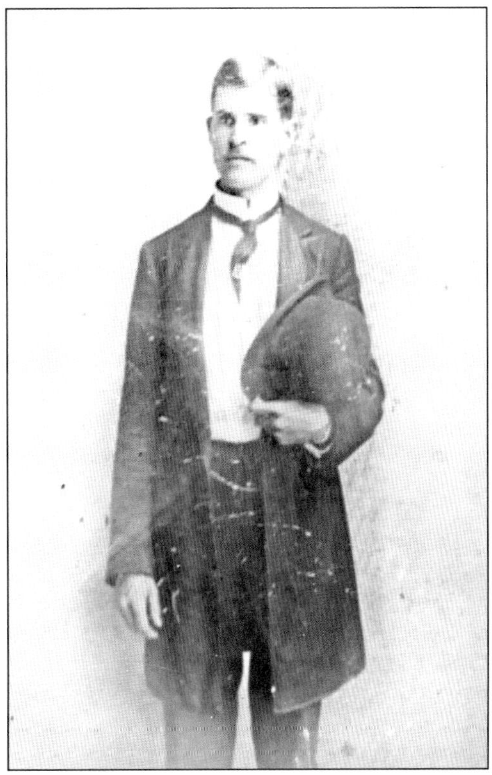

R. B. Nelson taught with his wife, Nannie King Nelson, at Glenwood and East Mountain before coming to Gilmer, where he entered the general merchandise business. He was later the president of the Gilmer State Bank until it merged with the First National Bank. He then bought a Dyke wholesale feed, which operates today as R. B. Cook and Sons. His only child, Kathleen Nelson, married Croley Cook, who established the Croley Funeral Home as a separate business from Cook Hardware. (GM.)

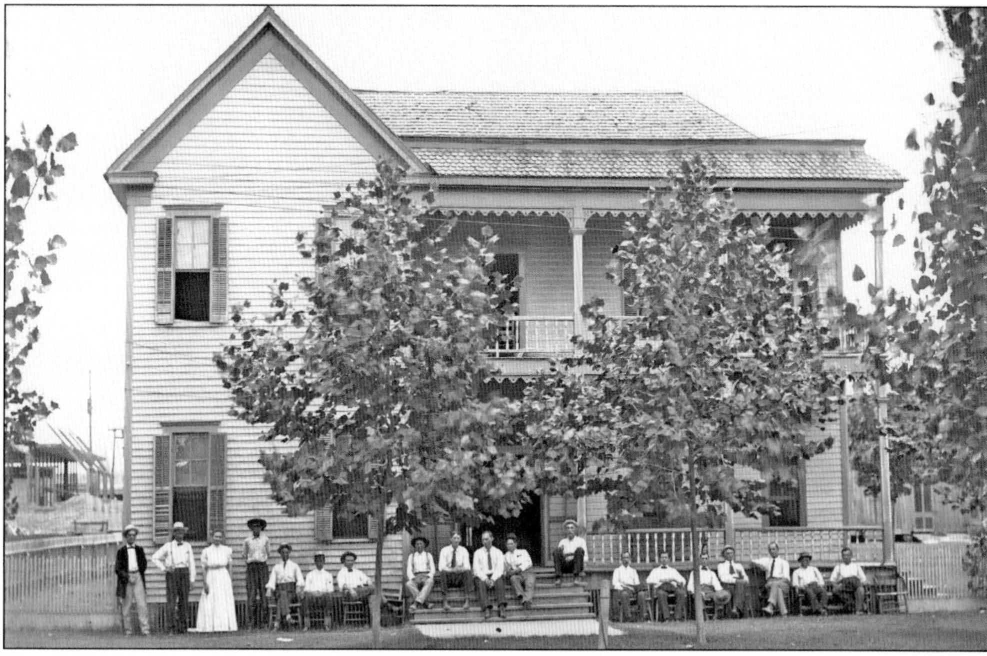

The Bell Hotel served as a second home for many single young men who were working in the booming lumber business or who had come to town to get a high school education. Mr. and Mrs. A. L. Bennett ran the hotel in the first quarter of a century before it was purchased by V. E. and Ella Briggs Todd, who ran it for several years. Located on the south side of Cass Street at the corner with Davis Street, the Bell had a reputation for fine family-style meals, which local people enjoyed alongside the guests. (HUM.)

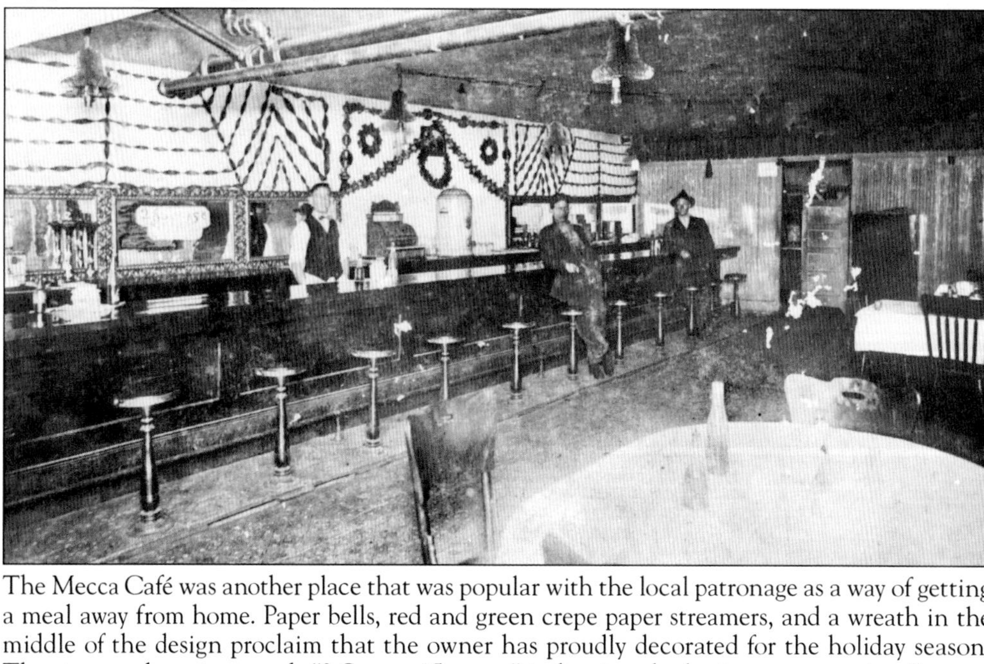

The Mecca Café was another place that was popular with the local patronage as a way of getting a meal away from home. Paper bells, red and green crepe paper streamers, and a wreath in the middle of the design proclaim that the owner has proudly decorated for the holiday season. The sign on the mirror reads "2 Syrups 15 cents," indicating the business was serving flavored sodas. (MLK.)

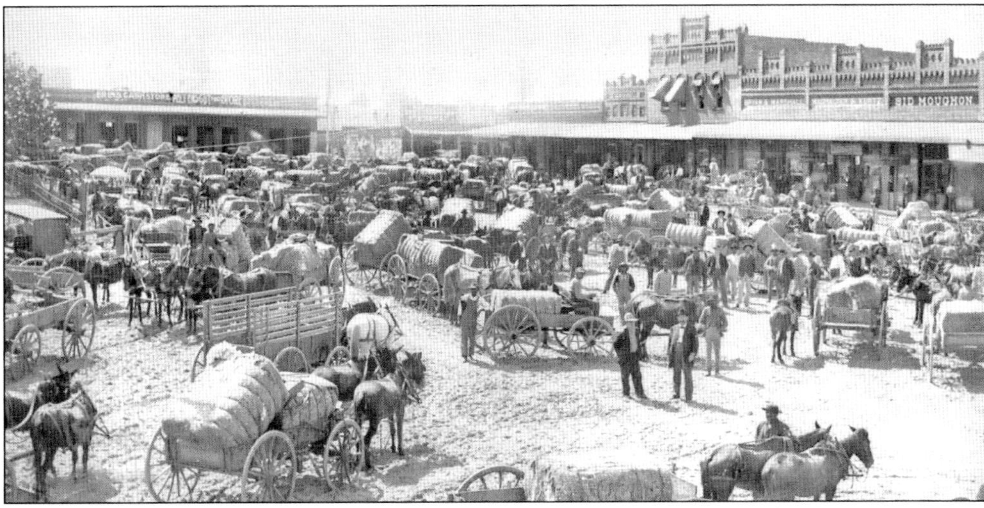

Traditionally, farmers would gather on the square after they left the gin and the cotton compress for a group photograph at a high point in the cotton harvest. Bales with a white patch indicate the cotton broker had cut away a section of the burlap to determine if the cotton was fine, fine to middling, or fair to middling, a term indicating the poorer grade. Although some copies of this photograph have 1902 written on them, the Oden Building on the west side of the square indicates it was constructed in 1903. The stores at Tyler Street and Silver Alley are restaurants, and Sid Moughon, who also served as a county judge, has a business to the right. (HUM.)

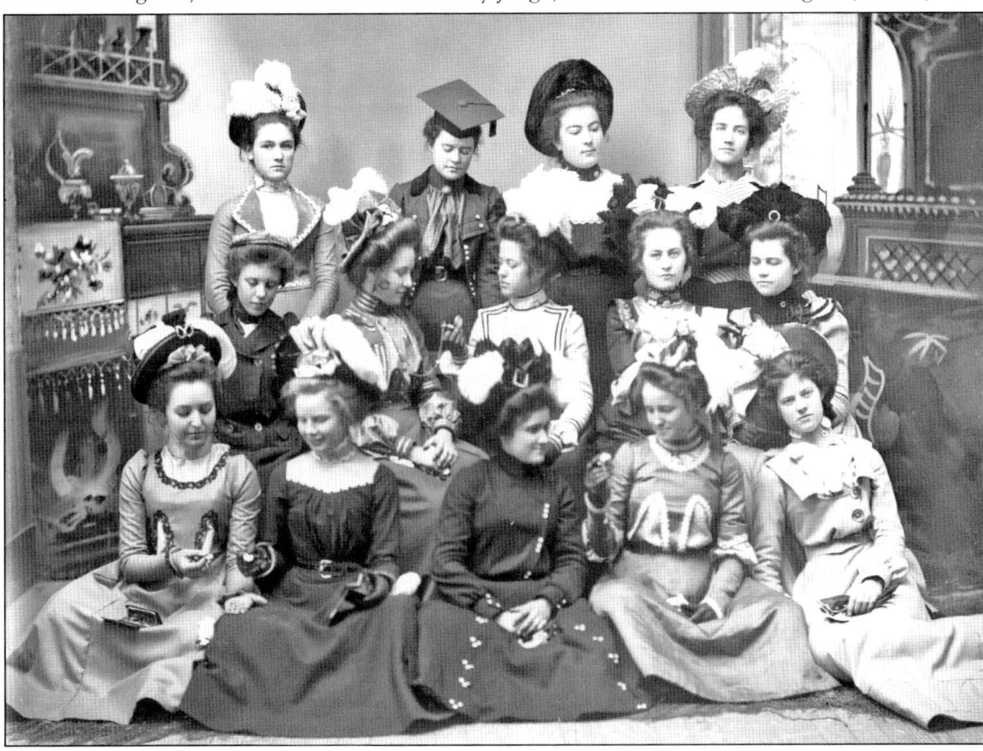

Fourteen young ladies dressed with diverse hats, perhaps in costume, went together to J. M. "Matt" Hays's photography studio to have their portrait made. Striking poses, which feign a lack of concern for the event, they carefully strike an air of nonchalance. (HUM.)

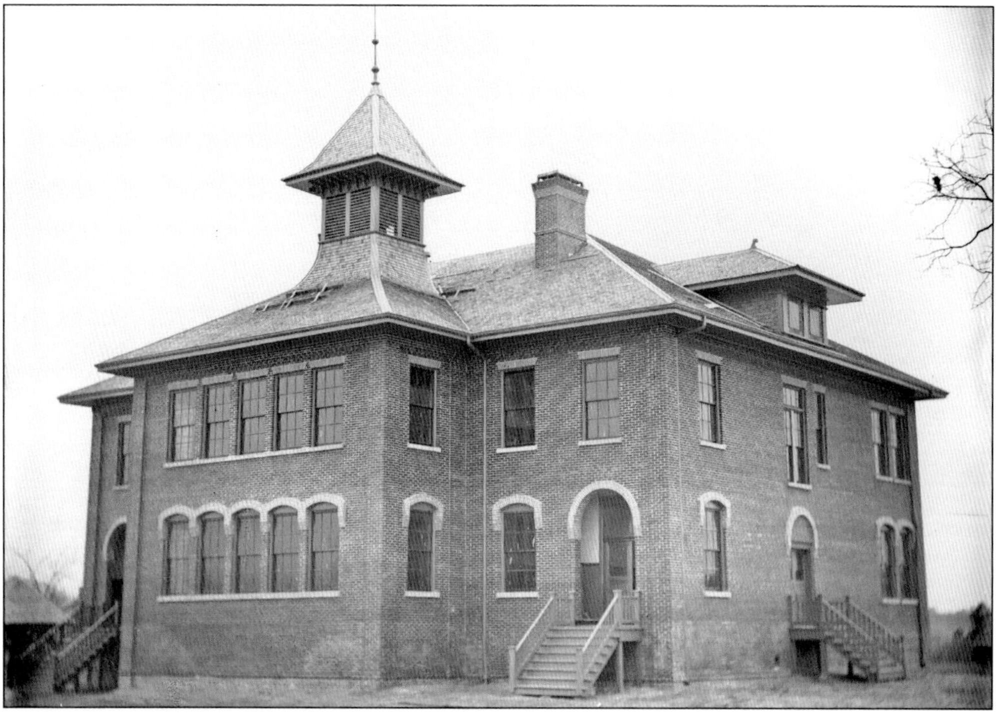

A two-story redbrick structure opened in 1905 as the first building constructed to house all 11 grades of the newly formed Gilmer Independent School District. An election on May 27, 1902, established the first free public school by a vote of 61 to 50. The school board established three campuses: the Gilmer white school using a frame building called "Seminary Hall" at Butler and South Montgomery Streets, a colored school, and a third school at the Dickson Colored Orphans Home. (HUM.)

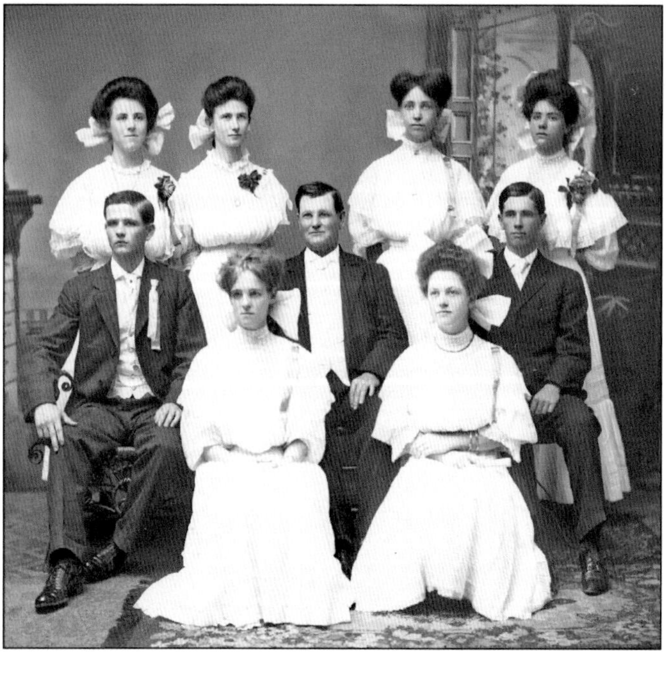

In an era when most people finished their schooling at the eighth grade, to finish high school was required only for entering the law, medicine, or teaching in the upper grades. From left to right are (first row) Curtie Schrum and Annie Thompson; (second row) Joseph Looney Fenlaw Sr., Prof. C. B. Christian (teacher-superintendent), and Vernon Jeptha Stephens; (third row) Mabel Epperson, Manie Ferrell, Eula Mae Cook, and Addie Elzora Pyle. Dr. Fenlaw became a dentist and died before he ever saw his son, J. Looney Fenlaw, M.D. (HUM.)

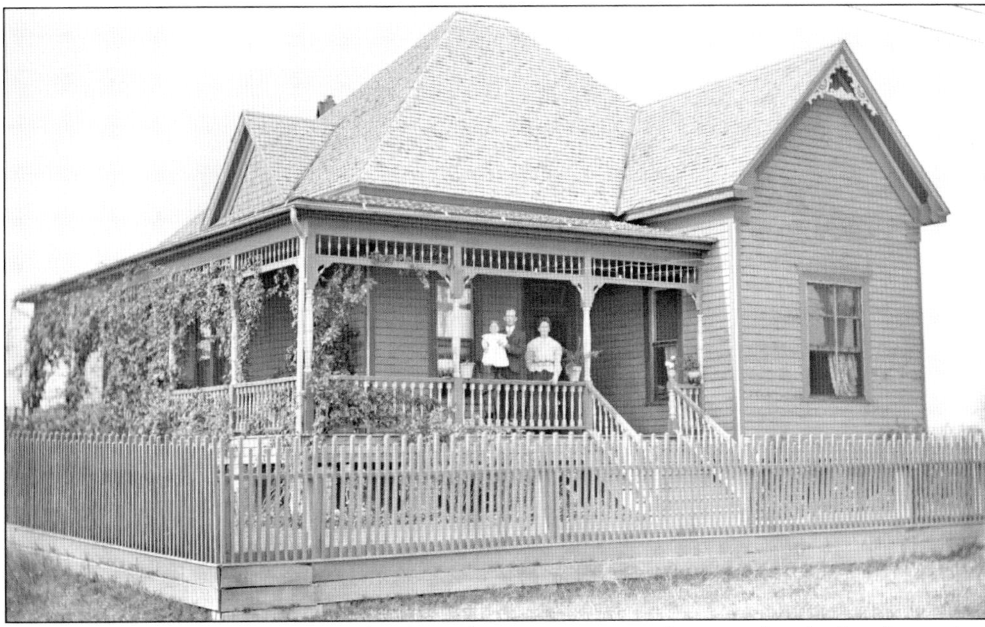

If early residents of Gilmer wanted to keep free-ranging animals away, they had to fence their yards. It was not until 1916 that Gilmer first voted on passing stock laws, and the measure failed by a small margin. The editor of the *Gilmer Mirror* wrote in the report, "If the ladies had been able to vote, it would have passed handily." From left to right, Frank, Effie Buie, and Jerry Marshall pose for this photograph of their new home, which stood at Kaufman and South Montgomery Streets into the 21st century. (HUM.)

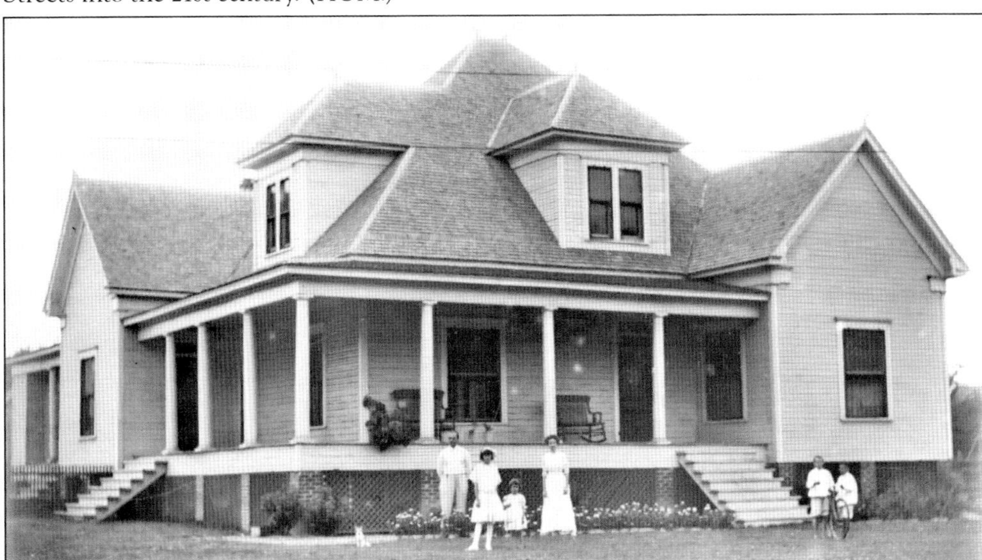

The W. T. Vaughn residence on Titus Street shows the first photographic evidence of a grass lawn with flowers blooming and no fencing. The magnolia tree the family planted still stands at the location of the McKenzie Family Clinic. In the image are, from left to right, William Tilden Vaughn, his daughters Mary Agnes Vaughn (Gill) and Hazel Reed Vaughn (Leard), his wife, Mary Whaler Vaughn, and their sons, William Afton Vaughn and Byron Houlton Vaughn with a bicycle. Tilden Vaughn was the Magnolia Petroleum Company distributor. (HUM.)

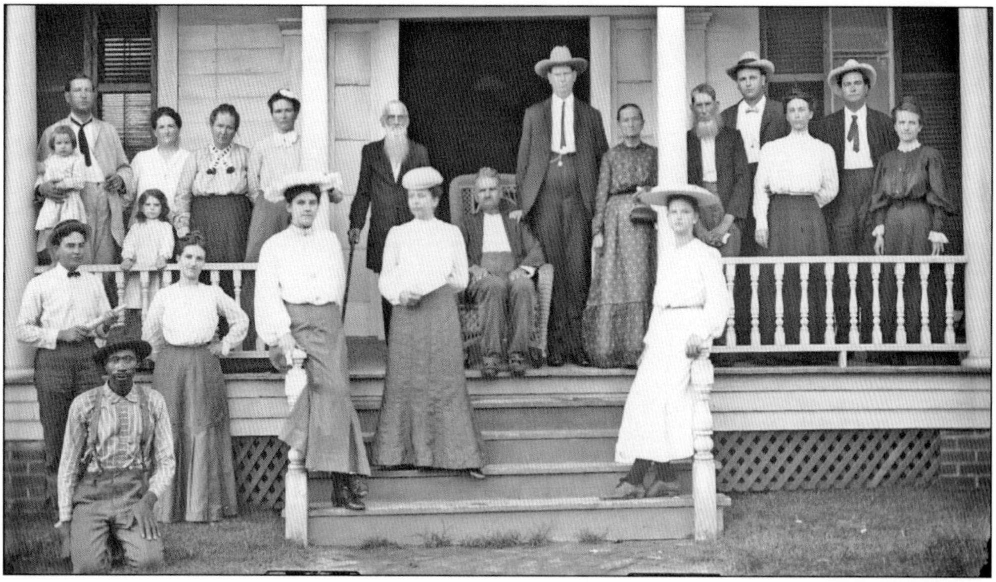

The T. H. Briggs family hosted a family reunion in August 1905. From left to right are (on the porch at left) Lizzie and Beulah Brigs with their parents, T. H. and Nona Briggs, Eliza Ervin, Ora Irvin Montgomery, the Reverend S. R. Chadick, T. H. Briggs Sr., J. J. Briggs, Nancy Niblett, J. M. Niblett, Dr. Charles Gregory, Minnie Gregory, M. B. Briggs, and Cordie Briggs; (in front) V. E. Todd, Ella Briggs Todd, Rosa Seagle Buie, Maggie Irvin, and Mamie Gregory (Harris); (kneeling) Houston Hawkins, the stepfather of Lonnie Turner and Thelma Turner Owens. Reverend Chadick established many Cumberland Presbyterian churches in East Texas. Tom Briggs served as mayor when the streets were covered with gravel, and Barney Briggs owned the first automobile. (HUM.)

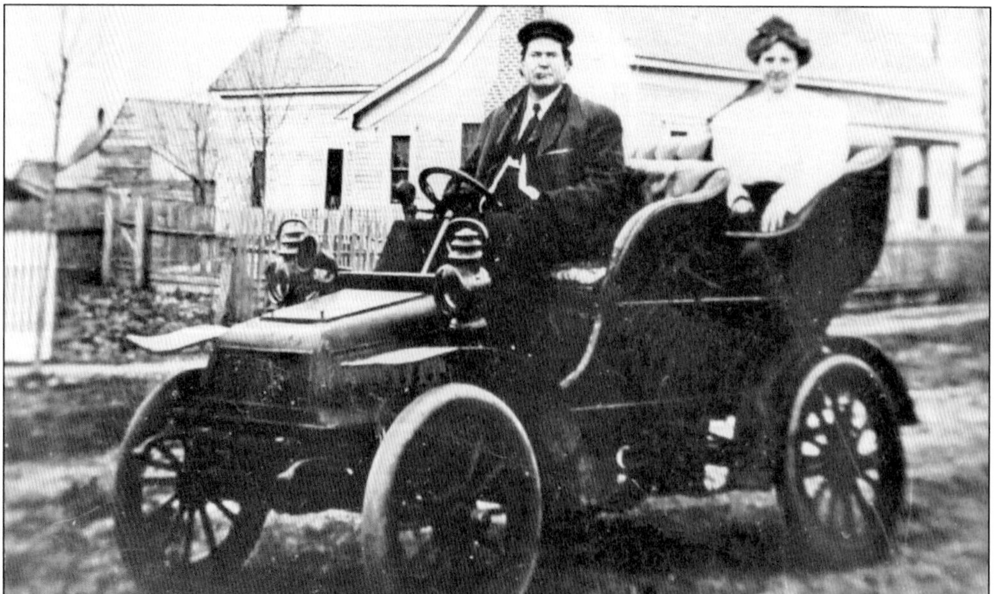

Judge Barney Briggs and his wife, "Miss Cordie," created a sensation when their new automobile arrived in the spring of 1909. The deep sand of Gilmer's streets proved to be an obstacle, requiring a mule team to pull the car to a blacksmith for repairs. (MLK.)

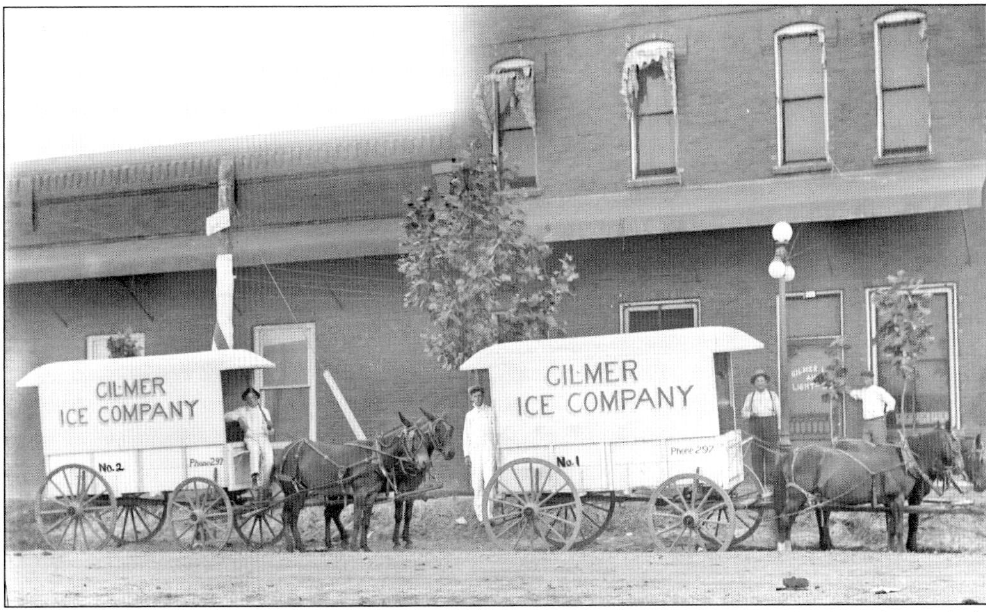

T. C. Mitchell brought electricity to Gilmer in February 1901 when he started the first electric light plant at Taylor and North Trinity Streets. To encourage customers to take the risk of electrifying their home, he put arc lights at his office of the Gilmer Ice and Light Company downtown to show the benefits of lighting at night. (HUM.)

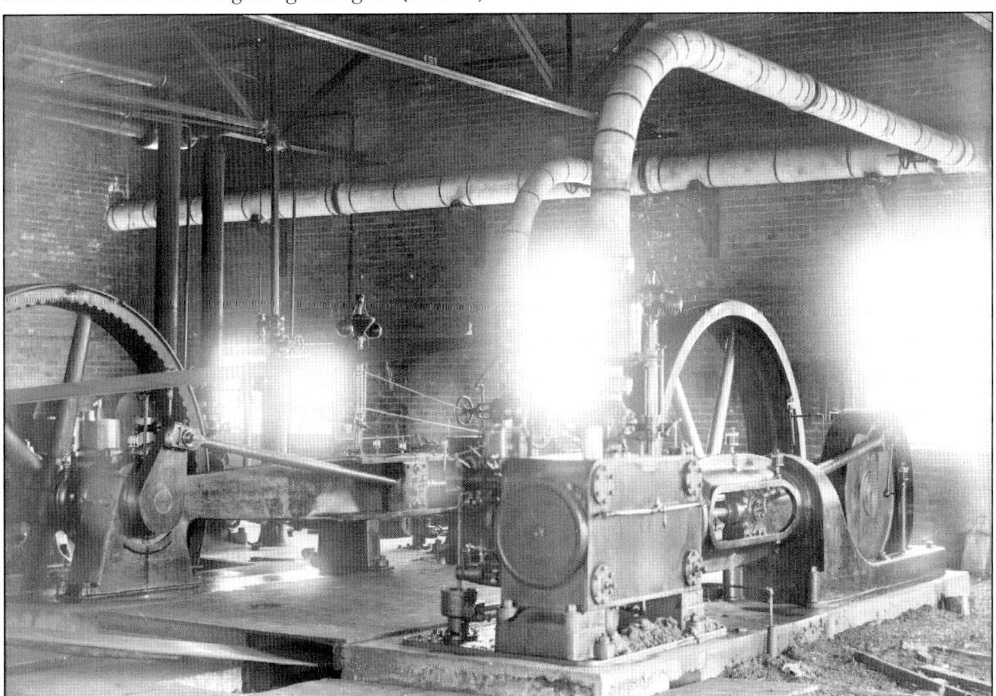

When the electric service proved popular, the Gilmer Ice and Light Company expanded to a new plant located on Mitchell's property west of the railroad, north of town. J. M. Hays photographed these generators in their new facility for the proud owner. (HUM.)

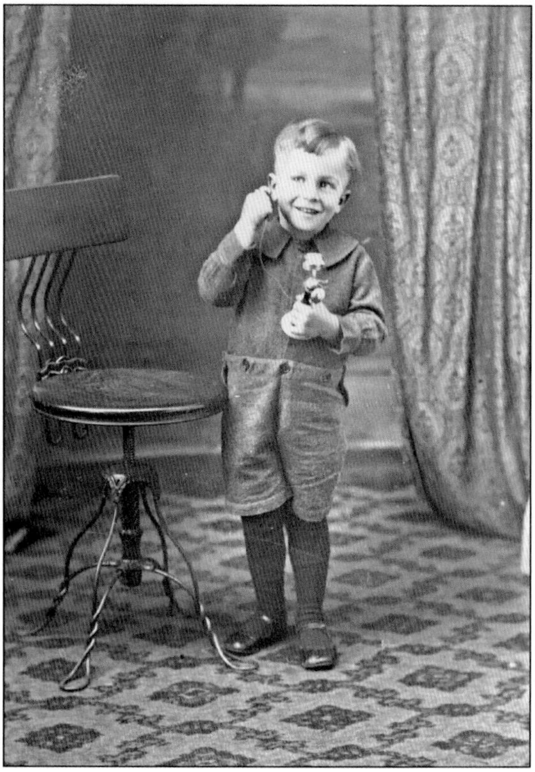

J. G. Wilson's boy enjoys use of a toy telephone during his portrait by J. M. Hays. Calling "Central" with a two- or three-digit number, Gilmer residents could make connections with their friends across town. (HUM.)

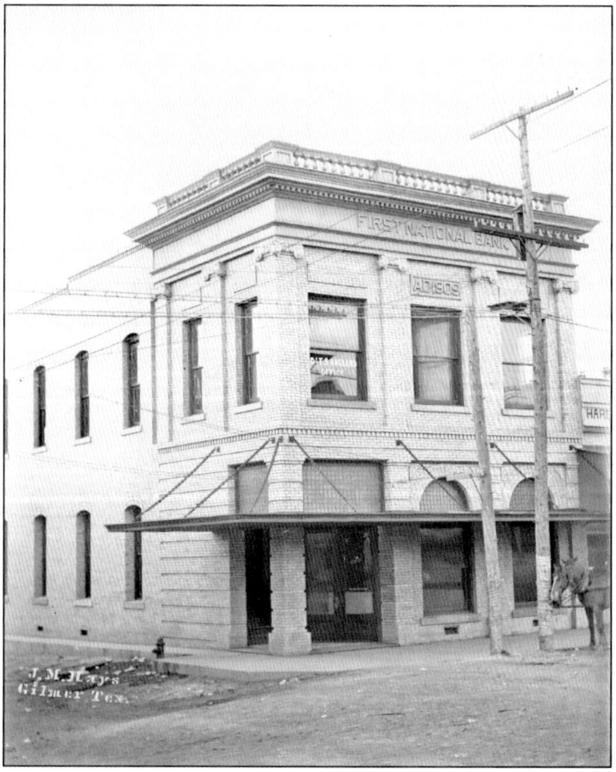

Texans distrusted banks after their experiences starting with the Panic of 1838. It was not until 1909 that new laws made state banks possible. Before that, the First National Bank was the first bank in town. This photograph of the new bank building at Buffalo and Davis Streets points out that Gilmer now had a public water system in place, that horses could be tied up to utility poles, and that the president of the bank, Dr. T. S. Ragland, had his offices over the bank. (HUM.)

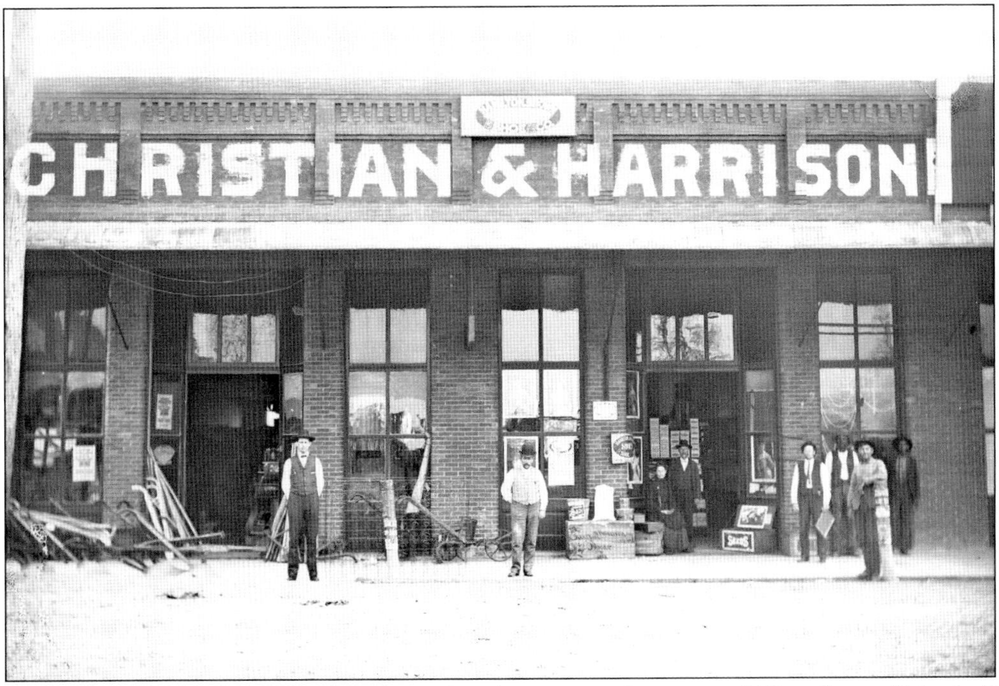

Christian and Harrison was a general merchandise store at the corner of Chandler and Marshall Streets, where some of the wares were on display on the sidewalk for all to see. The store sold Kelly plows, bed springs, tools, corsets for the ladies, and assorted other items. (HUM.)

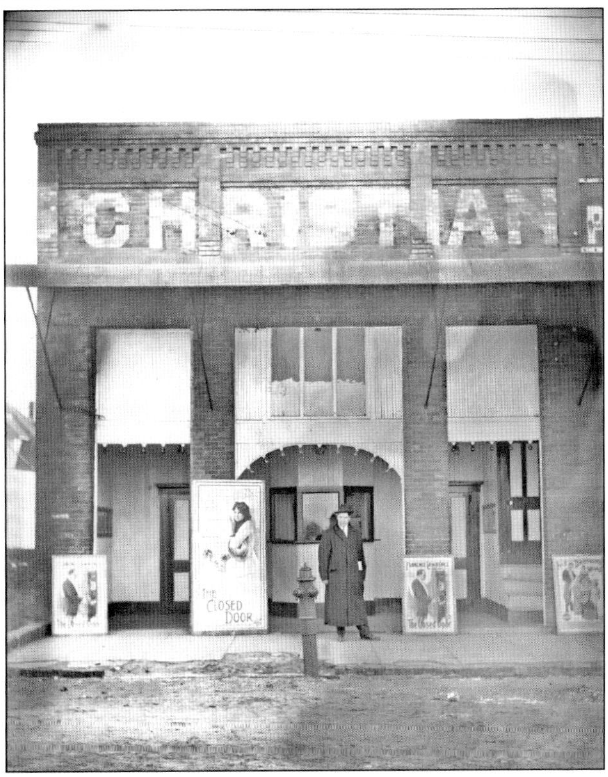

The eastern half of Christian and Harrison became Gilmer's first "picture show," the Rex Theater. Later renamed the Strand under the ownership of Cranfill Cox Sr., this corner remains a source of entertainment after a century under the ownership of D. P. Mooney with Gilmer Cable Television. (HUM.)

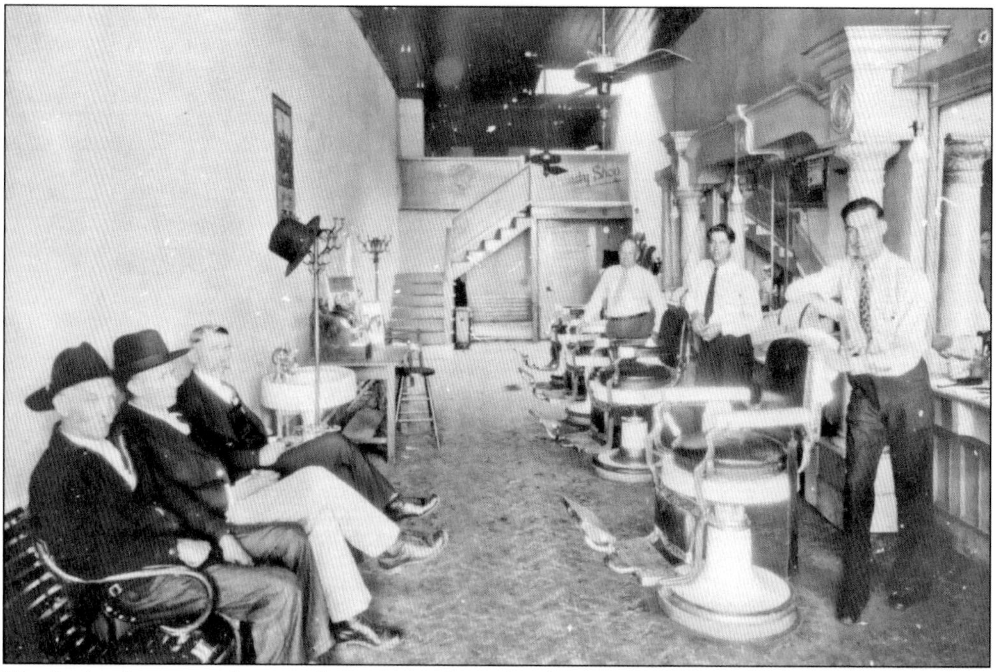

The barbershop served not only a practical use for the gentlemen of yesteryear, but it was also a great place to find out the latest information in politics and the daily happenings of the year. Bennie Bennett is the barber at the back chair. (MLK.)

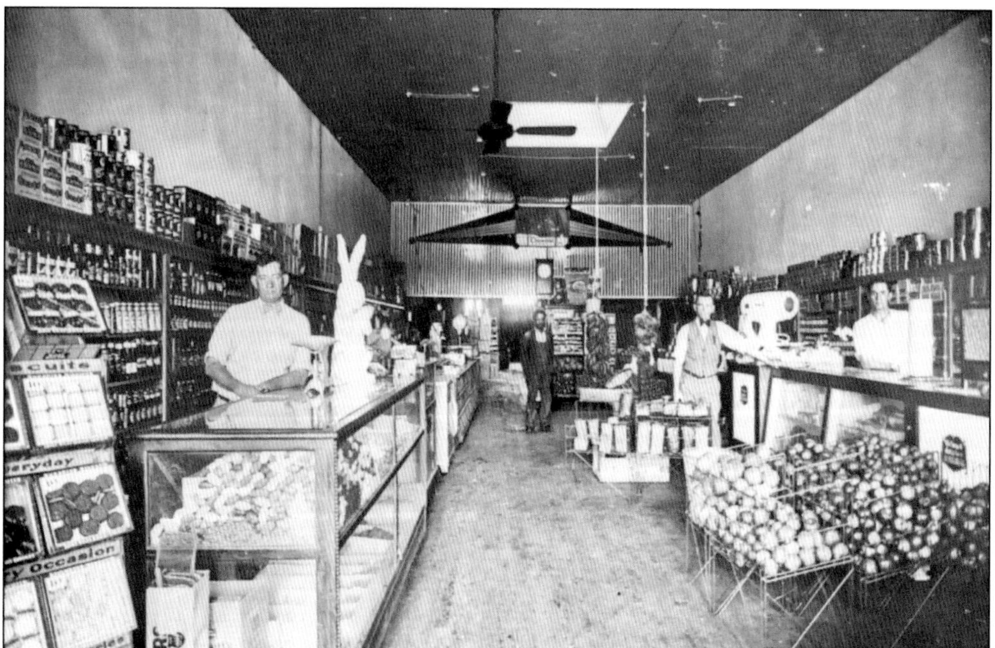

Store owner Vernon Stephens stands by the case where he can weigh the colorful candy eggs in the glass-fronted case at his store on the square. Two workers stand ready to select the merchandise for the customer. Bins contain apples and potatoes. In back is the customary black helper who will sweep up at the end of the day. (MLK.)

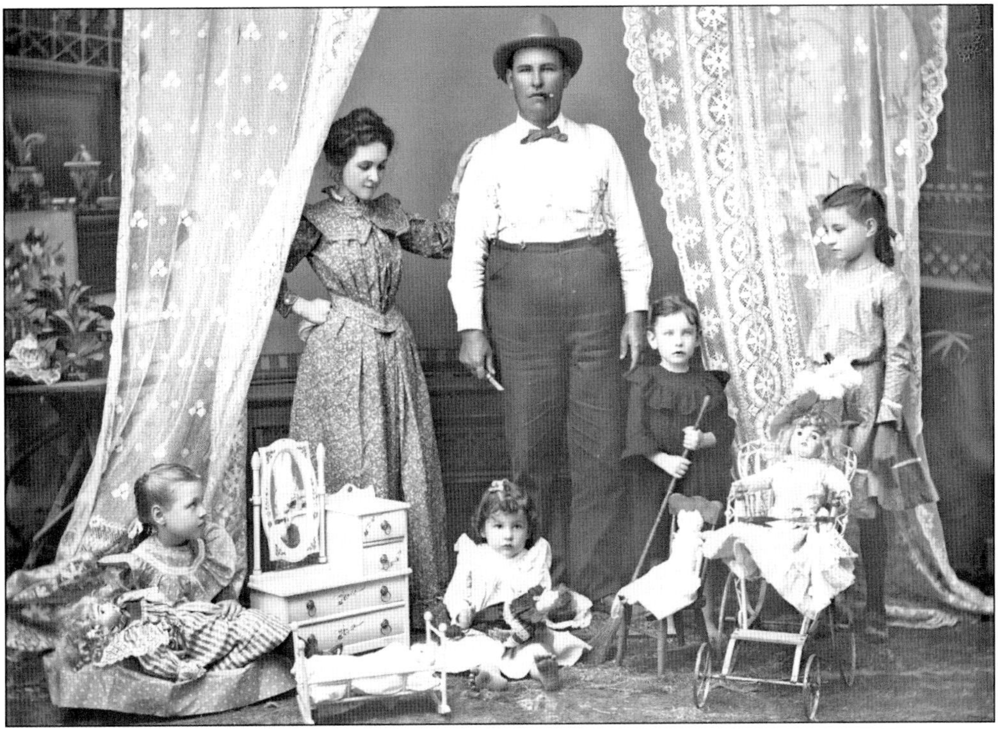

W. E. Crosby and his family came to the Hays Studio for this group portrait. The children brought their favorite toys, including the marvelous chest of drawers and dressing table, with them. The children are, from left to right, Clare Crosby (Murry), Lila Crosby (Baldwin), Boyd Crosby, and unidentified. The children's step-mother is Beulah Shrum Crosby. (HUM.)

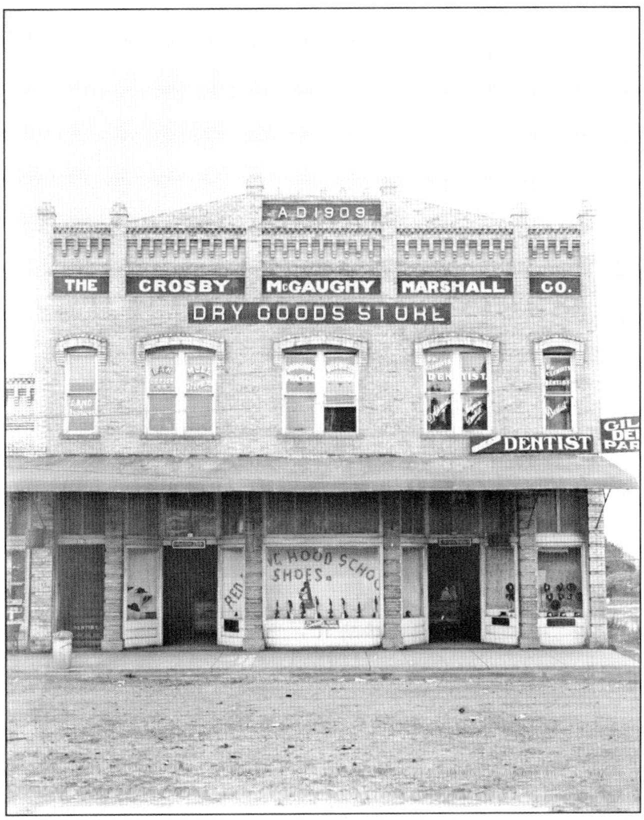

W. E. Crosby was a partner with H. P. McGaughy and J. W. Marshall in this two-story dry-goods business on the north side of the square at the corner of Buffalo and Titus Streets. A dentist, a business college, and M. G. Mell, an attorney, were all upstairs. (HUM.)

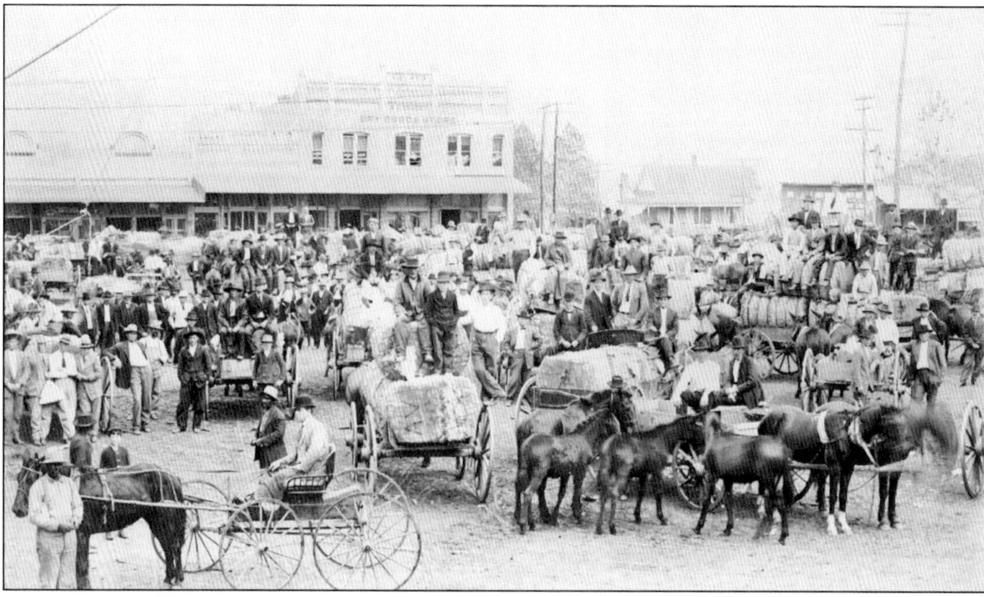

When the cotton crop came in in 1910, the wagons filled the open spaces for the traditional photograph. Old-timers sometimes said one could cross the square from one side to the other without touching the ground on peak harvest days. Everyone drove where they found empty space. Dividing the road between right and left driving came later. (HUM.)

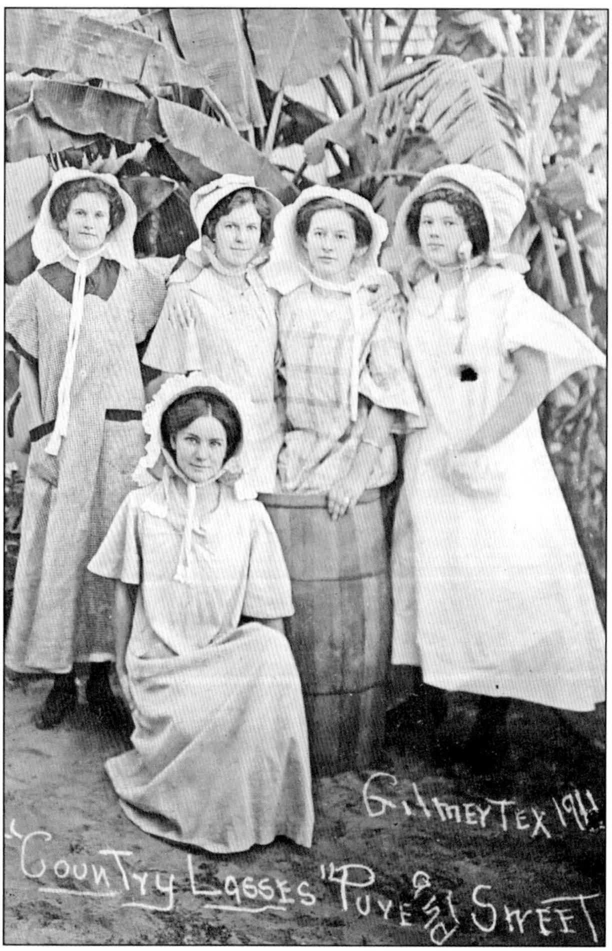

" 'Country Lasses' Pure and Sweet Gilmer, Tex 1911" reads the caption on this portrait of (seated) Pope Daniels and (standing, from left to right) Dora Swann, Sibyl McClelland, Kathleen Nelson, and Mildred Stapp.

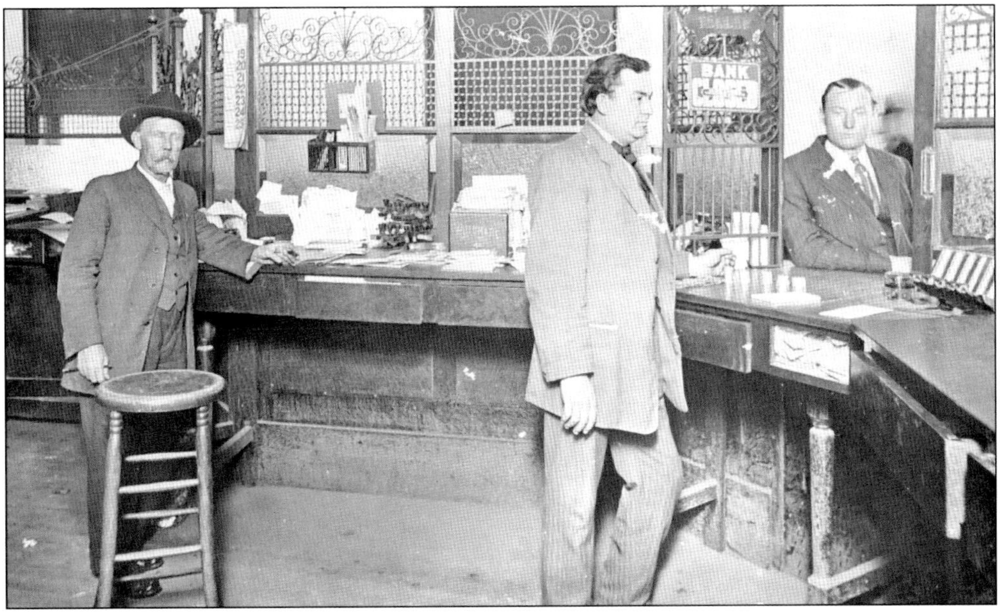

V. E. Todd stands at the teller's window in the Farmers and Merchants National Bank on the south side of the square. Todd was the cashier of the second bank in Gilmer from 1909 to 1911, when it was a single-story bank. N. M. Harrison, the bank vice president, stands at left. (HUM.)

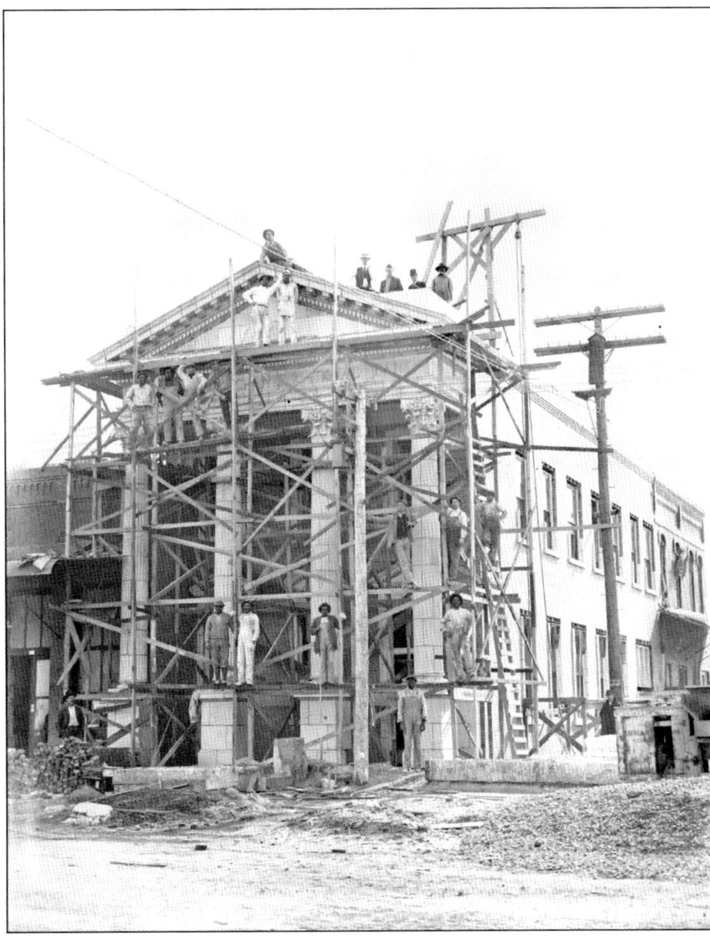

Even after the Commercial Lumber Company left town and business was slowing on the Marshall and East Texas Railroad, the building boom continued in Gilmer. After being successful as a single-story bank, the Farmers and Merchants National Bank in 1911 expanded into the two-story building that graces the square to this day. (HUM.)

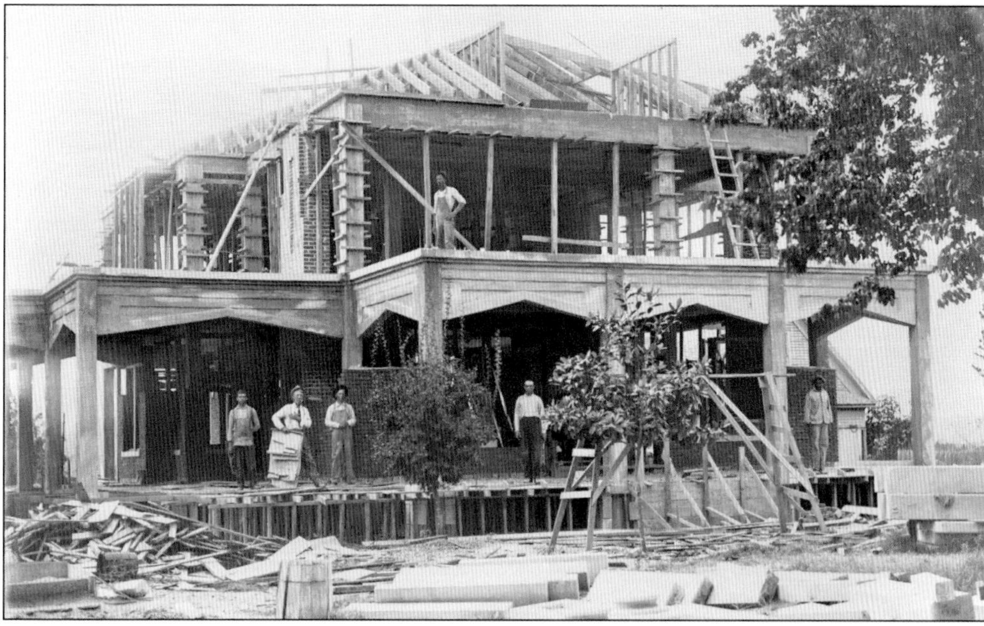

Four blocks west of the bank, at Tyler and Montgomery Streets, W. C. Barnwell began constructing his new home, a project that took three years, from 1912 to 1915. Barnwell was a strong promoter of diversification in agriculture and in growing sweet potatoes for a cash crop. His wife, "Miss Mittie," was the organist at the Methodist church into her 80s. They lived in their new home with their daughter, Evelyn. (HUM.)

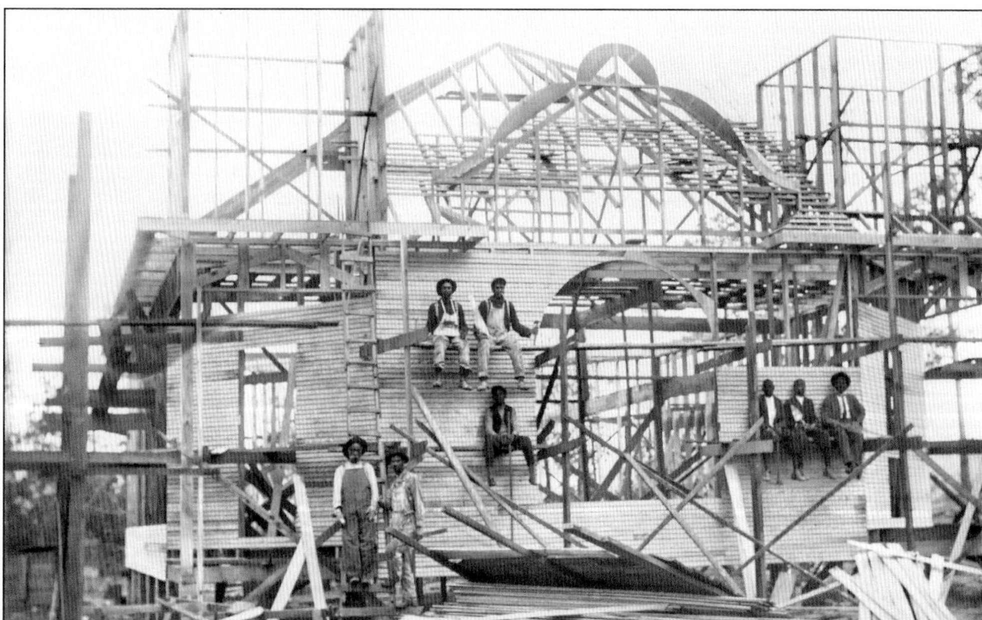

South of town, the African Americans were constructing a new home for Gilgal Baptist Church. The oldest church for blacks in the community, Gilgal was established in 1867 by a freed slave, John Baptist. While serving as pastor of Gilgal, the Reverend W. L. Dickson established an orphanage in Gilmer. (HUM.)

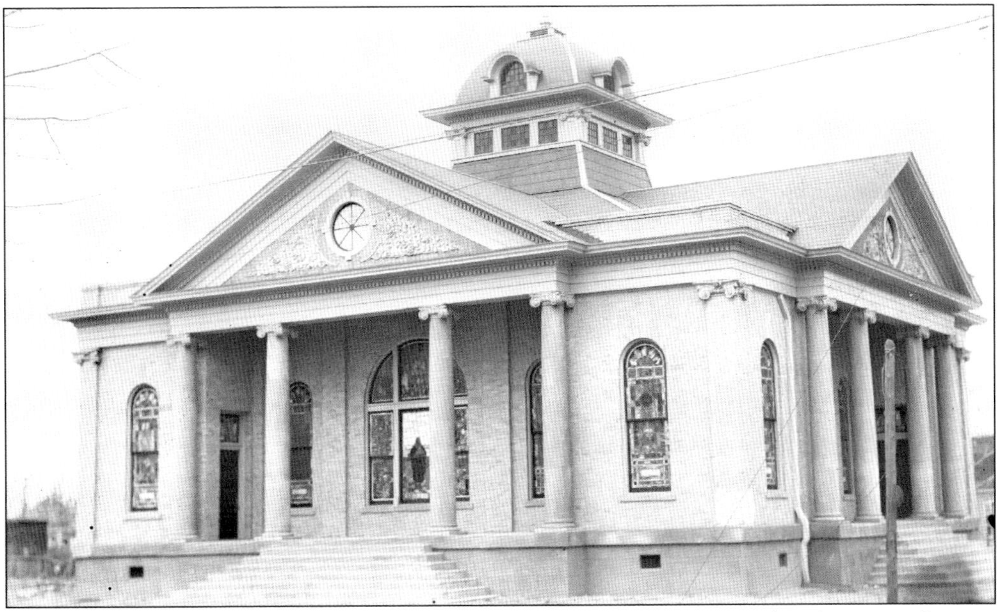

At the close of the January 3, 1909, service, the deacons of First Baptist Church proposed a new house of worship. The lot at Buffalo and North Trinity Streets, northwest of their current building, was purchased for $3,000. Architect George Lindsey designed the Greek Revival–style building that W. H. Pugh and Company constructed for $16,500. (HUM.)

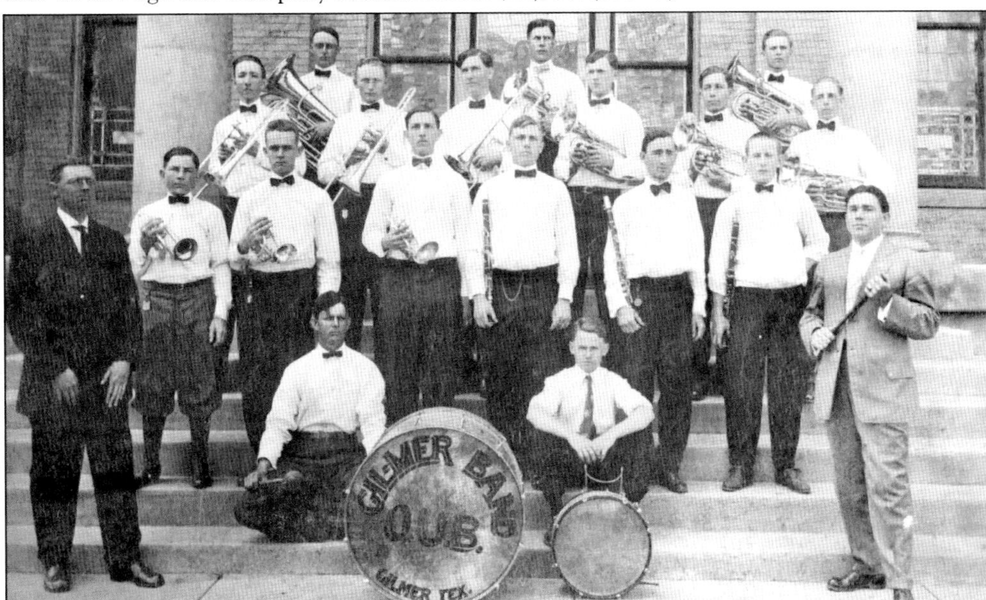

Our United Brotherhood Band in Gilmer served as a testament to the interest Gilmerites have long had in music. As exemplified in the musical *The Music Man*, travelling salesmen helped establish town bands. In front of the group stands T. H. Alcon, promoter, standing on left, and Joe Balero, director. Also pictured are, from left to right, (first row) J. M. Taylor and Dempey Brady; (second row) Frances Gipson, Sam Schrum, Sam Still, O. E. Oliver, Dr. ? Haney, and Claud Hart; (third row) Nolan Coe, Willis Reed McLendon, Will Clardy, Ed Buie, Ed Glezen, and Frank Jones; (fourth row) Lyn Moore, Happy P. Wright, and Gene Glazen. (MLK.)

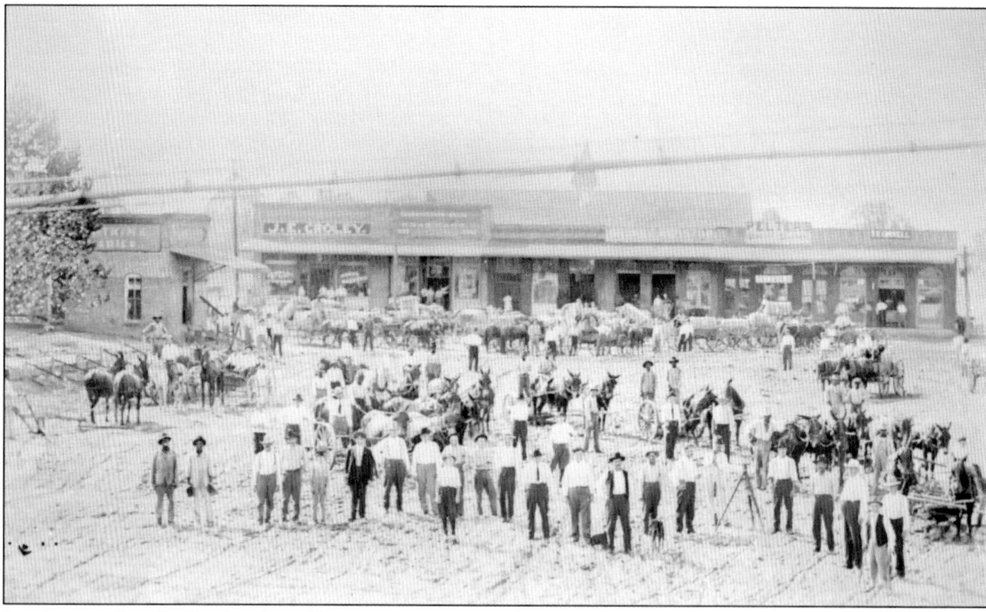

In 1914, under the leadership of Mayor Tom Briggs, Gilmer decided to improve the traction around the square. The surveyors and the graders are seen in front of the photograph; teams for hauling the gravel from east of town await instructions. The one-story building on the square housed the post office, and the long roof behind the business on the south side of the square stands as a silent witness to a major livery stable on Henderson Street. (MLK.)

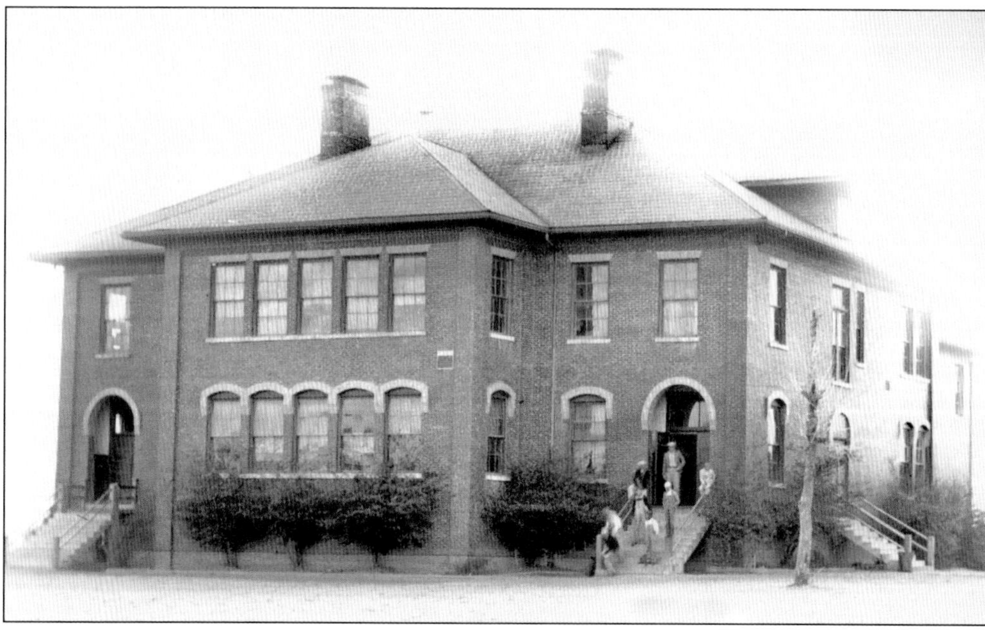

Boys hang out by the boys' entrance to the Gilmer Ward School with one about to slide down the railing. With the introduction of compulsory education laws and increased interest in attending high school, the school district had to consider additional capacity to meet their needs. By 1911, enough students had enrolled that an additional wing was added to the building, which still housed all grades. (HUM.)

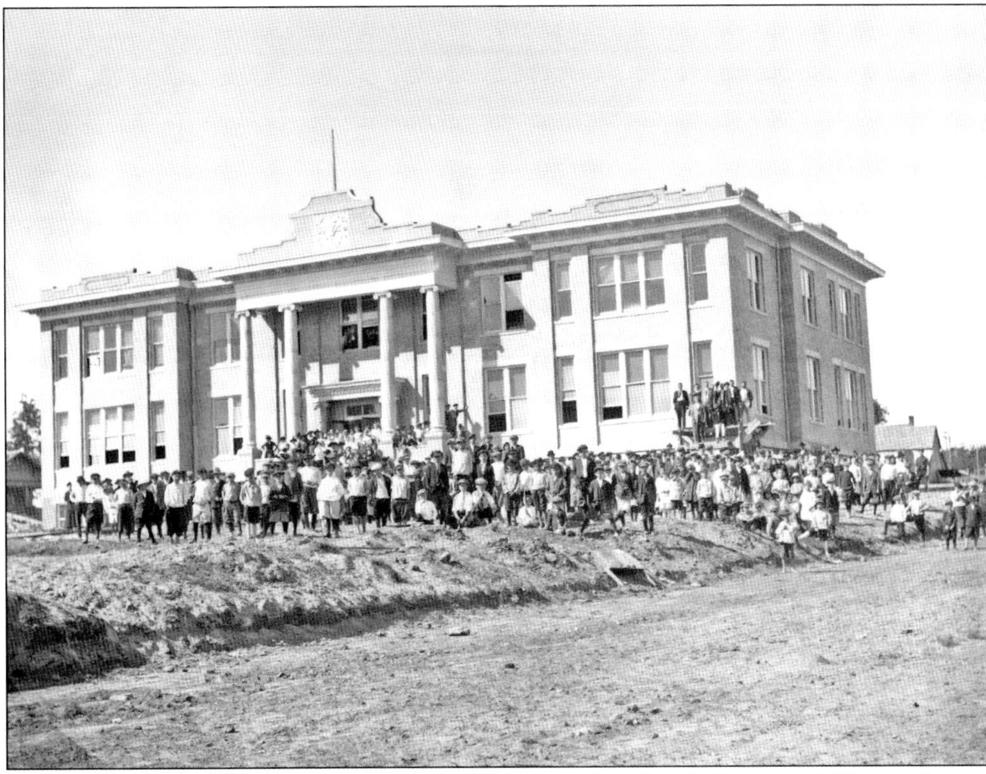

In 1915, people crowd up to the new Gilmer High School on South Trinity and Warren Streets. With Masons about to lay the cornerstone, the crowd turns to face J. M. Hays to document the event. The new building included an auditorium on the top story, new blackboards on the walls, and domestic science rooms for the girls to learn sewing and cooking. (HUM.)

Just before the new high school was built, these boys participated on the 1914 Gilmer baseball team. In the second row, third from the left, is William Berry Winn, and next to him is Curtis Hart. In the third row at center is John Colcman Winn. (HUM.)

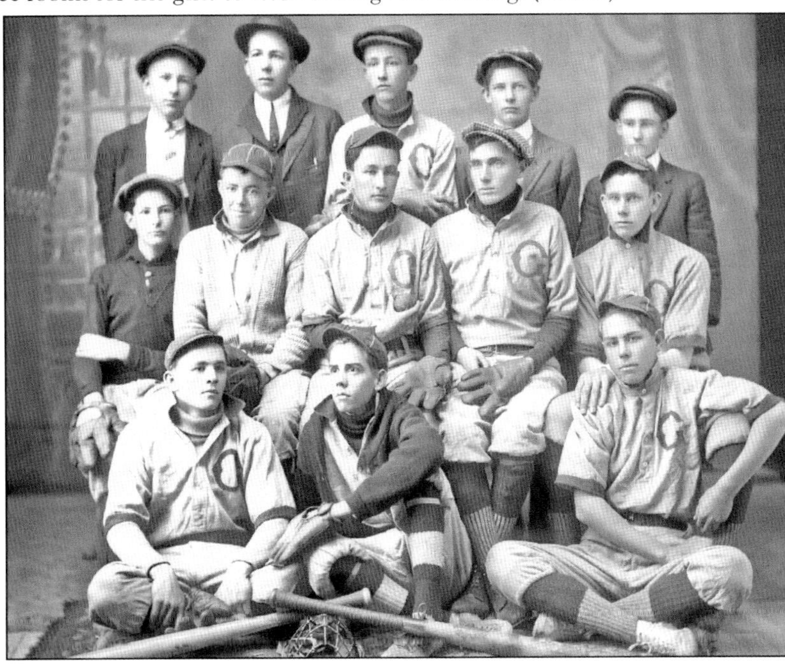

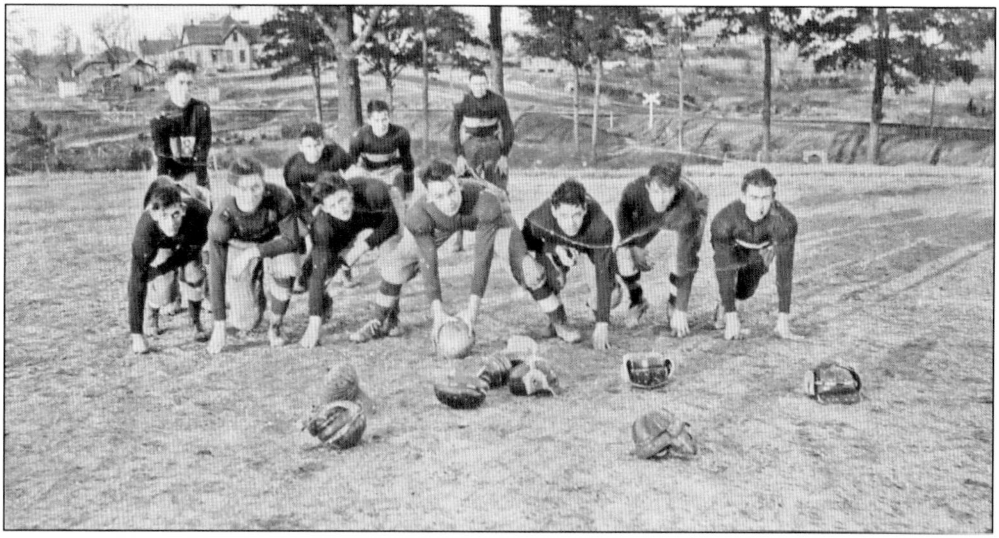

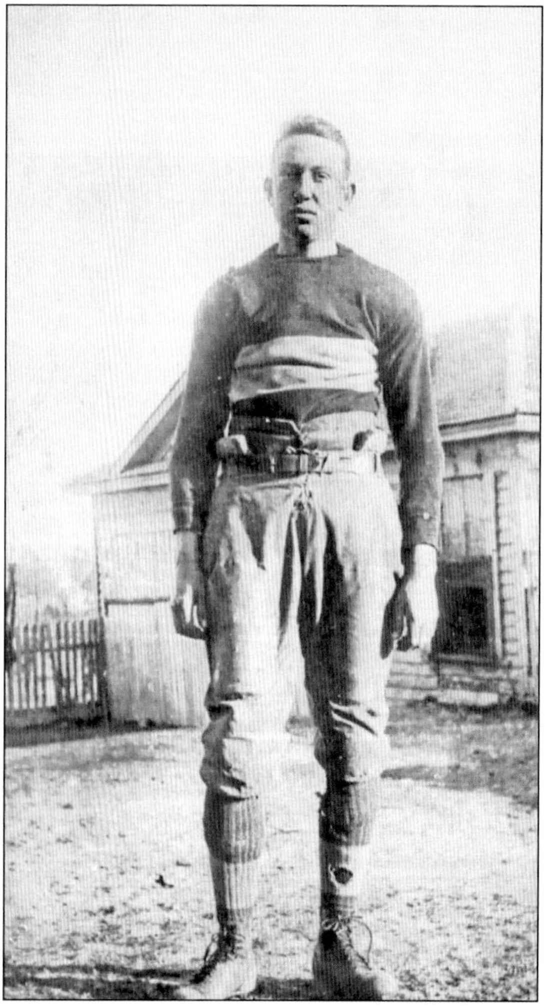

To the north of the new high school, where the Trinity Street Gymnasium now stands, the Gilmer football team of 1915 poses for the cameraman. Note the floppy leather helmets, which the boys have tossed aside while the photograph is made. Today dense greenery shrouds the view from the campus to the intersection of Butler and Trinity Streets. A park would be created with a swimming pool in the space in the left background. (MLK.)

In an era before the coach was a college graduate, often a recent graduate was the coach. Danily Warren was captain of the 1915 team, and after graduation, he remained in Gilmer, where he was a successful farmer and businessman. (MLK.)

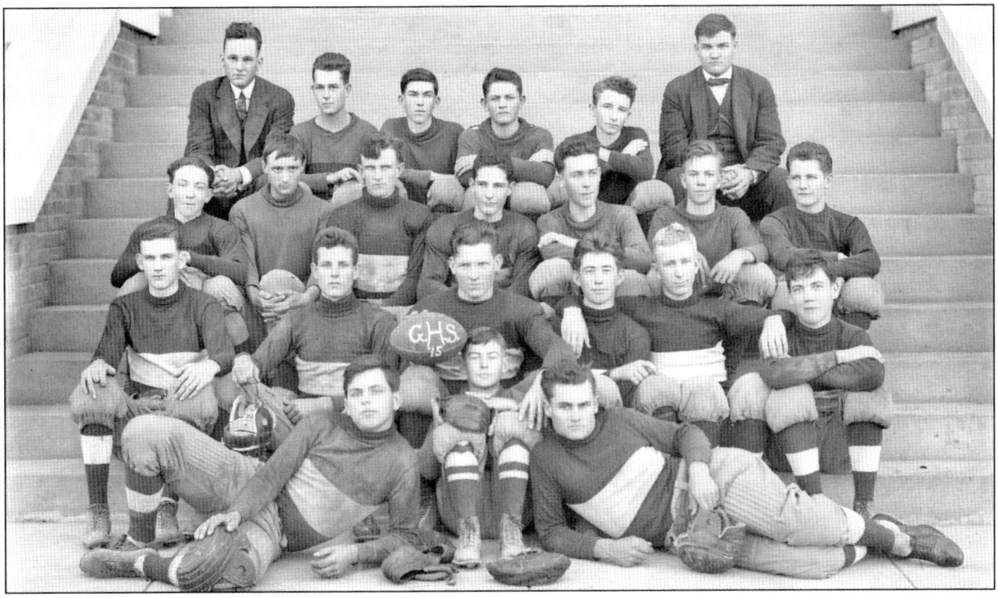

The Gilmer High School football team of 1915–1916 was coached by J. W. David, fourth row, far right. Eddie Marshall, front and center, was the mascot. The players were, from left to right, (first row) Howard Hart and A. B. Bullard; (second row) Newell Bennett, Lincoln McKinley, Jerome Reid, Jack Hogg, Carroll Connell, and William "Buster" Billingsley; (third row) Danily Warren, Oscar Douphrate, Grady McPeek, Raymond Crosby, Walter Roberts, Louis Harris, and Hugh Glezen; (fourth row) J. R. Reed, Robert Littlefield, Lawrence Rutledge, Glyn Stephens, and Hilton McClelland. (HUM.)

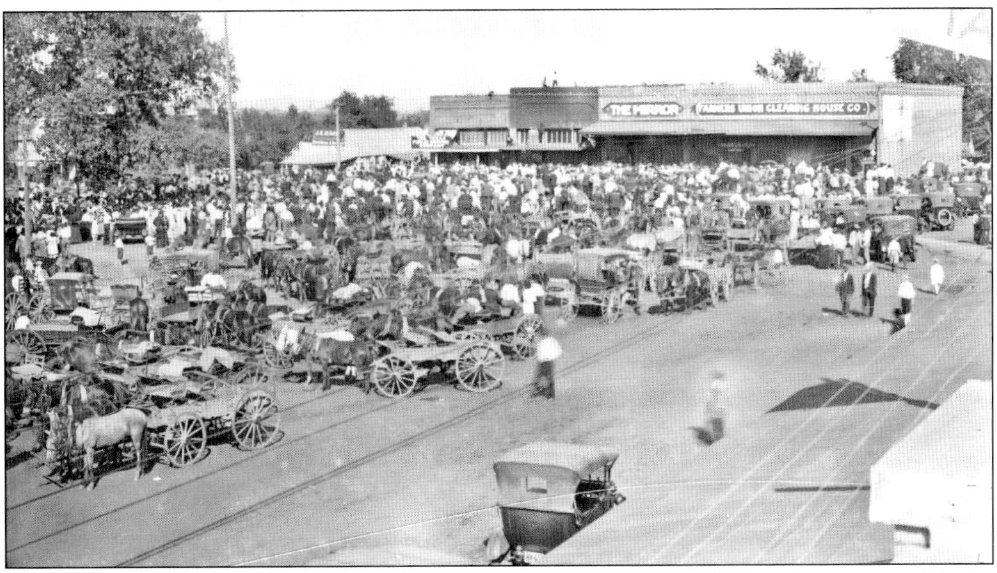

People crowded toward the northeast corner of the square in 1917 when a drawing on a Trades Day was held to give away a free automobile. In the eight years since Barney Briggs brought the first automobile to Gilmer, the new vehicle's popularity had increased. At least 10 are counted in this photograph, which was made from the roof of the Farmers and Merchants National Bank. In earlier histories, this image has been mislabeled as a Prohibition rally, but researching the original Hays negatives pinpointed the correct interpretation. (HUM.)

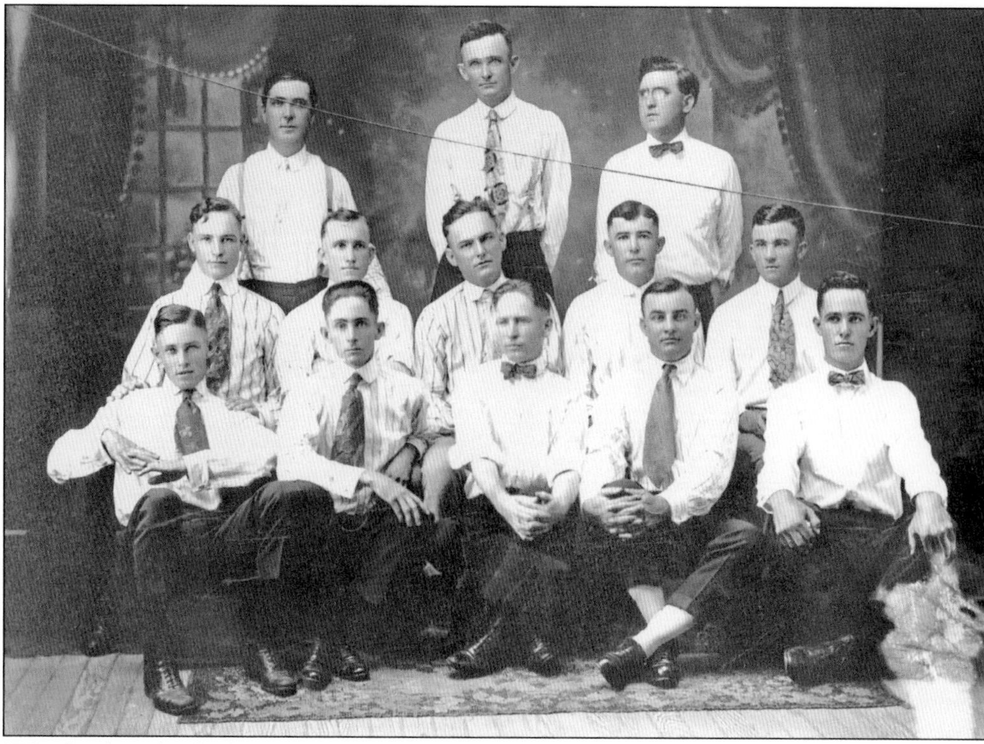

"The first bunch of volunteers" was the label J. M. Hays used to catalog this photograph of young men from Upshur County who came with the World War I draft board to the studio. Pictured from left to right are (first row) Leo Eberhart, Frank L. Futrell, Leo Hart, Ross McKissick and unidentified; (second row) Elwyn Crosby, Croley Cook, J. R. Reed, Alex Glass, and Frank Smith; (third row) the draft board members, Sam Waghalter, Dr. H. J. Childress, and Lewis G. Martin. McKissick came from Diana and was the first to be killed in the fighting in France in September 1918. (HUM.)

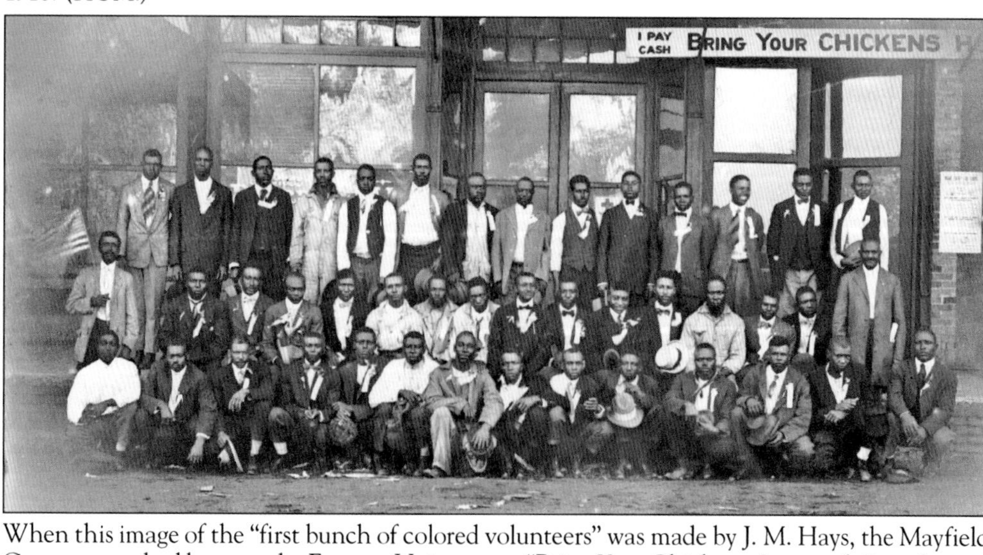

When this image of the "first bunch of colored volunteers" was made by J. M. Hays, the Mayfield Grocery store had become the Farmers Union store. "Bring Your Chickens, I pay cash," proclaimed the sign on the building. (HUM.)

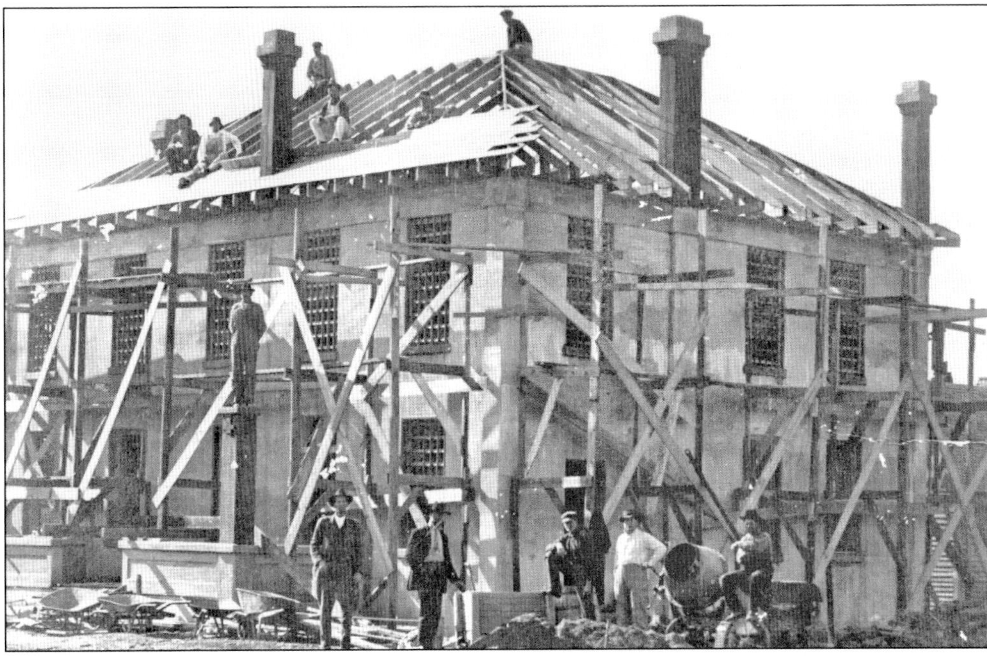

Joe Pickitt wrote on the back of this postcard in the collection of the Historic Upshur Museum about his work on constructing a new jail for the county on Silver Alley. He told how he spent $400 for the concrete mixer, but it was worth it. Pickitt is seen seated on the mixer at the far right, with Jim Denton to his left. Others standing are Dady Phillips, Jim Mechon, and Jackson Clayton (on the column). Carpenters were on the roof. Pickitt declared he would clear only $150 on the job, with $800 invested in tools for the job. (HUM.)

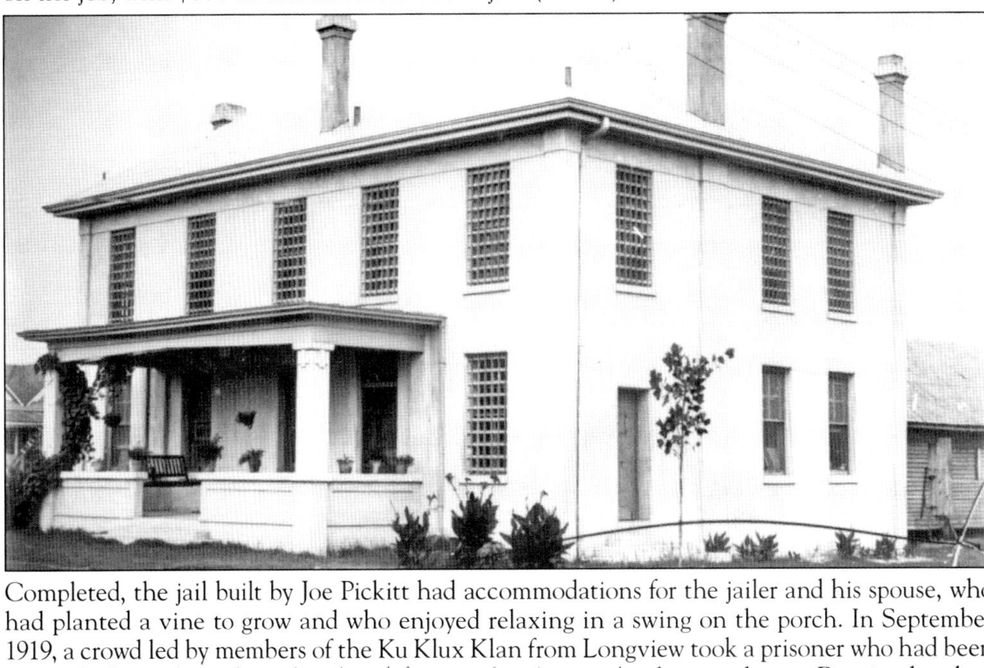

Completed, the jail built by Joe Pickitt had accommodations for the jailer and his spouse, who had planted a vine to grow and who enjoyed relaxing in a swing on the porch. In September 1919, a crowd led by members of the Ku Klux Klan from Longview took a prisoner who had been accused of rape from the jail and took him to the elm tree by the courthouse. Despite the pleas of Judge R. W. Simpson, the mob lynched the man. (HUM.)

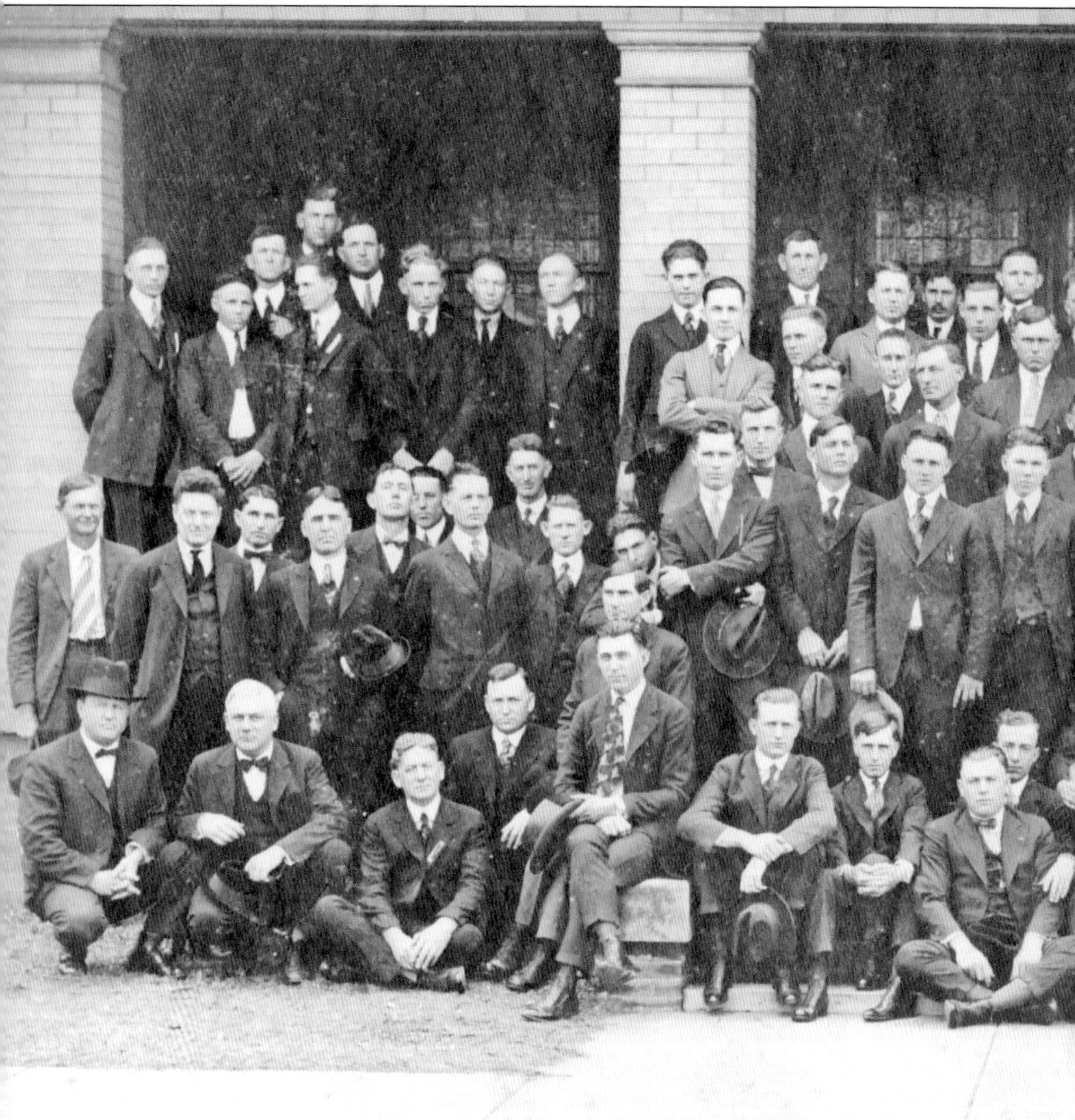

First Methodist men of the Wesley Bible Class posed at the conclusion of a Sunday school campaign held in 1921. From left to right are (first row) Will Chandler, Dr. J. C. Wood, Bob Barnwell, Croley Cook, Roy Cook, H. M. Prater, Nat Harrison, Rex Moughon, Roger Croley (behind Rex Moughon), Prof. ? Dodson, Edwin Aldredge, Frank Jones, unidentified, J. E. Boykin, Fred Hamm, Weldon Wheeler, Buck Childress, Chris Abney, J. B. Arnsby (behind unidentified man with hat on knee); (second row) Esta Farrow, H. P. McGaughy, Bill Bryce, Clyde Coleman, Wes Bryce, unidentified, Charlie Hill, George Anderson, Charlie Rider, Jake Smith (behind Roy Cook), Garland Patterson (behind Smith), unidentified, Will Smith, Oliver Yocom, L. Bellamy, two unidentified, Aubrey Foster, Joe Latch, Willie Still, Alvin Spencer, unidentified, Max Croley, Milton Greer Mell (in front of Croley), Jim Still, Henry Mings, Oscar Stropp, Reece Barnwell, Aubrey McClelland, J. E. Stephens, Dee Magrill, and J. E. Daley. The four men at the center are John H. Pearson, unidentified, Nolan Coe, and the Reverend Allen Tooke, pastor. The third row

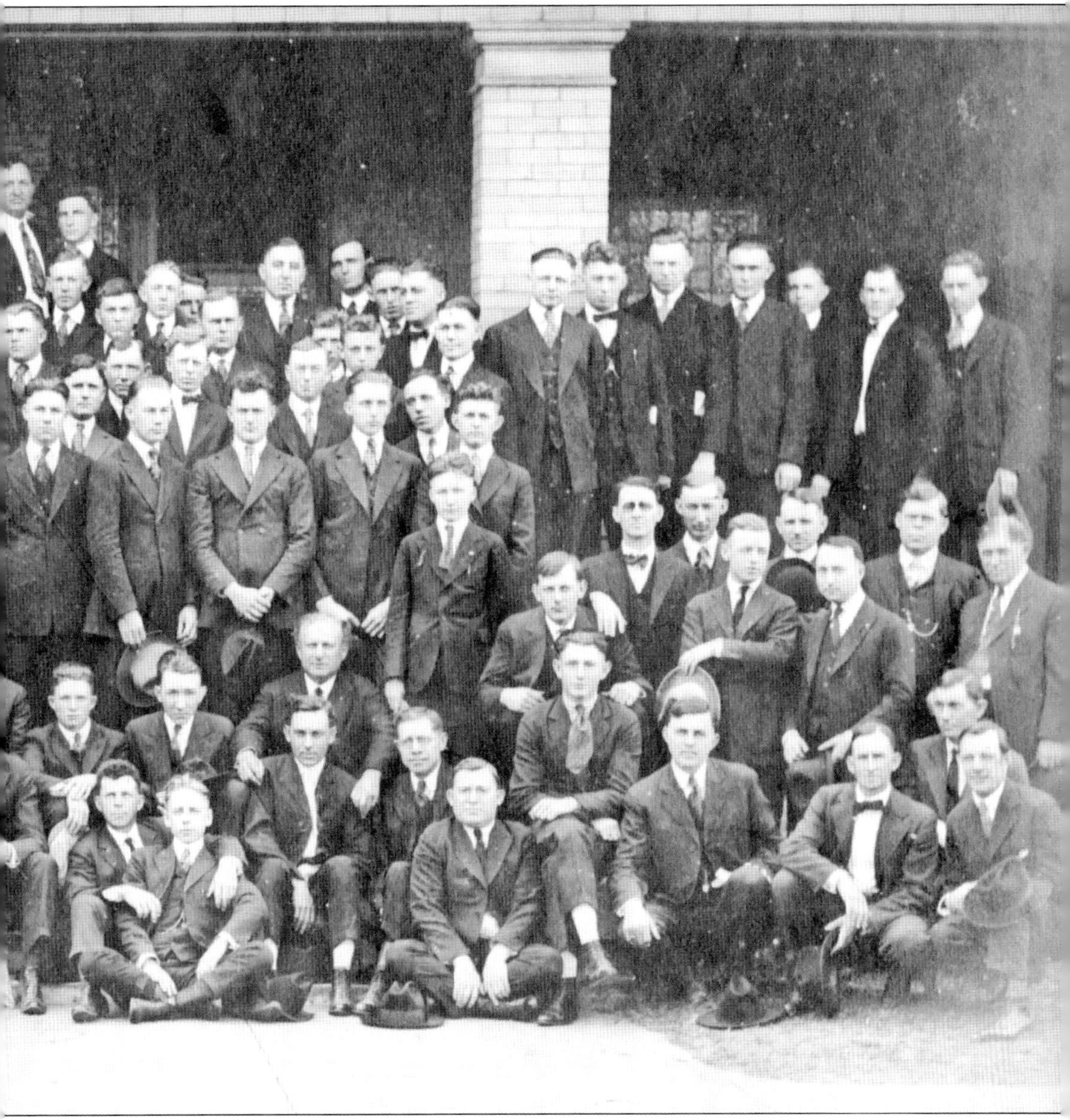

begins with Henry Lucas, arms folded, in front of pillar at left, Gene Glezen, unidentified, Leo Hart, Cay Richardson, unidentified, Lee Mings, Tom Bledsoe, Horace Bledsoe, Key Jones, Ross Buie, two unidentified, and Dr. E. C. McAlpin. Third from left, back row, with head turned, is Buford Robertson. The two men to his left and above him are unidentified. Above his left shoulder is Pete Chandler. Continuing left is Hugh "Babe" Jones, Fred Hogg, Fletcher Lovell, unidentified, Floyd Carroll, Edgar Croley, Granville Glezen, Len Moore, John Chandler (center, top), and E. R. Knowles. The two men in front of Knowles are unidentified. Next are Reece Buie, two unidentified, Jerry Dean, Eddie Moughon, Tom Baxter, Leo Eberhart, Hugh Glezen, unidentified, Jack Hogg, Hugh Brawley, Lee Quinn, Henry Lee Davis, Albert Tucker, and unidentified. Some of these men also attended gatherings of the Ku Klux Klan, which met in the basement of the church, and were witnesses of the lynching in 1919. The Klan was reaching the height of its popularity in 1921. (GM.)

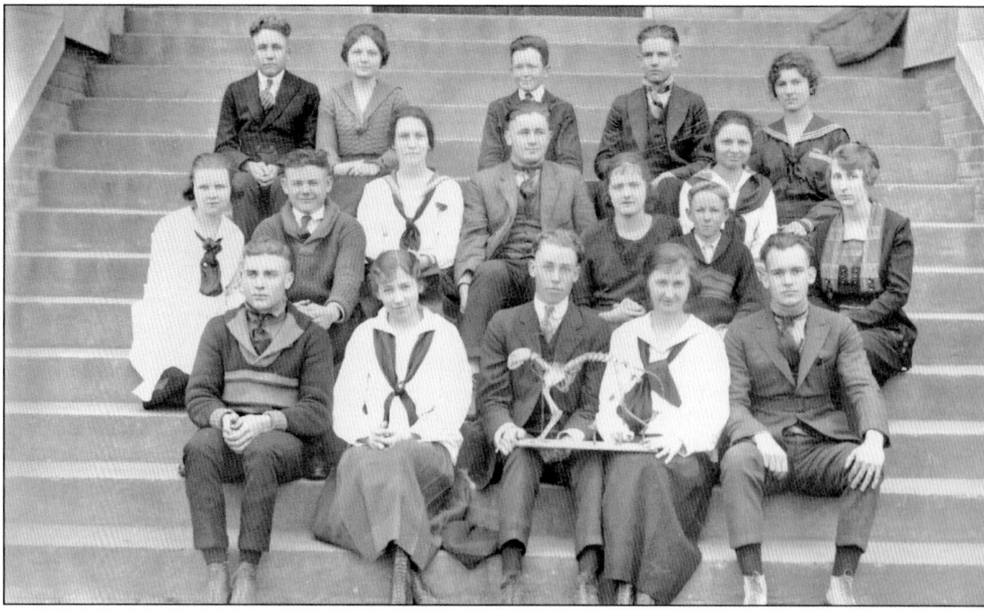

The Gilmer High School Biology Club for the school year 1919–1920 pose on the front steps. From left to right are (first row) Hardy Hart, Leta Moughon, Malcolm Smith, Cecile Ragland, and J. T. King; (second row) ? Lockhart, Milton Stephens, Vera Mitchell, Gus Morris, ? Childress, Ross Hogg, Rosalee Herring, and Virge Connell (sponsor); (third row) Leon Walker, Elizabeth Harrison, Truman Warren, Frank Marshall, and Laverne Busby. (HUM.)

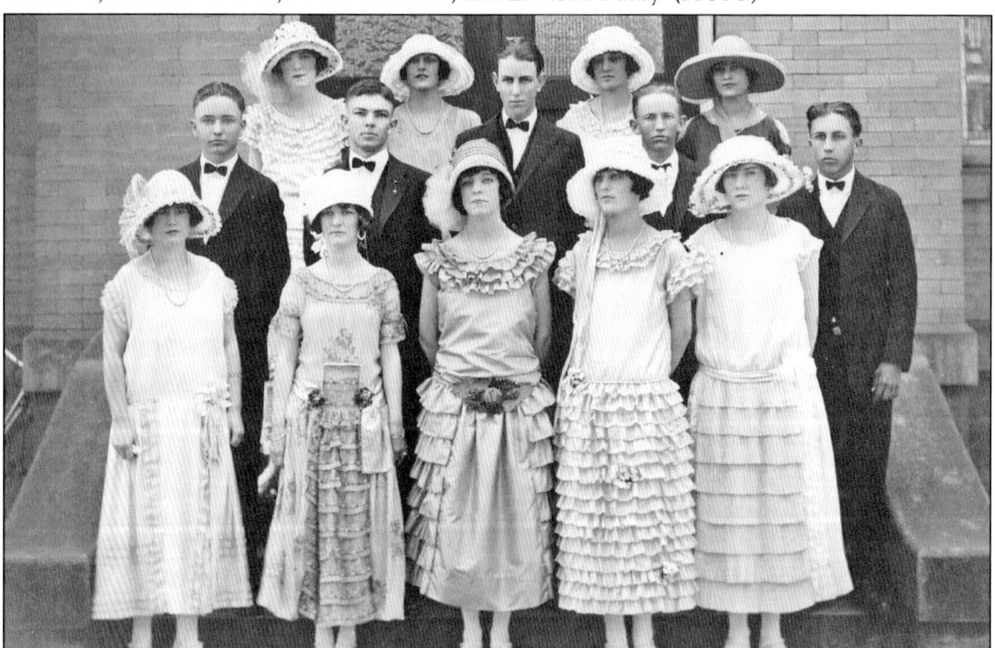

The Gilmer graduating class of 1920 included, from left to right, (first row) unidentified, Elizabeth Marshall, Ruth Sheppard, Doris Lindsey, and Ruby Hart; (second row) Wayne Fenlaw, Harvey Crawford, Cecil Bradford, unidentified, and ? Ray; (third row) Evelyn Wheeler, Leone Childress, Winnie Spencer, and Rayvon Moon. (GM.)

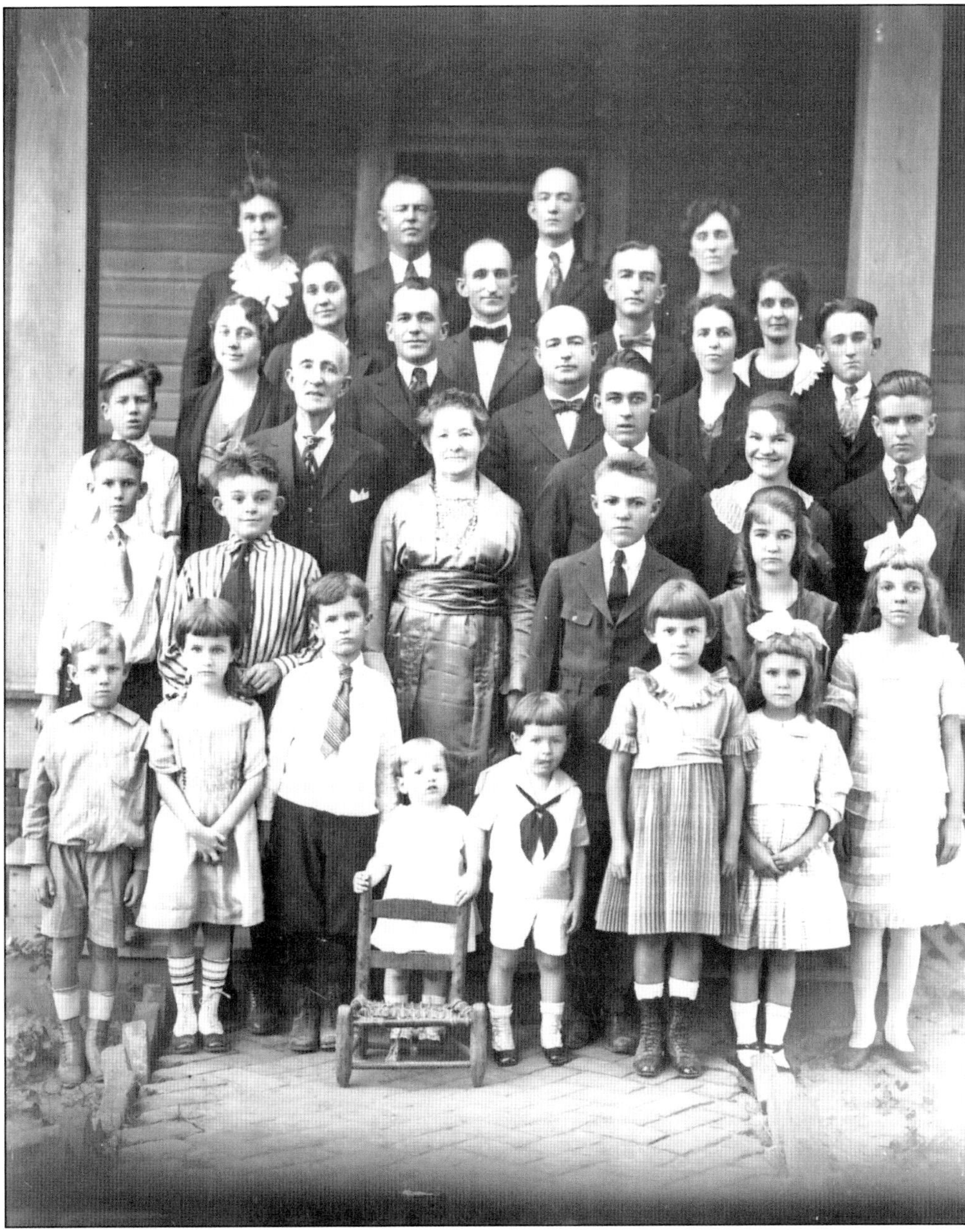

Family surrounds J. M. and Lavina P. Boyd Marshall (center left) on their 50th wedding anniversary at their home on South Montgomery Street. From left to right are (first row) Thomas Arch Marshall, Ruth Marshall, Jimmie Marshall, Mitchell Marshall, William Marshall, Madge Quinn, Louise Marshall, and Mildred Quinn; (second row) Neal Marshall, Jack Quinn, Marshall Quinn, and Elizabeth Marshall; (third row, on each side of their grandparents) Berry Luther Marshall, Hugh Quinn, Faye Marshall, and Frank Marshall; (fourth row) Virge Crosby Marshall, Will Marshall, Frank Marshall, Effie Buie Marshall, and Jerry Marshall; (fifth row) Edward Aubrey "Eddie" Marshall, Winnie Hill Marshall, J. Walter Marshall, and May Hart Marshall; (sixth row) Harry "Pat" Marshall, Ollie Hill Marshall, W. Arch Marshall, and Myra Mitchell Marshall. Winnie and Ollie Marshall were Hill sisters who married Marshall brothers. (HUM.)

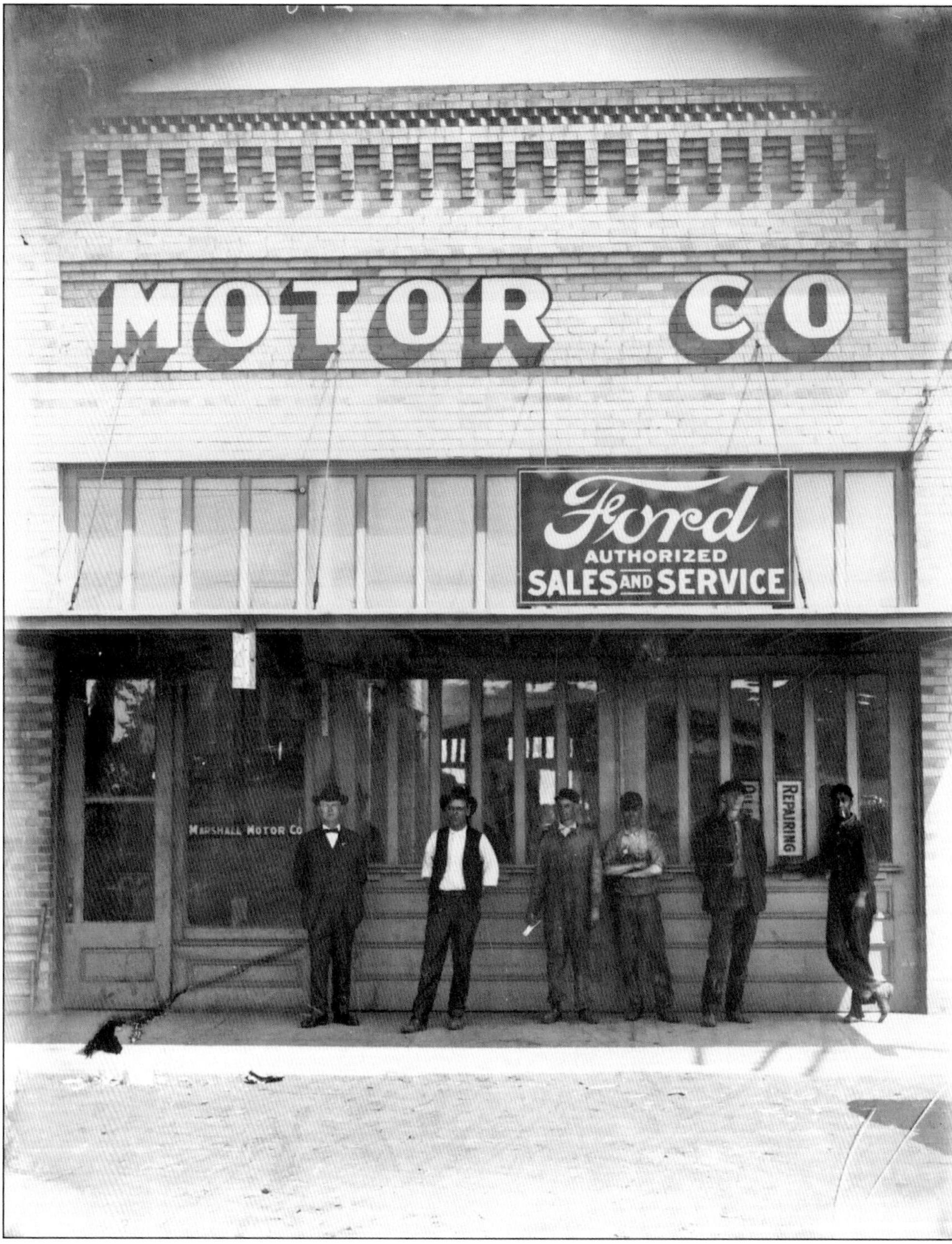

Will Marshall (left), owner of the Marshall Motor Company on the north side of the square on Jefferson Street, had all his employees come out front for a photograph. All stood under the awning on a hot summer's day. The black employee casually takes a cigarette break while J. M. Hays counts off the seconds. (HUM.)

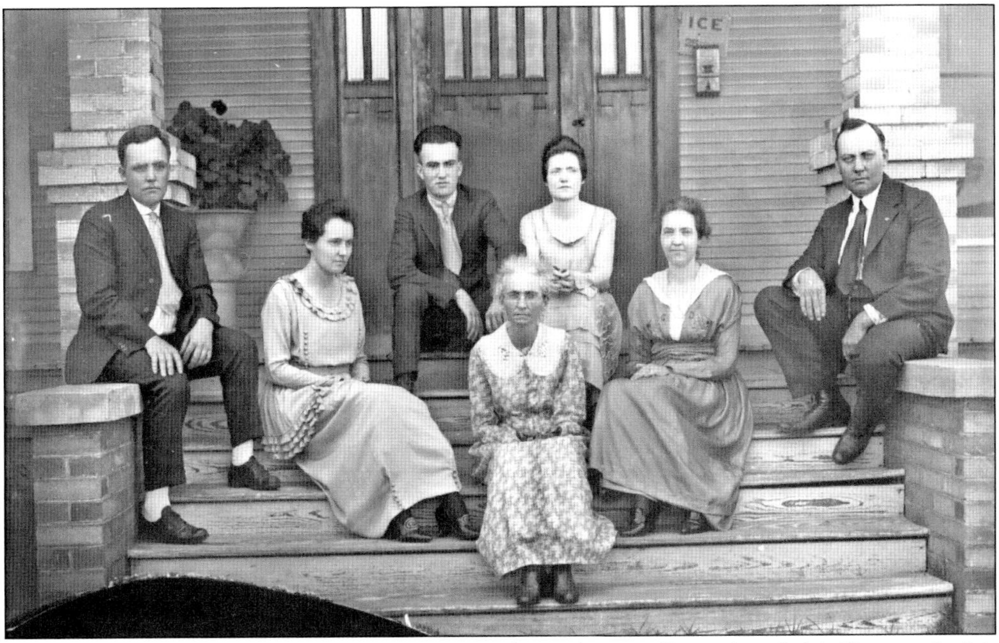

Rosa Petty had the "ICE" delivery sign propped over her mailbox when J. M. Hays took this photograph of her with her children at her home on South Montgomery Street near Kaufman Street. Included from left to right are (first row) Daisy Petty Dyer, Rosa Petty, and ? Ray; (second row) Joe Petty, Aubry Petty, Lollie Petty Coe, and Hardy Petty. (HUM.)

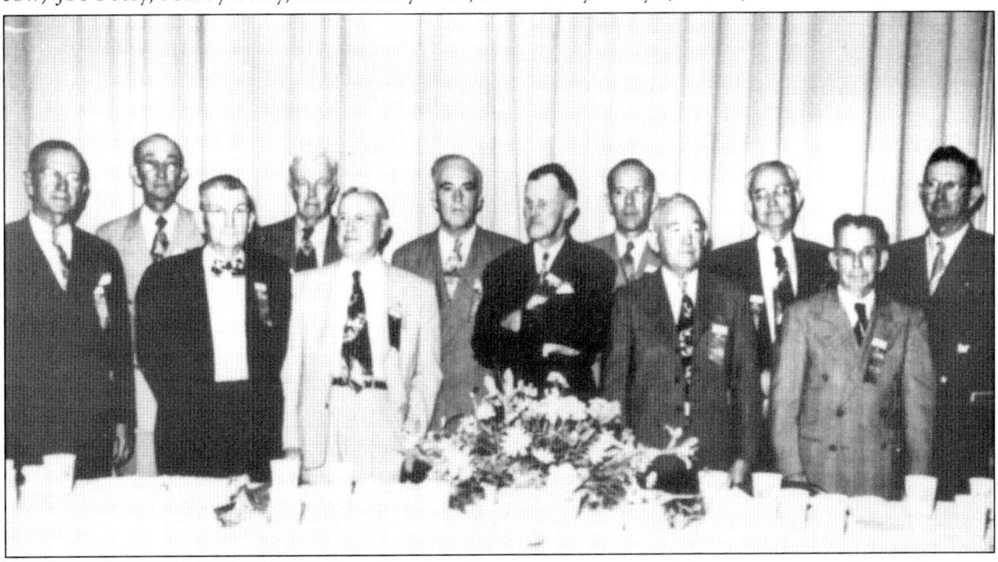

The year 1925 stands out in Gilmer history for several reasons. The government built the new post office at the corner of Jefferson and Simpson Streets, the people voted to pave the square, farmers harvested a cotton crop of 41,000 bales (the largest ever), and businessmen organized the Rotary Club, including these charter members photographed 25 years later. Among the charter members were, from left to right, (first row) Cranfill Cox Sr., Dr. J. G. Daniels Jr., John A. Mathis, Richard "Dick" Denman, Fred Hamm, and Edwin Aldredge; (second row) Nolen Coe, Allen McClelland, Redwood Taylor, John Brogoitti, Virgil Todd, and Horace Davis. Dick Denman was the first president, and Dr. J. G. Daniels Jr. was the second president. (MLK.)

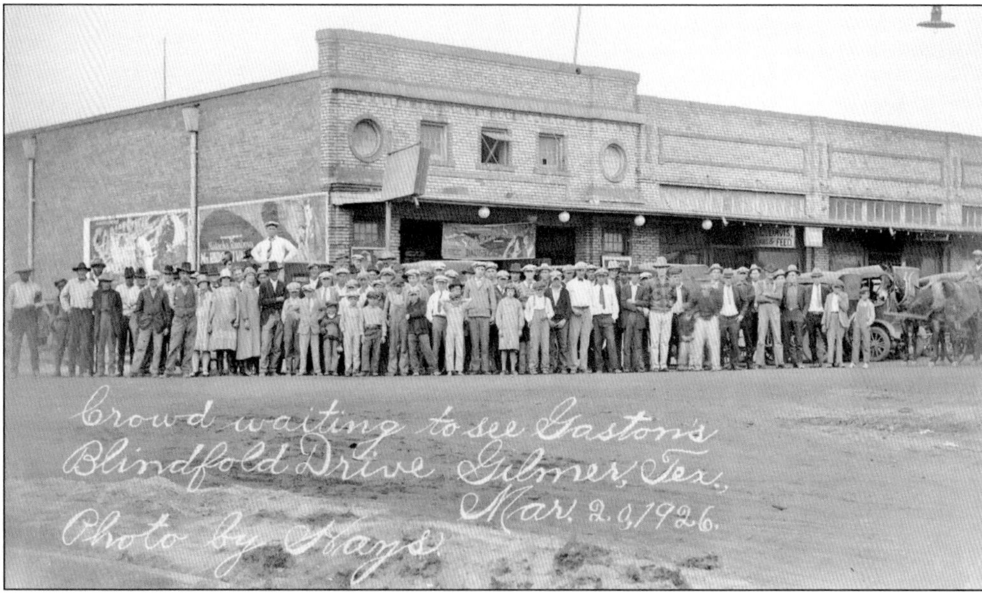

In 1926, a crowd gathered in front of the Crystal Theatre to watch a demonstration of blind driving. For four decades, the Crystal joined the Strand Theatre as the centers for entertainment in Gilmer. The Crystal often featured the major films, while the Stand had Westerns and the classic serials on Saturdays with their cliff-hanging endings each week. (HUM.)

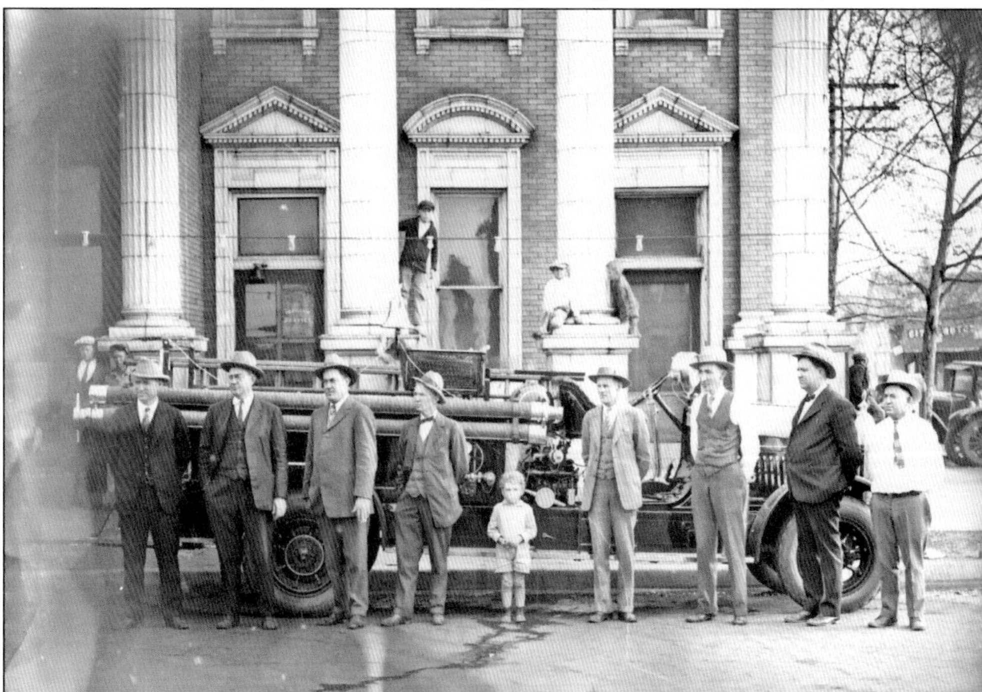

Volunteer firemen gladly posed with the first new fire truck bought for the Gilmer Fire Department. From left to right are Richard Dedman, the mayor of Gilmer at the time; Nolan Coe; unidentified; and Fred Hamm, the department's secretary. Trucks the department had used previously had been used models owned first by other departments. (HUM.)

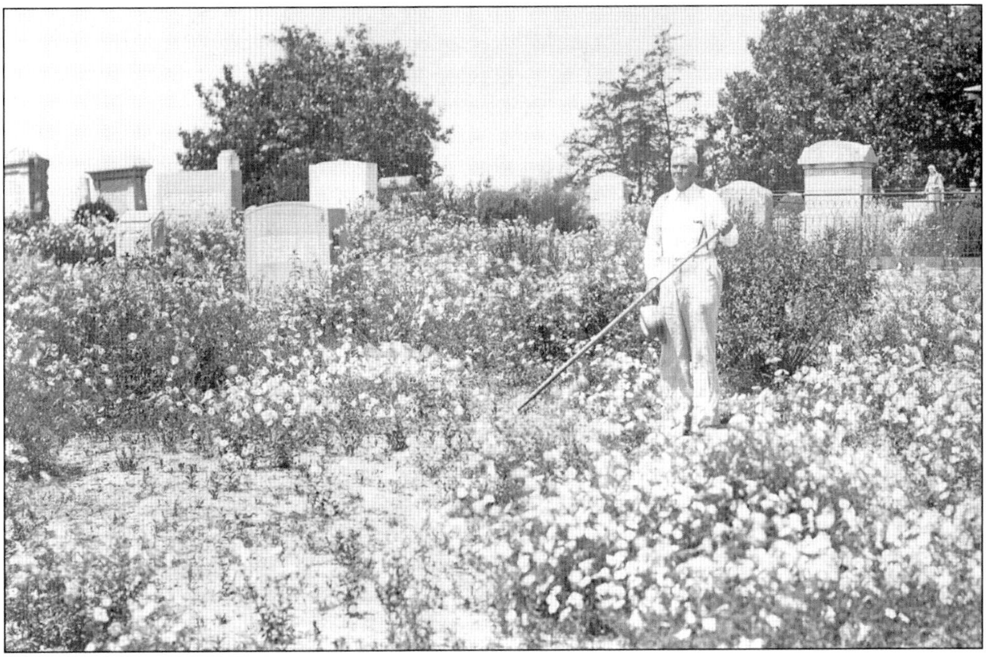

J. J. Stephens, owner of the *Upshur County Echo*, pauses from his labors at the Gilmer City Cemetery, where he served as the sexton in his retirement. Periwinkles bloom at Stephens's feet. The heat-loving annual was often one of the first flowers to be used in landscaping. (HUM.)

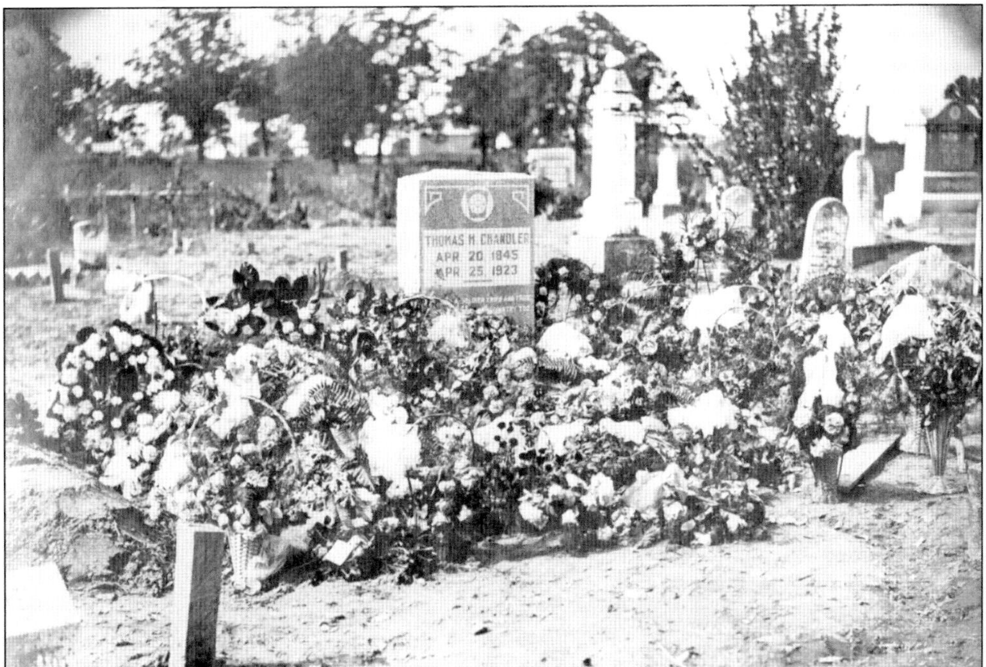

Tom Chandler, a graduate of the Looney School and a Royal Arch Mason, lay at rest in the Gilmer City Cemetery when his wife, Emma J., a Looney School alumna, died on October 31, 1928. Note the scraped earth burial, a practice common in the South that is believed by some scholars to have come to the United States from the practices of the African slaves. (HUM.)

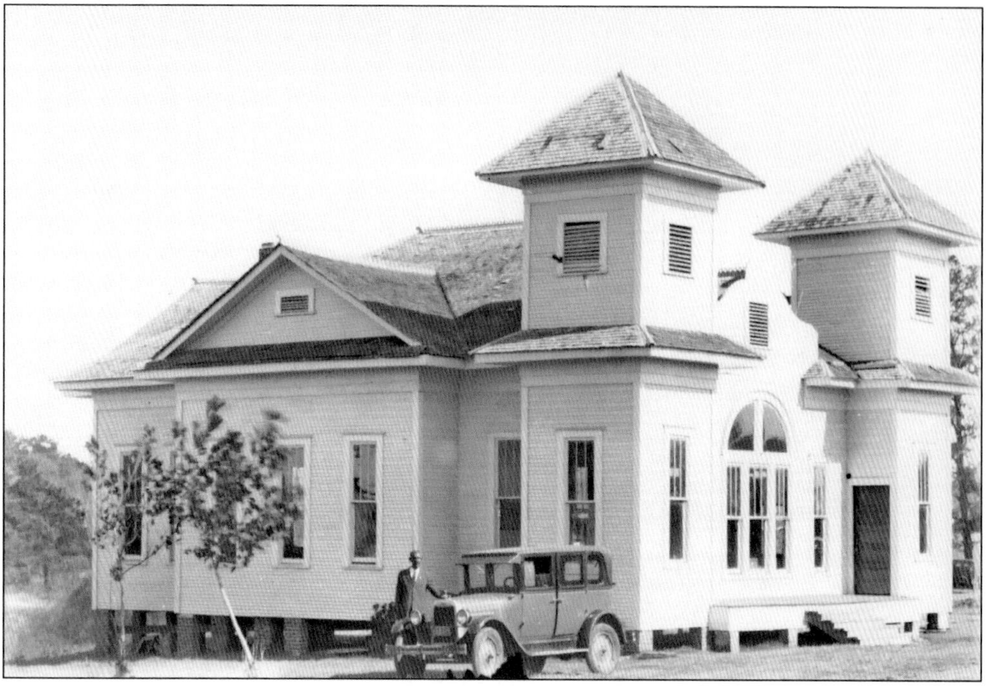

Moses Chapel Christian Methodist Church at Taylor and Roberts Streets had its first pastor who owned a car when Brother Palmer was the minister in the 1920s. The building was later remodeled into its current brick format. (HUM.)

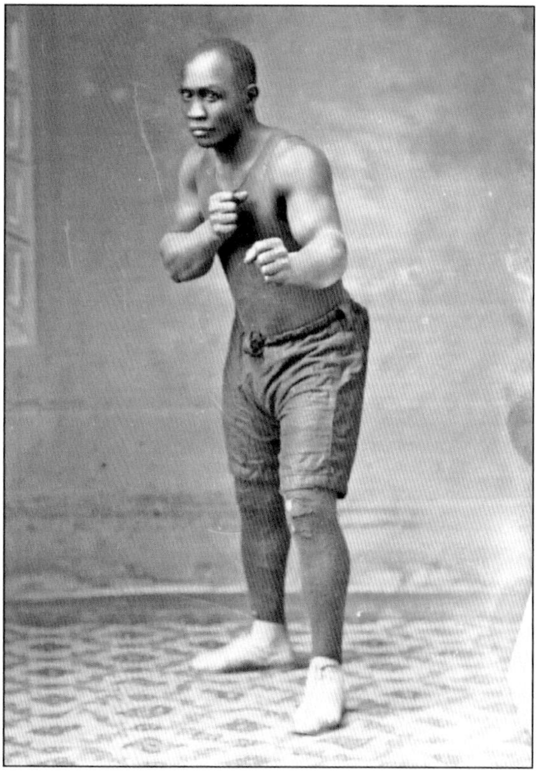

Whites and blacks alike took interest in the accomplishments of Manna Turner, who was known by his nickname, "Cyclone," when he was in the ring. In 1928, at Bruce High School, the heavyweight knocked out Battling Hunter in the fifth round of a planned 10-round bout. For an encore, he knocked out Jim Collins in the third round of a four-round bout. The *Gilmer Mirror* reported there was a good crowd of white and black men to witness the exhibition. (HUM.)

Appropriately for a woman who was among the first graduating class of Gilmer High School and a charter member of the Twentieth Century Club, Myra Mitchell (Mrs. Arch) Marshall became one of the first women to serve on the Gilmer School Board. Her terms overlapped the school years of 1926–1928. (HUM.)

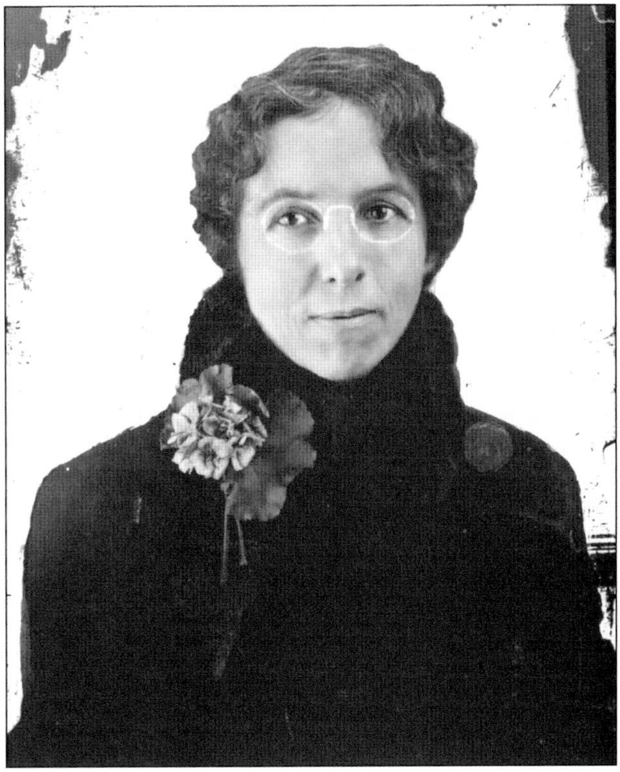

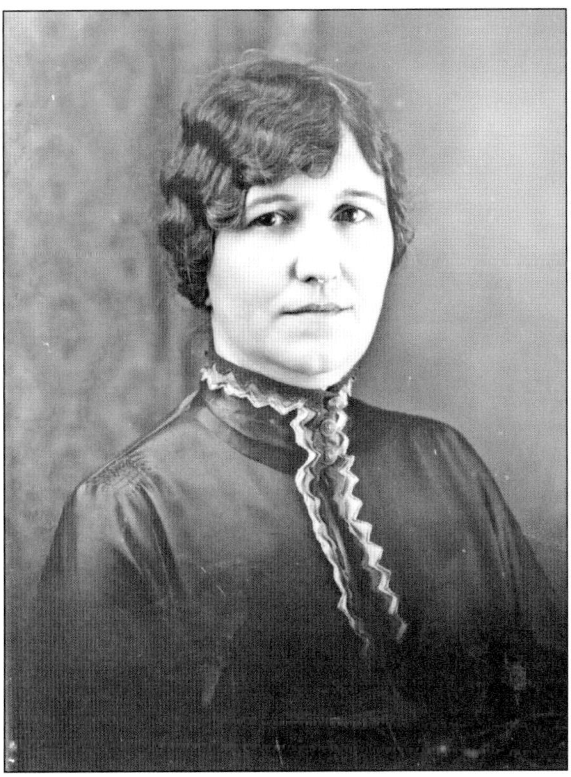

With politics in her blood and with the urging of her fellow Twentieth Century Club members, Ella Briggs (Mrs. V. E.) Todd joined Myra Marshall on the school board. As president of the Twentieth Century Club in 1935, Todd would oversee the creation of the first free public library in Gilmer. (HUM.)

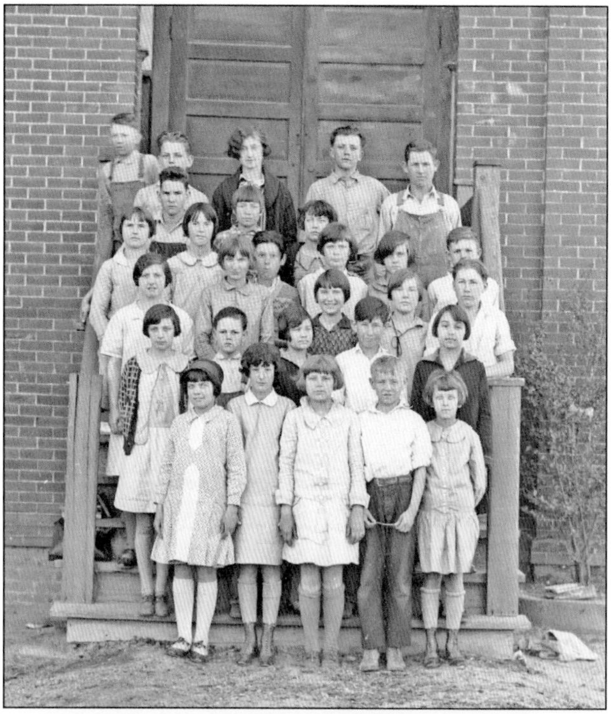

Another Gilmer High graduate, class of 1920, returned to her hometown after furthering her education at Baylor University in Waco. First, Cecil Ragland shepherded a new group of fifth graders through Gilmer Ward School, as shown here. Later she opened a successful gift shop on the east side of the square, where Coldwell-Banker Real Estate is currently located. (HUM.)

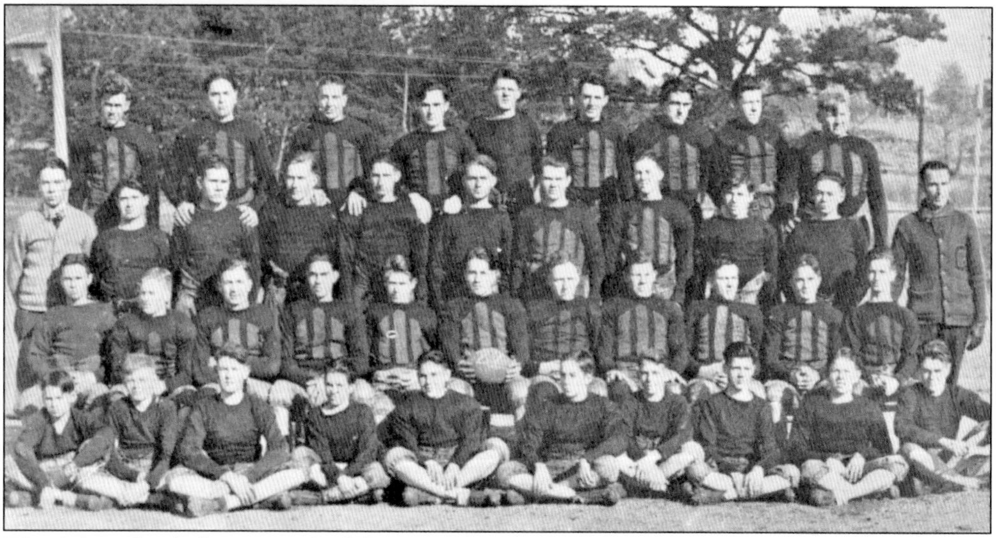

The Gilmer football team in the fall of 1927 hit the field wearing school colors orange and black with Henry McClelland as the coach. From left to right are (first row) Charles Edward Stephens, Alfred Jasper, Paul Vandiver, Jimmy Sheppard, Frank Denman, Grayson Ray, Pat Duncan, Sydney Martin, Thomas Arch Marshall, and Hunter Ennis; (second row) Jimmie Phillips, Milton Hinson, Harris Daniels, Briggs Todd, Osborne Powers, Louie D. Hill (captain), Rex Hudson, Bernice Wallace, Kermit Nation, J. T. Baird Jr., and Jimmie Marshall; (third row) C. T. Crosby Jr. (manager), Sidney Waghalter, Buster Wallace, Truman Ray, Ramah L. Matthews, ? Wilson, Leonard Duggar, Maurice Hinson, William Glass, Easley Nation, and coach Henry McClelland; (fourth row) Dennis Wyatt, Clovis Patterson, Willie D. Quinn, Buster Bullard, Boyd Stephens, Andrew Boyd, Leonard Pickitt, Brunelle Moon, and Roland "Puny" Vivian. The team racked up a record of 7-2-1. (HUM.)

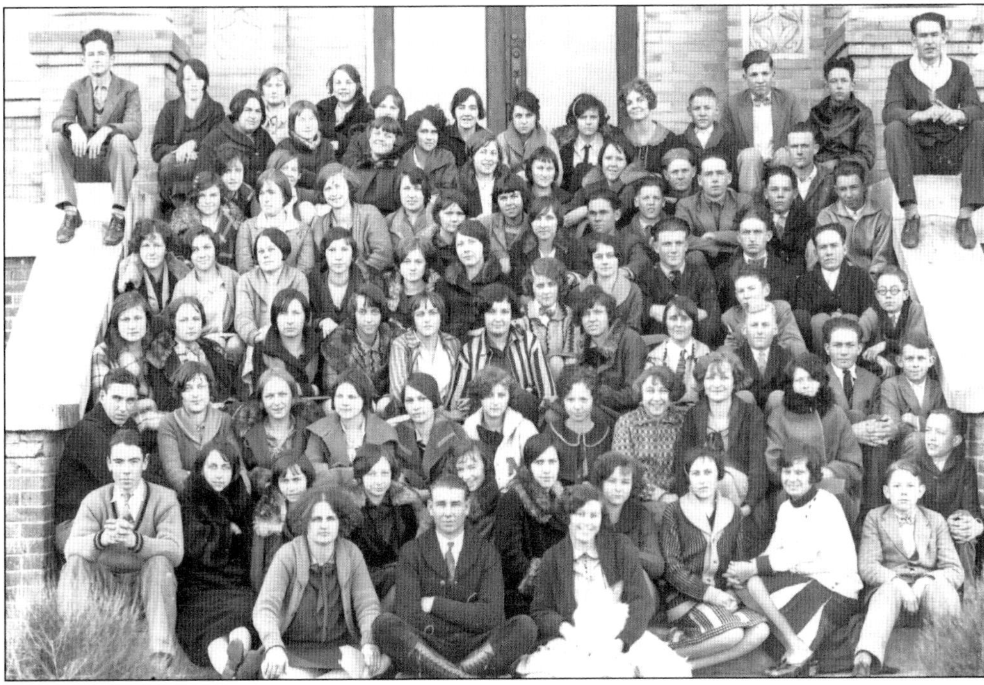

With the success of the 1927 football squad, Gilmer students wanted to support their team. Following the tradition of Texas A&M, the school Henry "Doc" McClelland attended, the pep squad had four yell leaders: Albert Douglas, Juanita Wallis, Lula Elder, and Troy Ledbetter. (HUM.)

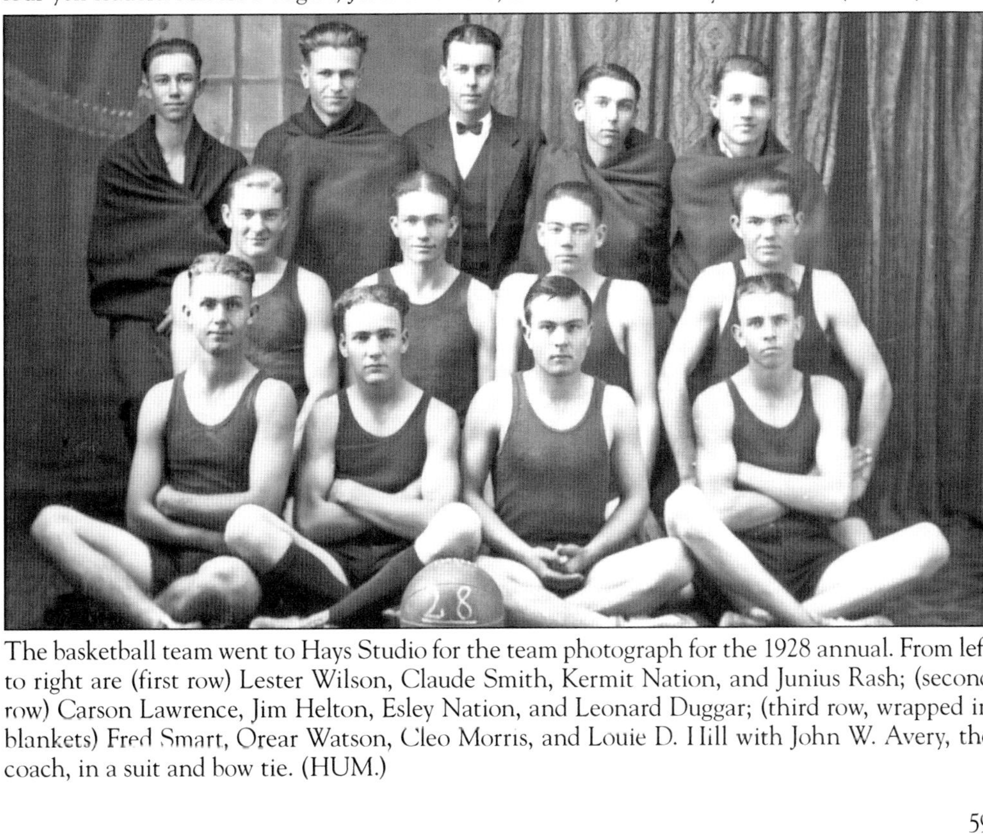

The basketball team went to Hays Studio for the team photograph for the 1928 annual. From left to right are (first row) Lester Wilson, Claude Smith, Kermit Nation, and Junius Rash; (second row) Carson Lawrence, Jim Helton, Esley Nation, and Leonard Duggar; (third row, wrapped in blankets) Fred Smart, Orear Watson, Cleo Morris, and Louie D. Hill with John W. Avery, the coach, in a suit and bow tie. (HUM.)

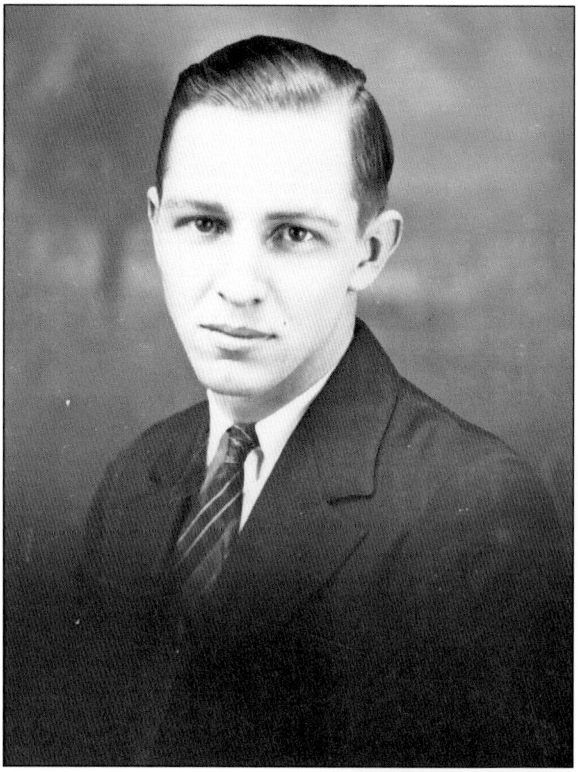

Warren Whittlesey left his permanent mark on the history of Gilmer High by creating the first band. At first, the musical group allowed adults from the community, but once the East Texas Yamboree started, the band donned orange and black capes to wear over white shirts and slacks as a marching band. Whittlesey left to answer the call of World War II, never to return to Gilmer. (HUM.)

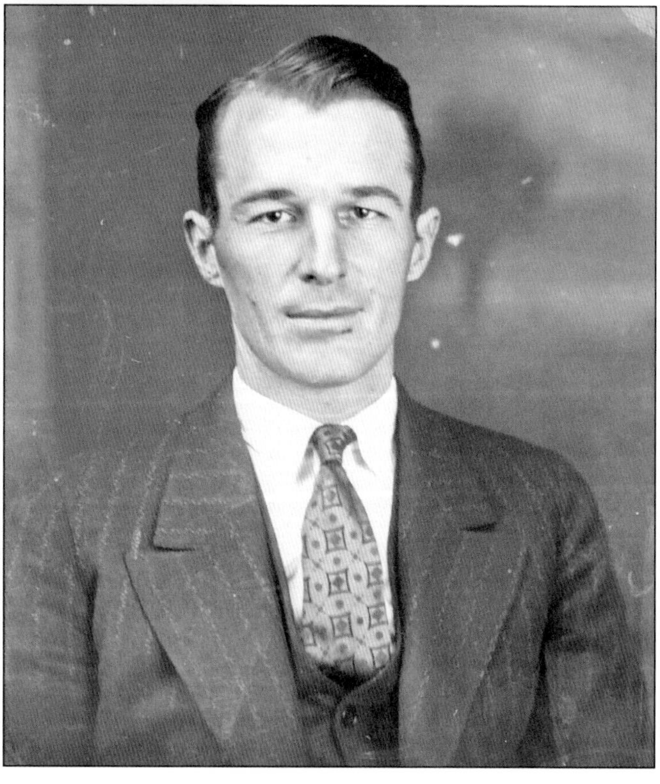

Not only did Henry McClelland play football for Gilmer High School, but he was the first college-trained coach to attend Gilmer. "Doc" McClelland, as the 1927–1928 annual called him, used the skills he learned under D. X. Bible when the team from Texas Agricultural and Mechanical College defeated Centre College in the game where the Twelfth Man tradition was born. McClelland was one of the 11 on the field. At Gilmer High, he taught vocational agriculture when he was not coaching. (HUM.)

South of the city limits, several hundred students of all ages lived at the Dickson Colored Orphanage. Following the principles established by Booker T. Washington, the Reverend W. L. Dickson emphasized teaching the girls domestic science and the boys agricultural skills. When the board of directors came for the annual meeting, the girls and their instructor prepared the meal. Dickson stands with the girls and their teacher by the Domestic Science Building. (HUM.)

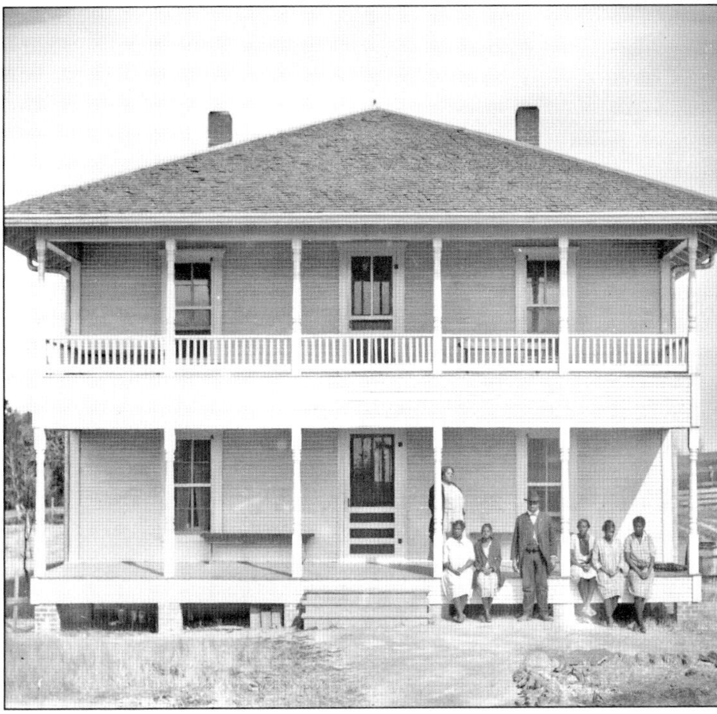

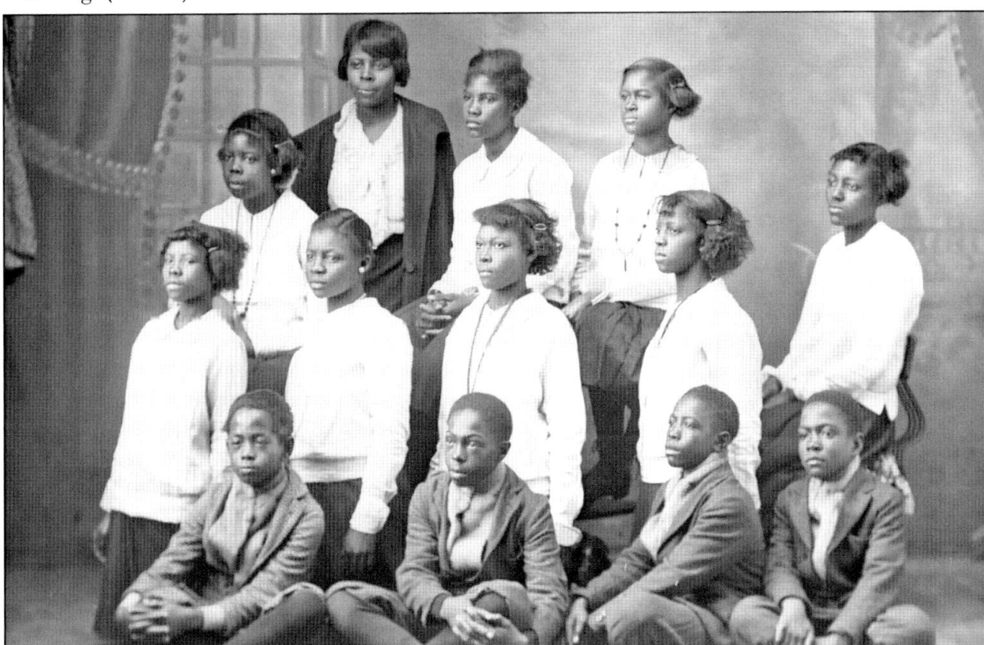

One of the principal ways that the Dickson Colored Orphanage could raise money was to entertain people with the vocal prowess of the students under the leadership of Odessa Josey, the assistant superintendent and a former member of the Fisk University Jubilee Singers. The First Methodist Church in Gilmer hosted a gathering where the children sang classical music and spirituals. More than $1,000 was raised in the collection that Sunday evening, according to the *Gilmer Mirror*. (HUM.)

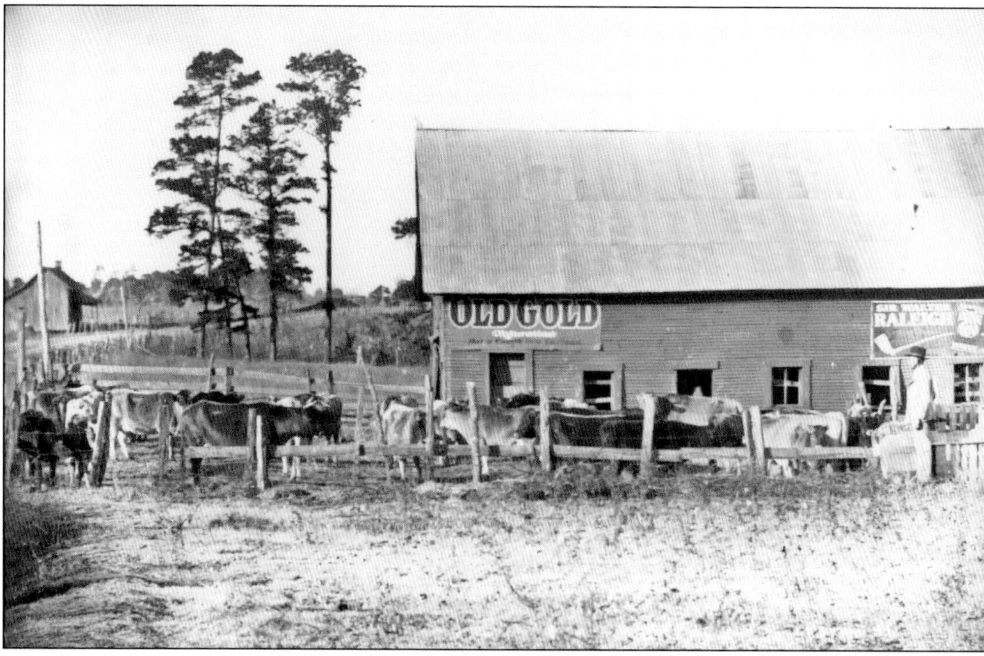

Another source of income came from using the side of one of the outbuildings for cigarette advertisements. The acreage of the school extended from the vicinity of Dean Street to the Gilmer Municipal Airport and beyond. The road to the left in this photograph was called the Old Jefferson Highway and is known today as U.S. Highway 271. (HUM.)

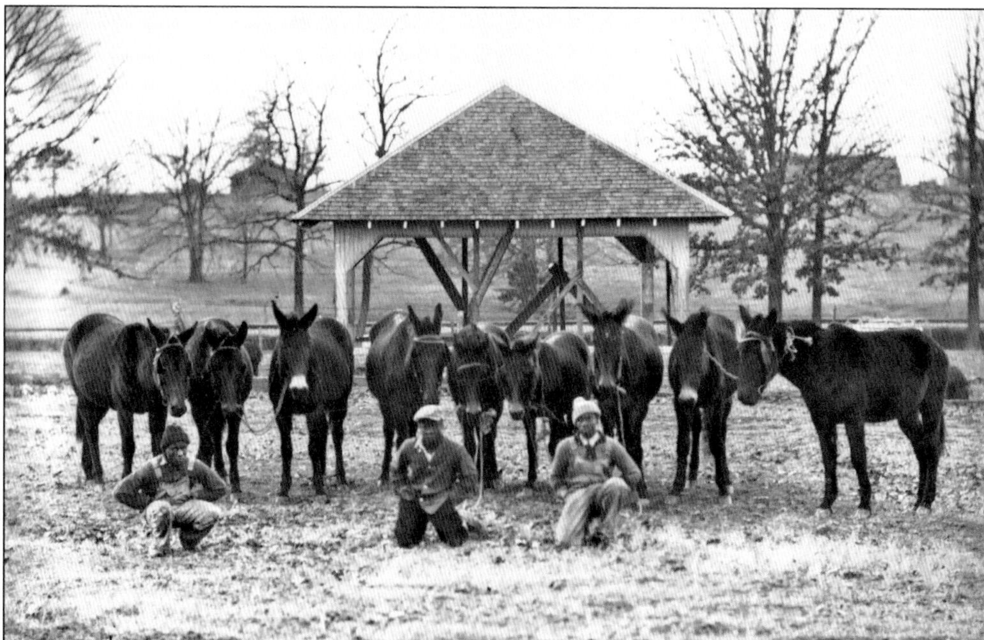

In this view looking toward the west, the boys have halted with the mules near the well on the property. In the background appear the railroad tracks of the Cotton Belt, but there are no roads connecting the highway with Montgomery Street. The sawmill that Denman and Williams would initiate had not yet been established. (HUM.)

Four

Depression and World War II 1930–1946

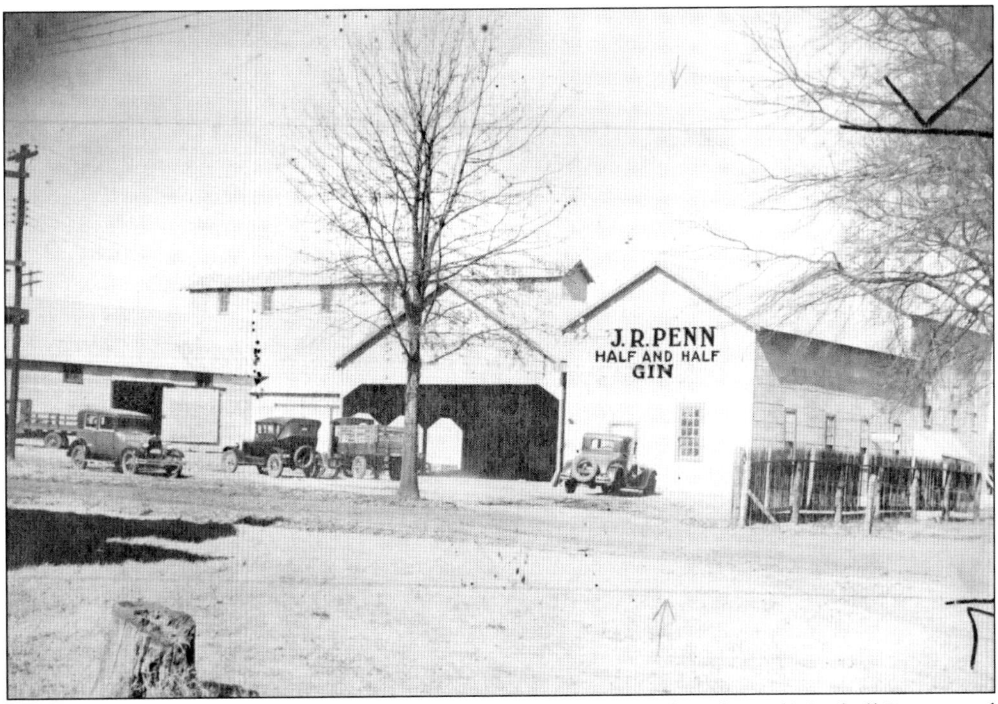

J. R. Penn moved his cotton gin to property adjoining the railroad tracks and Mitchell Street, and hired Otis McHenry to serve as caretaker of the area. Even though the cotton crop was under assault by boll weevils, no one in 1931 would have anticipated an era when not a single stalk of cotton was grown in the county. Penn adapted to growing sweet potatoes and converted some of his property into curing barns. Today trucks bring gravel and lime as raw materials in place of cotton, and truckloads of cement depart for the surrounding areas. (Otis McHenry.)

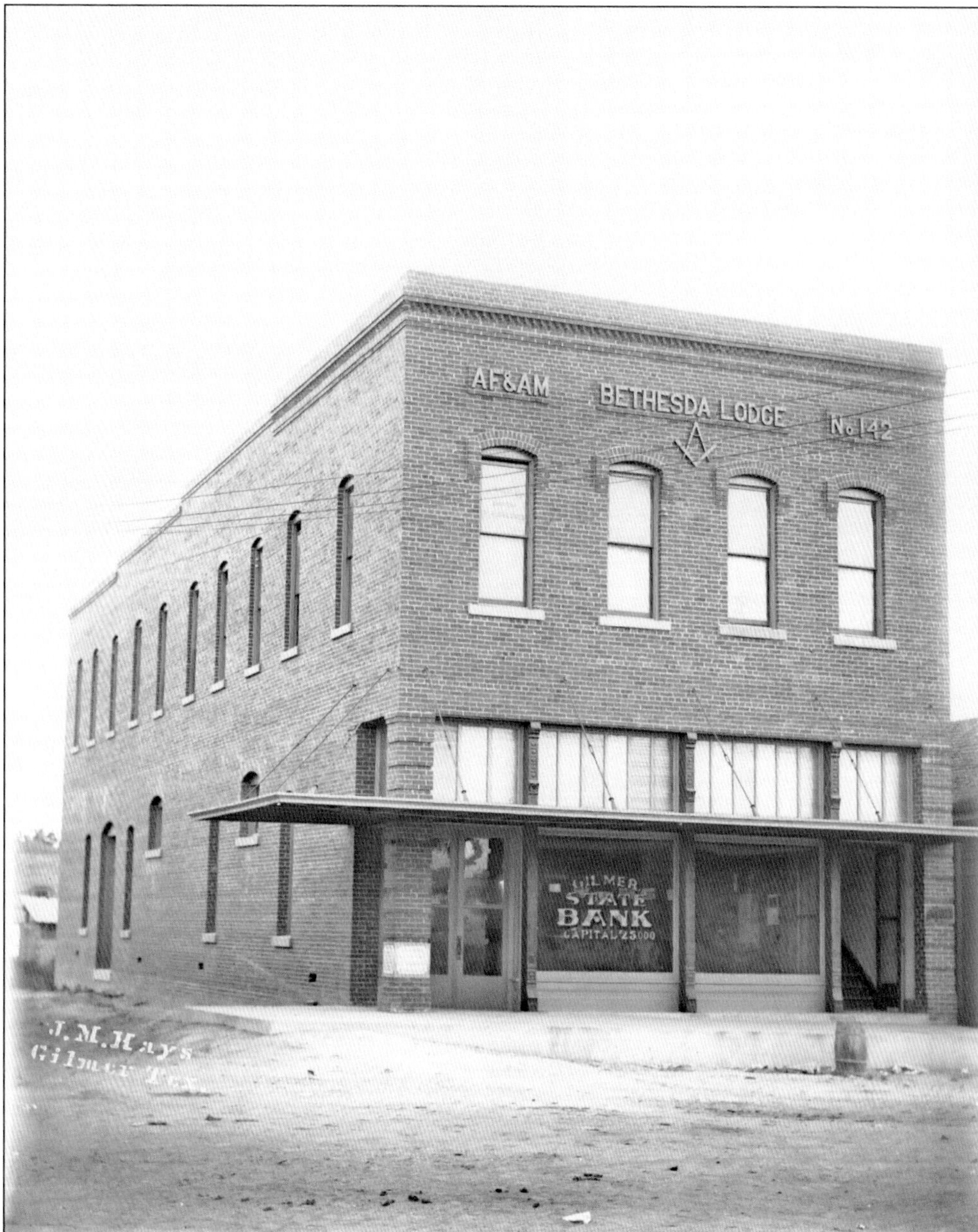

Shortly after the East Texas oil boom hit in Rusk County, oil was discovered closer to home. Neither event prevented the run on the banks in March 1933, which led Pres. Franklin Roosevelt to close all the banks in the country for a few days. When they reopened a few days later, the assets of the Gilmer State Bank and its loans had become the property of the First National Bank, and state banks all over the county never reopened. The building, which opened in 1912 to house the post office in the rear, the Bethesda Lodge of the Masons on the second floor, and the Gilmer State Bank, had only the lodge as its remaining tenant. The Kurtz Store would become the new first-floor occupant. (HUM.)

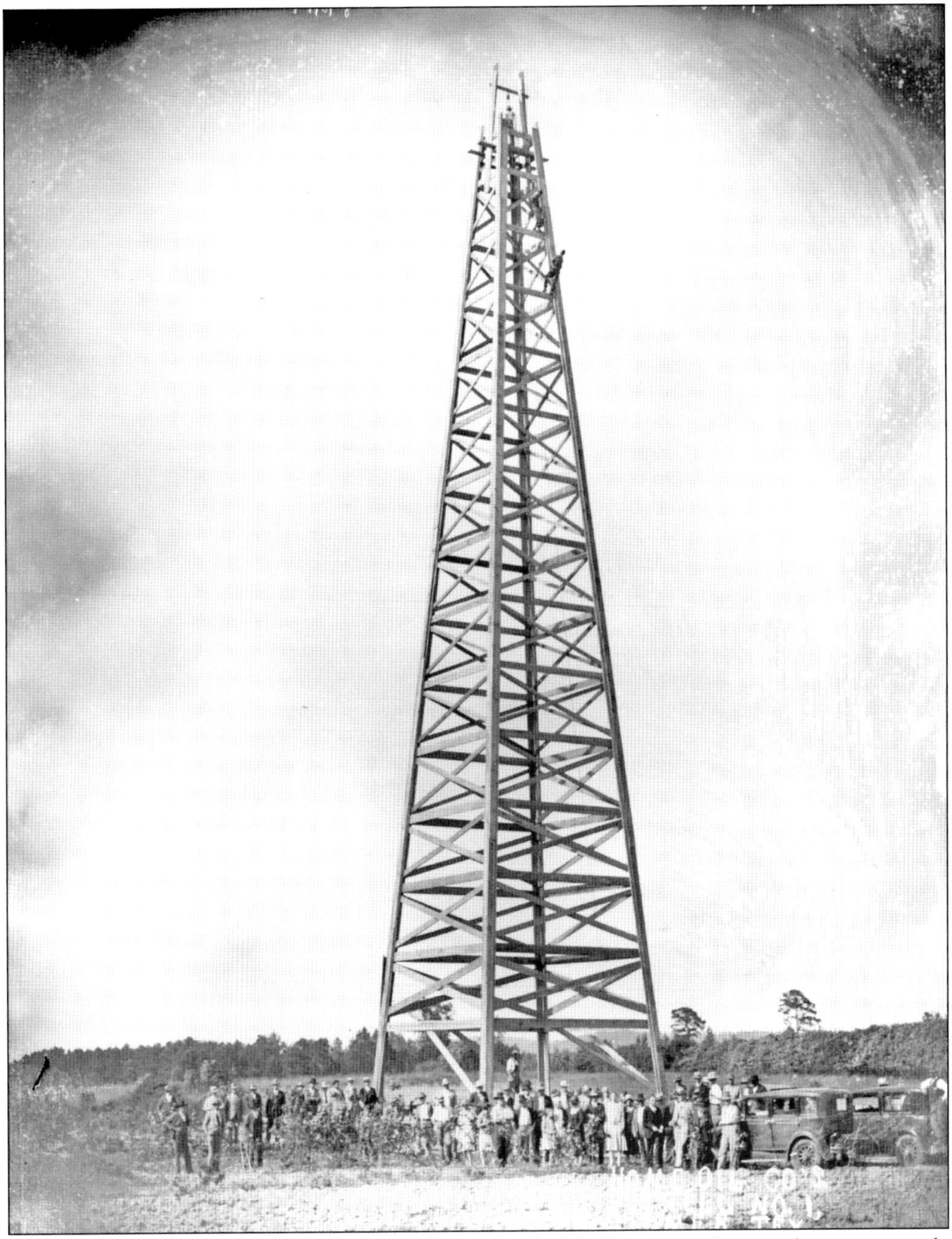

The new lifeblood for the county would come from the black syrupy substance known as crude oil. While many on the farms did not reap the benefits of this new infusion of cash into the economy, the businesses in Gilmer began to thrive when the rest of the country fell into the depths of the Depression. In this image, J. M. Hays recorded a group of businessmen and oil field workers joining B. D. Futrell at his rig, Futrell No. 1. (HUM.)

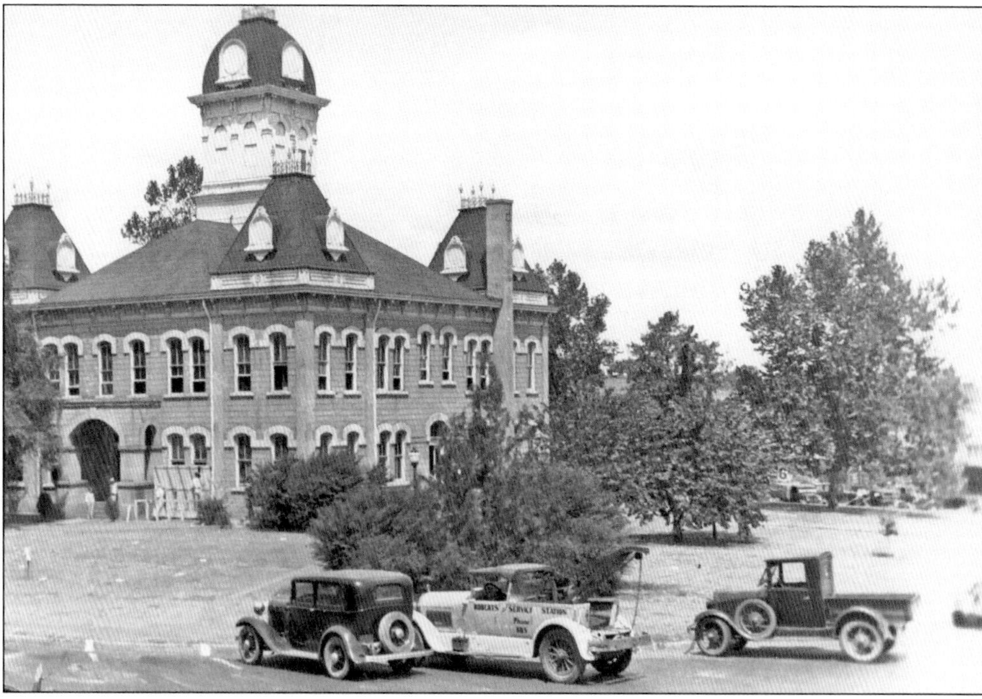

The courthouse had been remodeled in 1916 and the balconies removed, so the walls were pushed forward for more interior space. A new entrance had poured concrete columns. Plaster was applied over the bricks and scored to appear like stone. Despite appeals of the Twentieth Century Club ladies, public restrooms were not added, but the county commissioners did allow the women to landscape the grounds. By 1935, the fifth courthouse was bursting at the seams as the lease men came to the county clerk's records to find owners of minerals rights. Note the light-colored roadster advertising, "Roberts Service Station, Phone No. 185." After connecting with "central," the callers gave the two- or three-digit number of the party they were calling. (RHL)

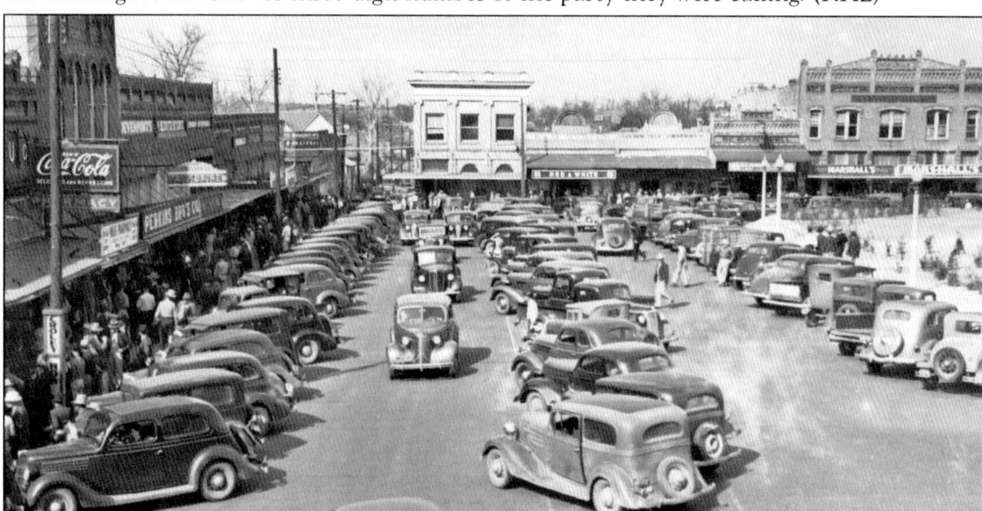

Parking was allowed in the middle of the street on the west side of the square on a busy day in the 1930s. With the activities of the lease hounds and other researchers of the deeds, this busy scene did not necessarily take place on a Saturday but was a more frequent occurrence. (RHL)

With the cash flowing into the community when others had few funds available, Gilmer became the location of new businesses, such as 3 Beall Brothers 3, a chain of dry-goods stores out of Jacksonville, and Safeway, a chain of grocery stores headquartered in California. In 1935, Safeway sold oranges for 19¢ per dozen and drew customers to the attractive produce. (HUM.)

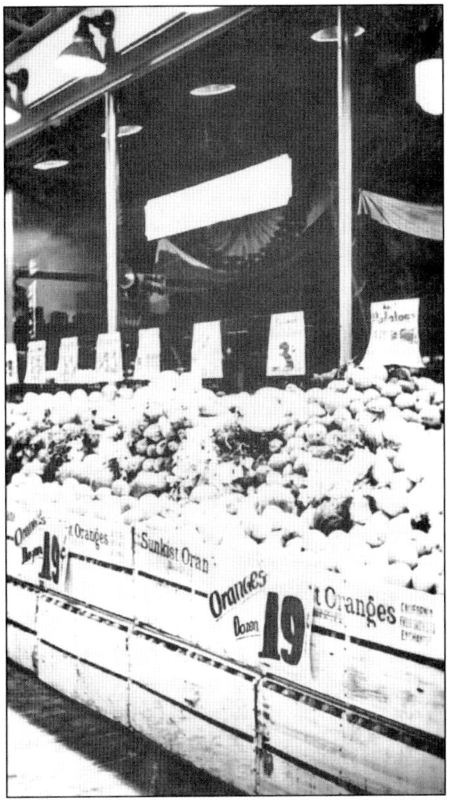

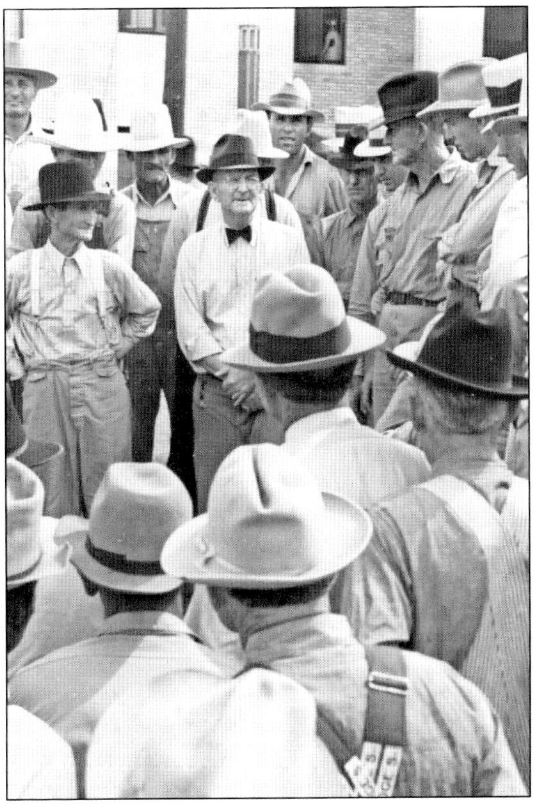

Dr. J. Gilbert "Gib" Daniels Jr. (center) was well respected both as a family doctor and as a civic leader who was the second president of the Rotary Club. He persuaded Gilmerites and residents of the surrounding countryside of steps they needed to take to improve the health of their families. A generation of children all over the county knew him as the public health officer who came to the schools to give them free vaccinations, which would protect them against typhoid, a disease endemic in the county at that time. In 1951, Dr. Gib and his nurse, Ruby Gravley, gave almost 4,000 typhoid boosters, 584 whooping cough shots, 617 diphtheria vaccinations, and 385 smallpox vaccinations, and examined the children's vision and hearing as well. (RHL.)

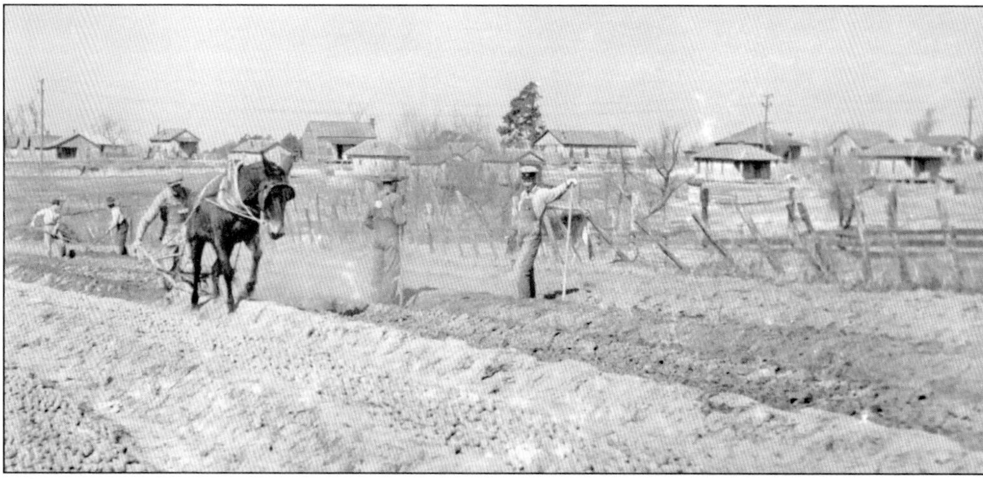

When the ground began to warm in the spring, Otis McHenry (right) and other employees of J. R. Penn would begin to turn the sand over the sweet potatoes to start them sprouting. Once sprouted, the potatoes would be planted in rows for the harvest of another crop of sweet potatoes. In the late 1920s, a sweet potato weevil in the crops led to a quarantine, preventing the farmers from shipping their crops. In 1935, the quarantine was lifted, a cause for celebration. (MLK.)

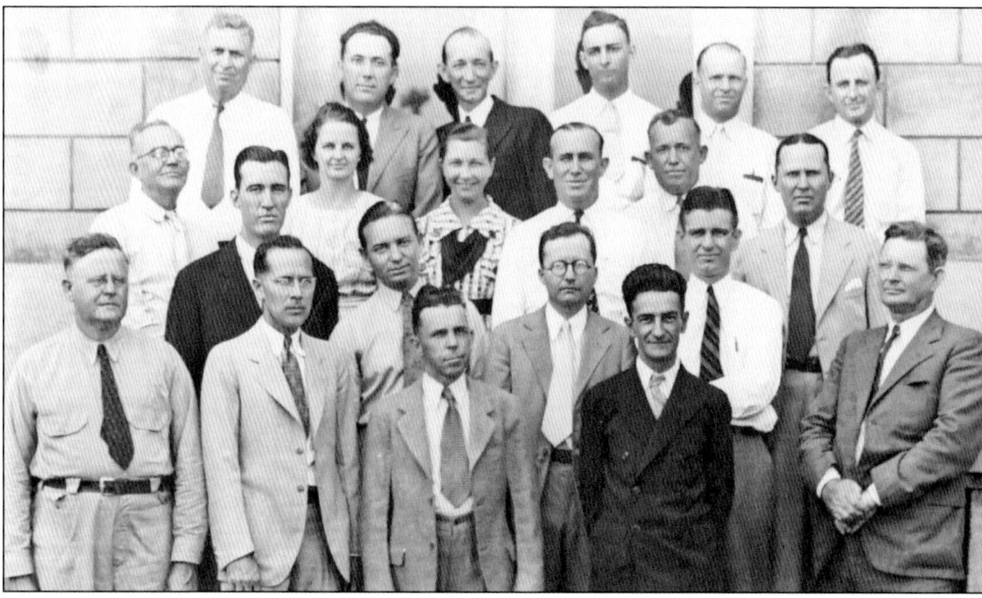

County agent W. D. "Bill" Seals and chamber of commerce secretary John Brogoitti began urging local leaders that an agricultural festival similar to a county fair would be an appropriate way to celebrate the lifting of the quarantine. An advertising executive in Dallas came up with the East Texas Yamboree name, and plans were rapidly made for an October celebration. The first board of directors included, from left to right, (first row) W. A. Terry; secretary John A. Brogoitti; Edwin Aldredge, president of the chamber of commerce; R. H. Laschinger; and Horace Davis, mayor; (second row) John Mac Brooks; Cranfill Cox Jr., publicity chairman; Milton Greer Mell; and Frank Marshall; (third row) V. E. Todd; Elizabeth Crosby, chairman of the pageant and queen's court; Georgia Laschinger; Elwin Quinn; Fred Hamm; and J. C. Fleetwood, parade chairman; (fourth row) Oscar Moore; Fred Covin; L. N. Coe; Douglas Matthews, city marshal; county agent Bill Seals; and Jake Long. (MLK.)

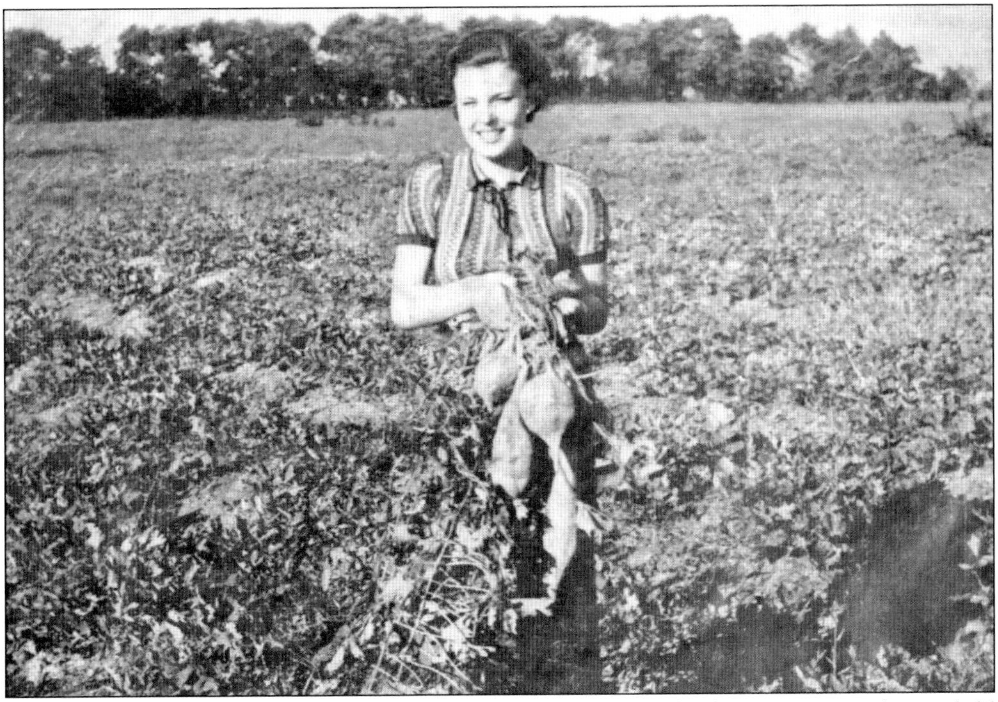

Queen Yam Jane Tuttle of Union Grove willingly gathers a bunch of sweet potatoes from a field of the productive tuber in a publicity photograph for the magazine of the East Texas Chamber of Commerce. The first queen was selected by voting at a penny a vote. The next year, the sale of tickets to various events, including the coronation of the queen and a queen's ball, replaced the counting of pennies. (MLK.)

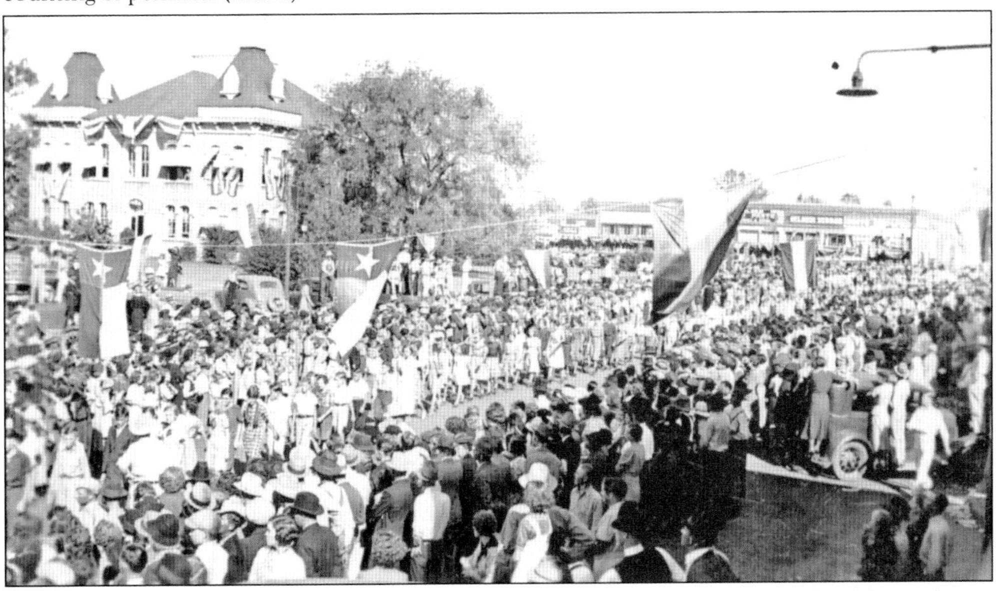

The first Yamboree Parade proceeds around the square, the only parade when the old courthouse still stood. The next month, demolition of the structure, built in 1889, and construction of a new courthouse both began. In the confusion of this first parade, no one notified the people with the float carrying Queen Jane Tuttle, so she missed the parade. (HUM.)

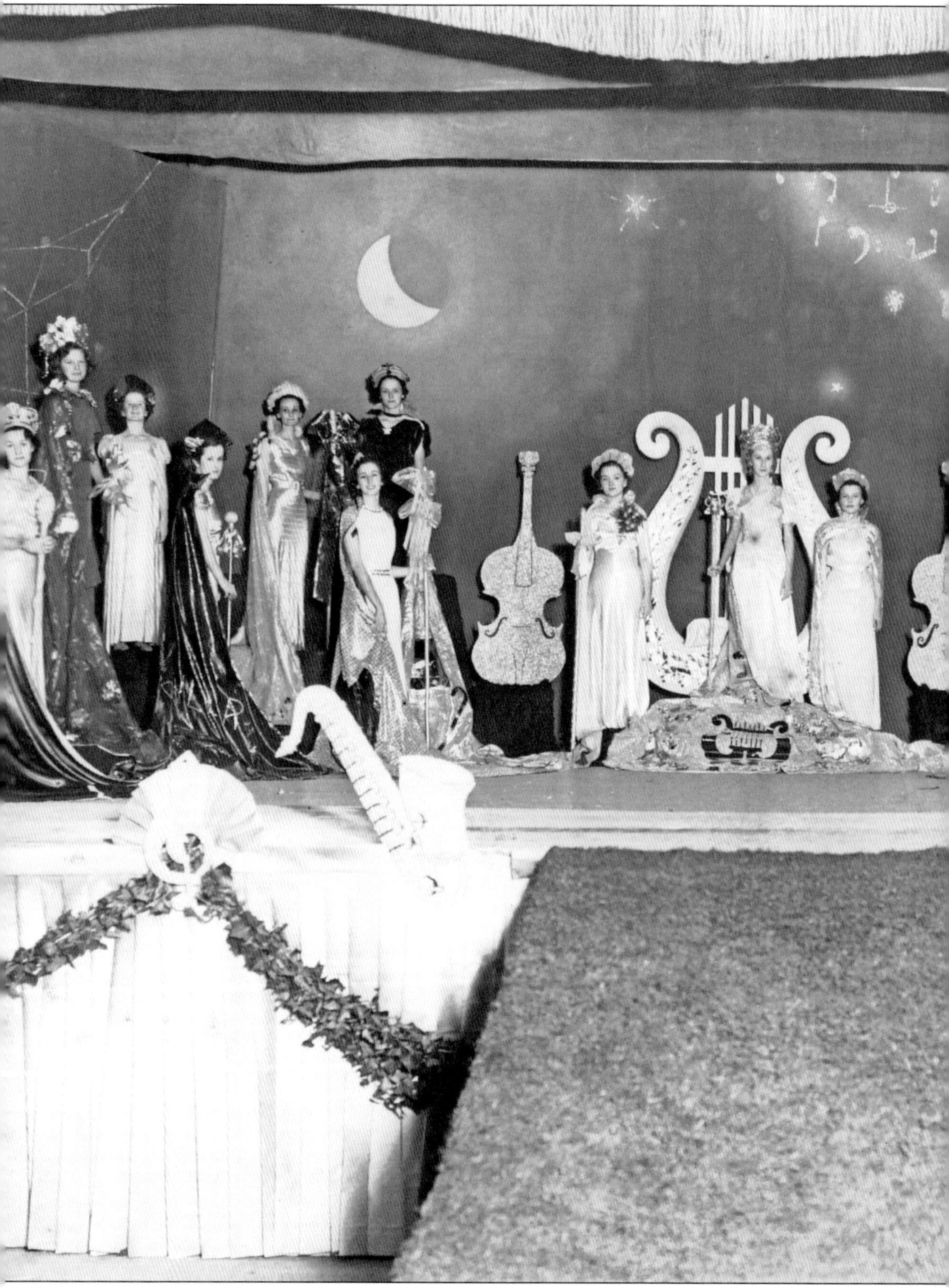

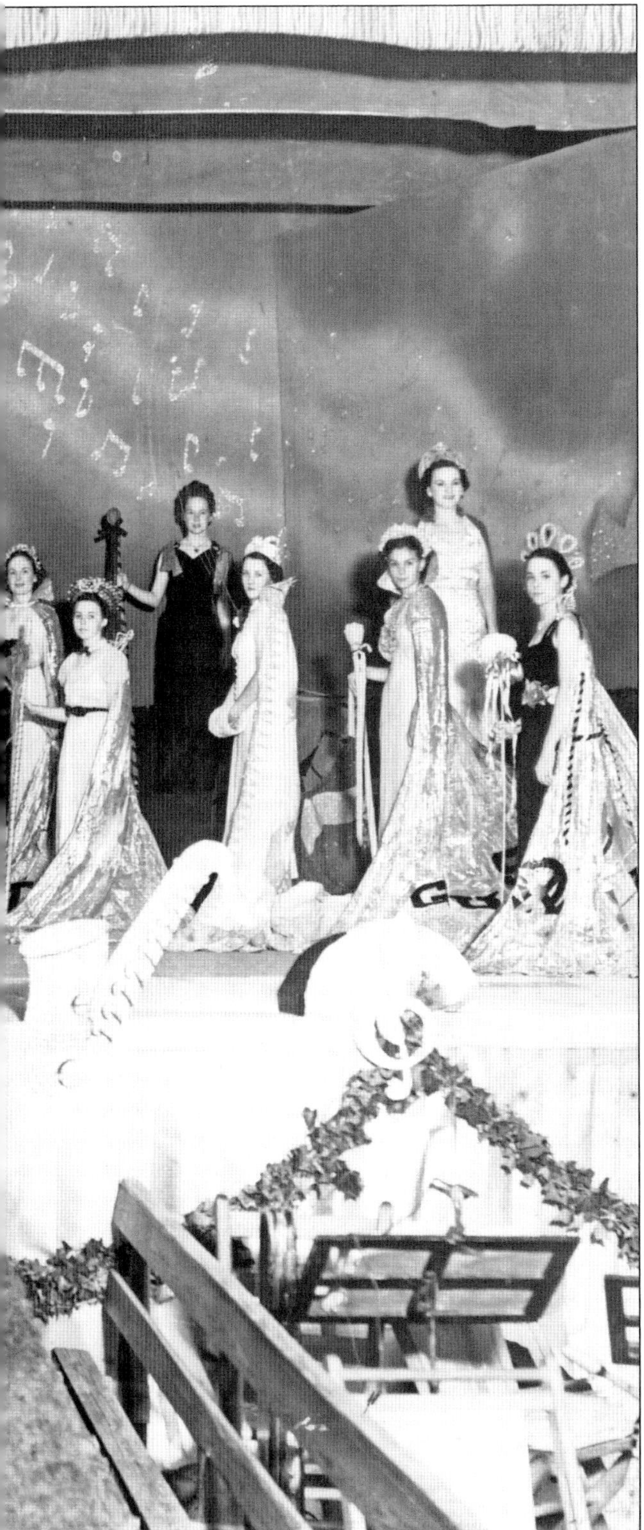

For the third coronation, 28 communities sent representatives to join in the celebration. In the second row, from left to right, are Emmalee Byman, duchess of the Eastern Star; Betty Jo Myers, Rotary Club; Ruth Boyd, fire department; Queen Yam II Marjorie Coe; Queen Yam III Ruth Hogg; Queen Yam I Jane Tuttle; and (far right) Mary Jo Cox, duchess of the Twentieth Century Club. The other young ladies represent the Court of Colleges, with each representing a different area college. The Swingtime set was designed by J. B. Wallace. (MLK.)

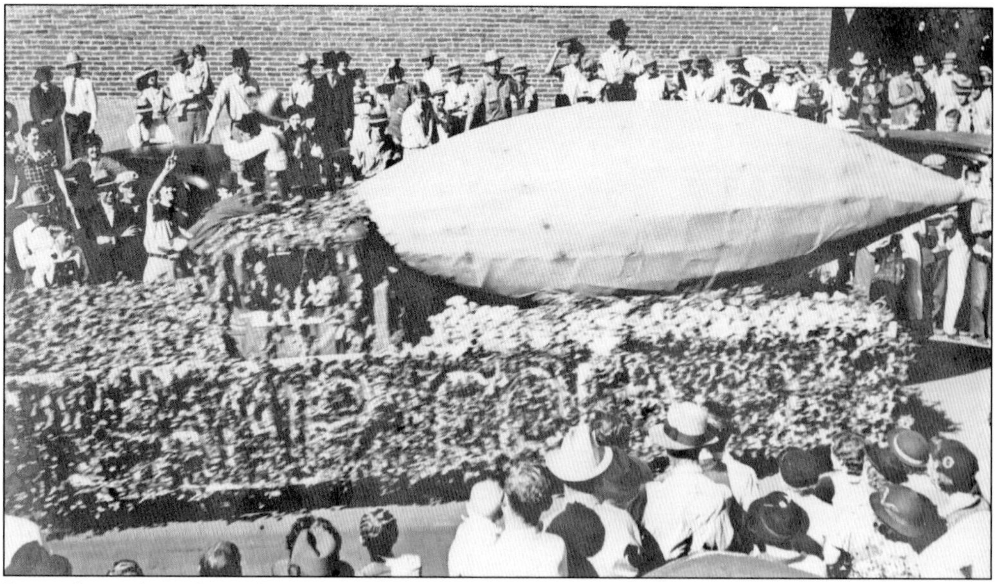

From the earliest days, the East Texas Yamboree has included participants from communities outside Upshur County. In the first Queen's Parade, Camp County sent this giant representation of a sweet potato as its entry. (HUM.)

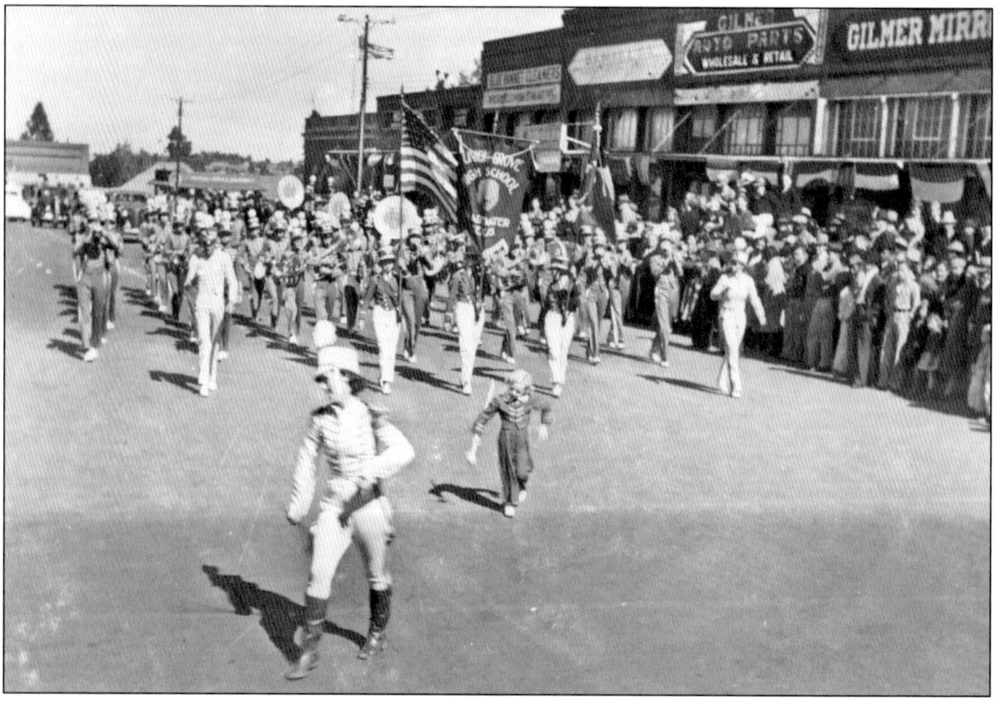

Bands in uniforms were rare during the first Queen's Parade in 1935. Union Grove had used funds received from the oil royalties to outfit their students. Gilmer wore white shirts and pants and a black cape with orange lining. Jack Mahan, the band director at Union Grove, persuaded the East Mountain Schools to get uniforms for their band, and the movement grew. Every one of the seven school districts in Upshur County proudly wears their uniforms as they participate more than 70 years later. (RHL.)

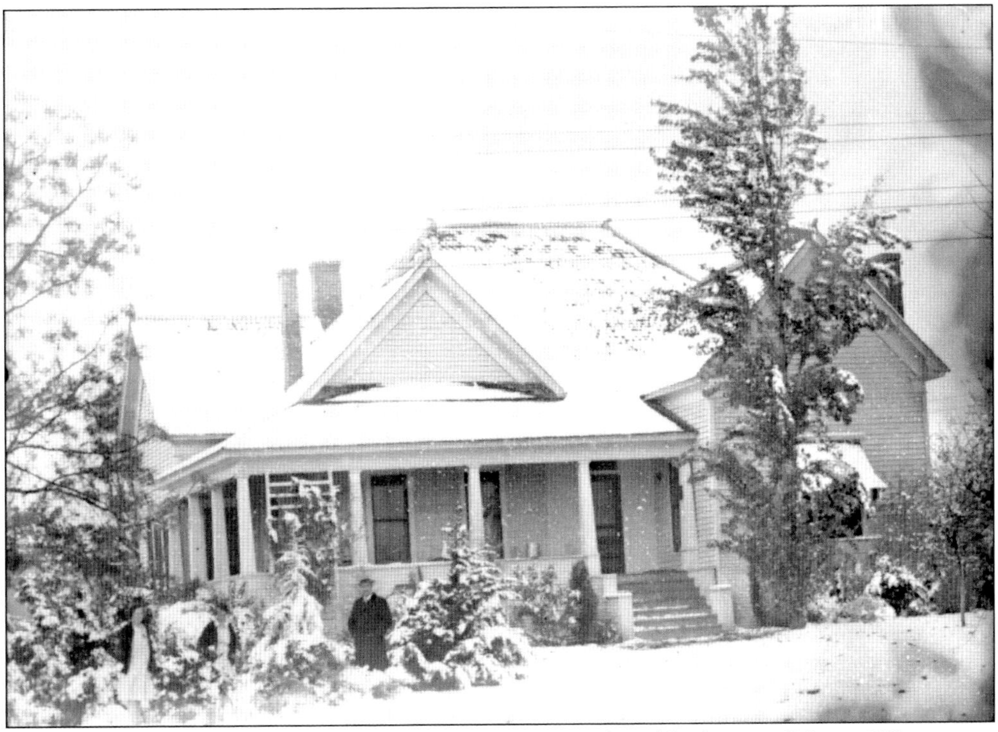

In the 1930s, probably 1939, several deep snows cast a white blanket on Gilmer. When snow blew in from the north, James M. and Cornelia Shepperd contacted J. M. Hays to make their photograph in the drifting snow. The third person seen standing by the plants on the left is unidentified. (HUM.)

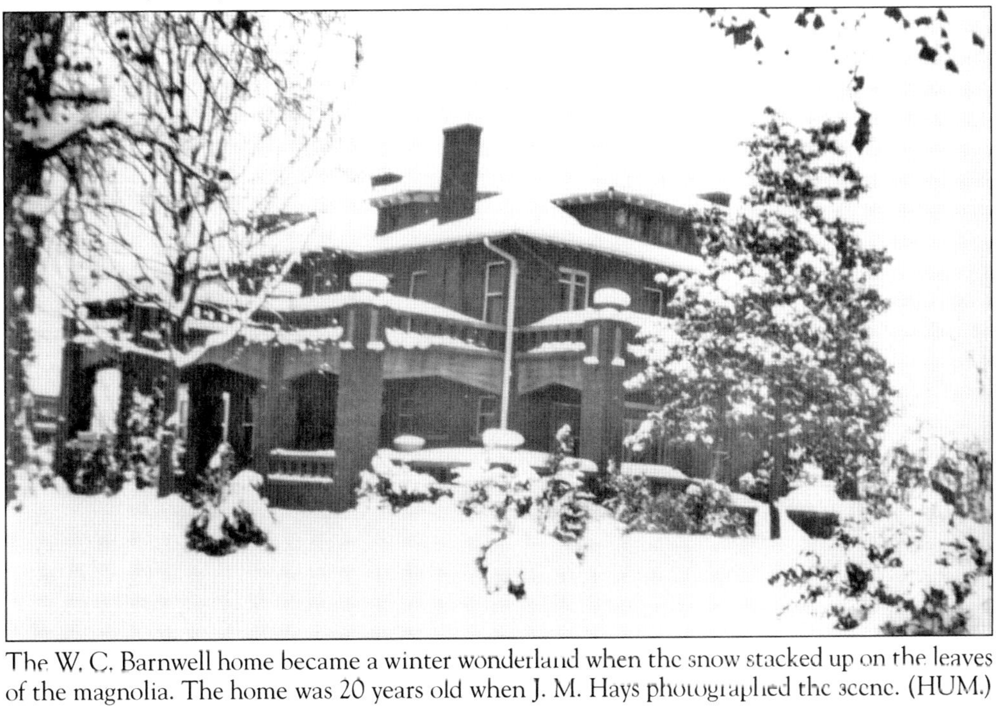

The W. C. Barnwell home became a winter wonderland when the snow stacked up on the leaves of the magnolia. The home was 20 years old when J. M. Hays photographed the scene. (HUM.)

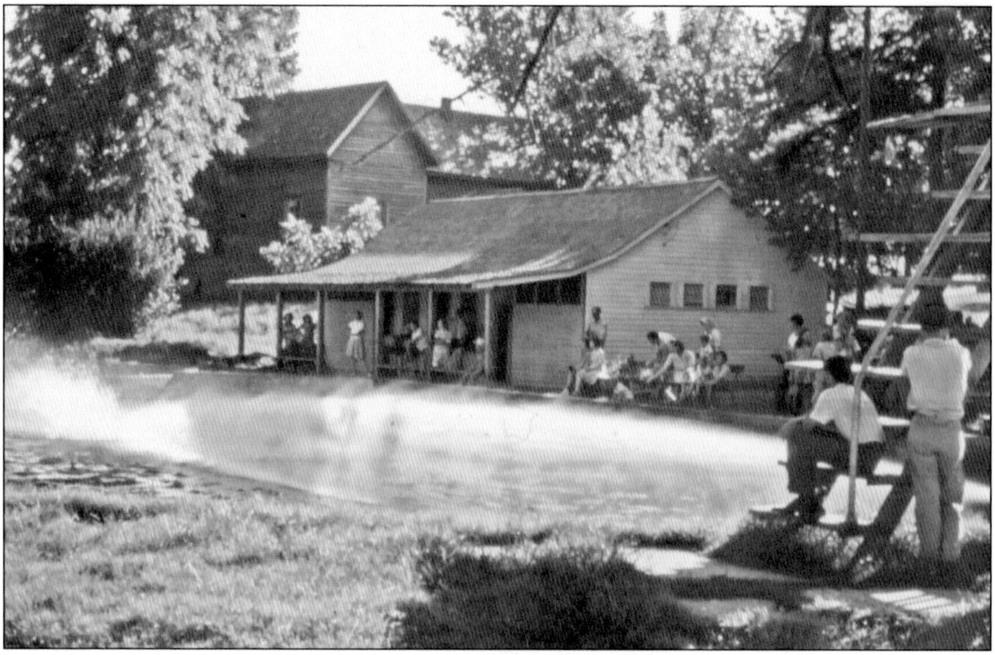

As the Great Depression continued, the City of Gilmer called on the Works Progress Administration to convert swampy lands by the railroad tracks into Roosevelt Park between Harrison and Kaufman Streets. When the swimming pool on the south end of the park was filled with water, it was an occasion worthy of celebrating. (RHL.)

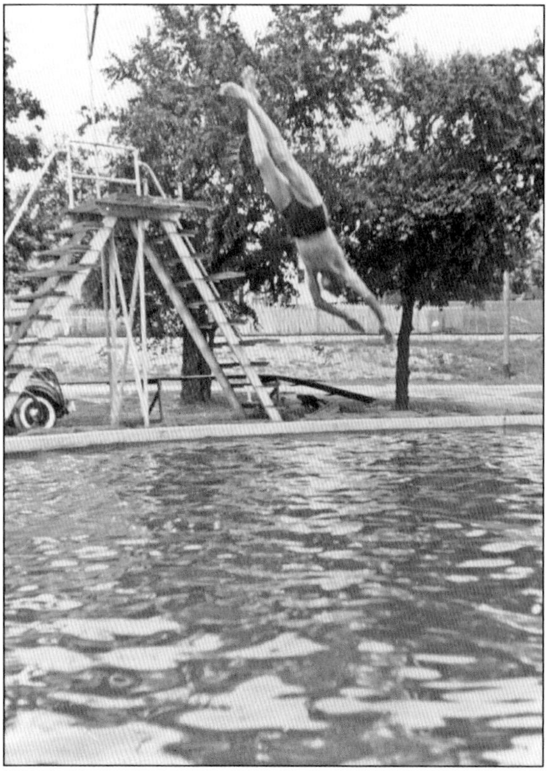

The swimming pool in Roosevelt Park was the source of summer fun for Gilmer children for more than 50 years. A generation of youths learned how to swim under the tutelage first of Leonard Pickitt and later of Truitt Rattan. Ann Bates was the last director before the second pool in the park was closed for technical reasons. (RHL.)

Juanita Nelms shares conversation with Edwin Aldredge in 1937 when the Rotary Club went to Friddle Lake for an outing. Most of the barbeques of the era were chicken, with a half a chicken slow-cooking over coals and being basted with barbeque sauce for hours until the meat practically fell off the bones. Nelms played the piano at Rotary meetings for more than a half century. (RHL.)

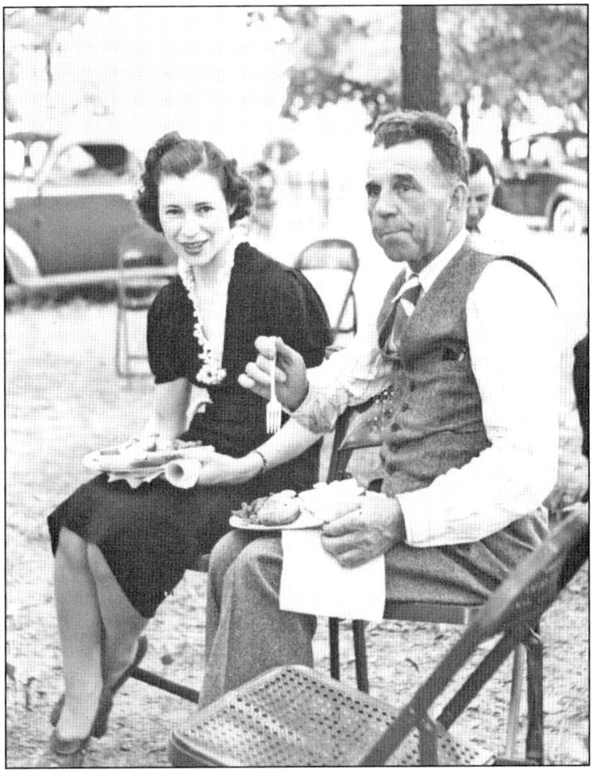

At the same 1937 gathering at Friddle Lake, a group of Rotarians posed for Russell Laschinger after they finished their barbeque. From left to right are (first row) M. G. Mell, Royce Hogg, Harry Aldredge, and Frank Marshall; (second row) C. T. Crosby Sr., Arnold Anderson, John Mack Brooks, and Dr. Harris Daniels. (RHL.)

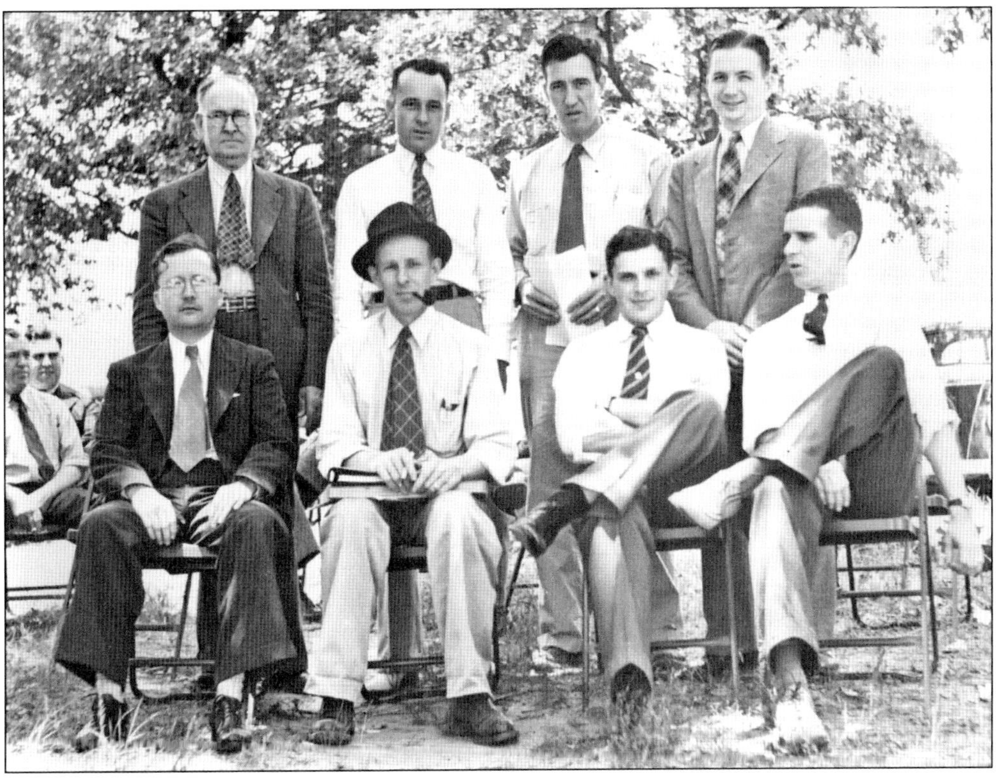

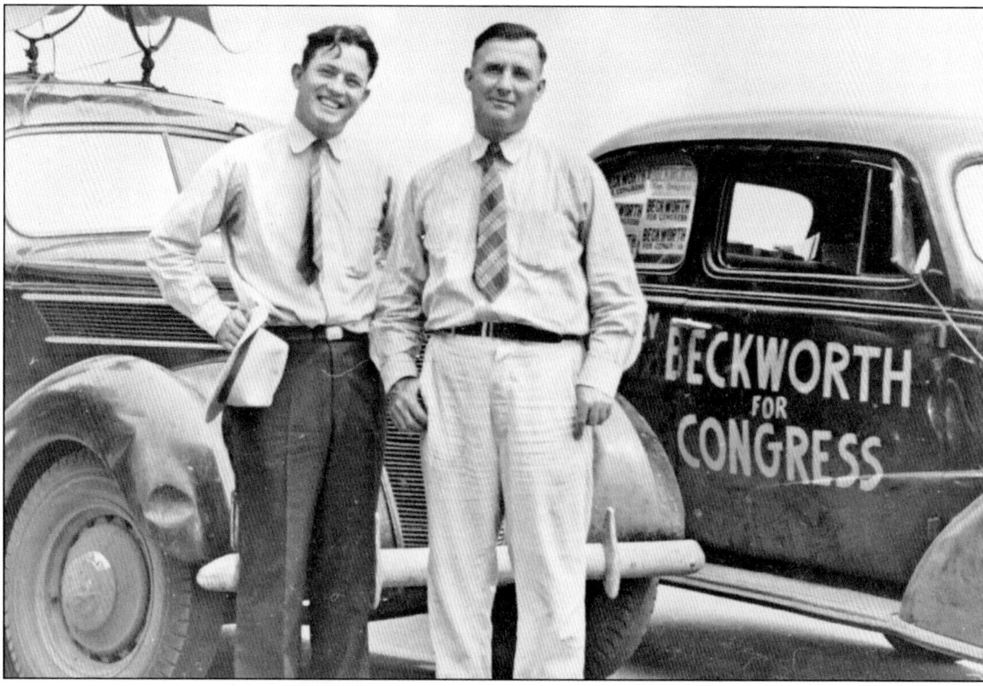

Lindley Beckworth (left) and his father, O. J. Beckworth, of Gilmer paused on the campaign trail of 1938 when Lindley made his first race to be the Congressman from the Third Congressional District. When he took the oath of office in 1939, the Upshur County Democrat was the youngest member of the U.S. House. He served from 1939 to 1953 and from 1957 to 1967. (GM.)

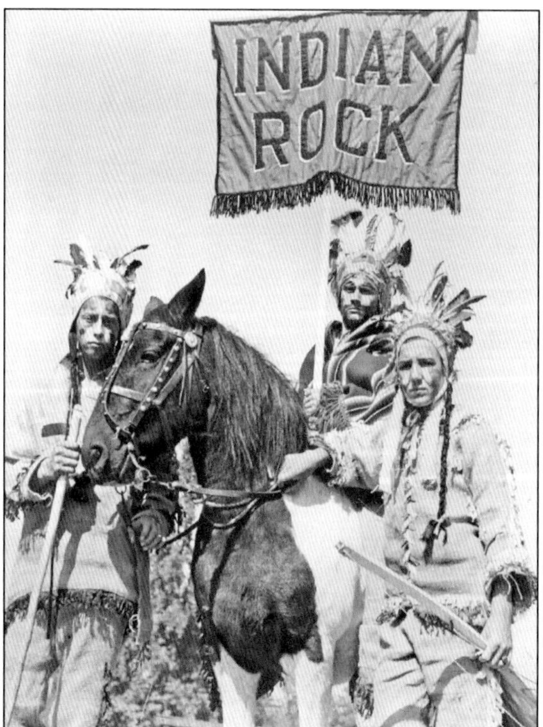

For the 1938 Yamboree School Parade, organized by Fred Covin, the students from the Indian Rock School enthusiastically donned war paint and dressed like the Hollywood Indians with whom they were most familiar. (GM.)

Dr. T. S. Ragland (center) was joined by his sons, Dr. Hugh M. Ragland (left) in 1934 and Dr. Madison S. Ragland in 1929, in the general practice of medicine. The first units of the Ragland Clinic-Hospital at the corner of Cass and Davis Streets opened in 1933. (HUM.)

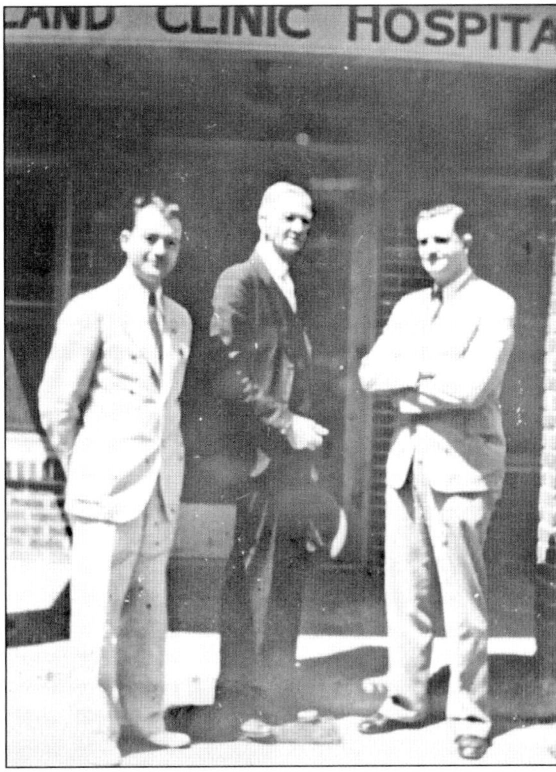

With a large west wing as a new addition to the hospital, the Ragland Clinic-Hospital had 25 beds after 1935. In 1939, Dr. J. Looney Fenlaw joined the group. (RHL.)

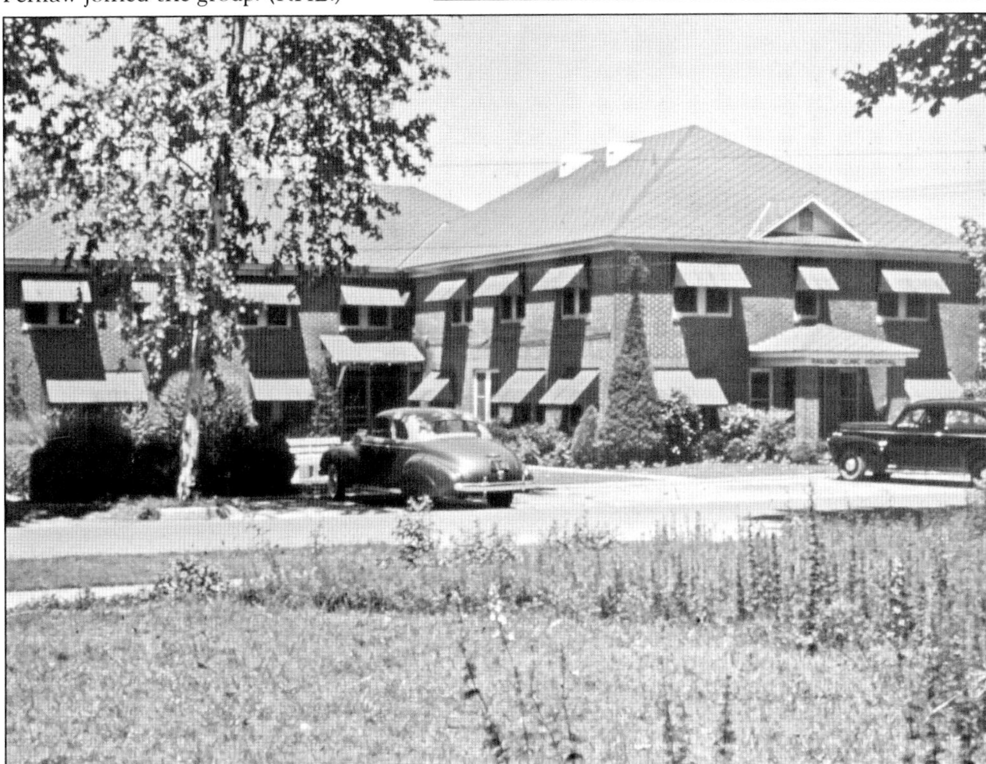

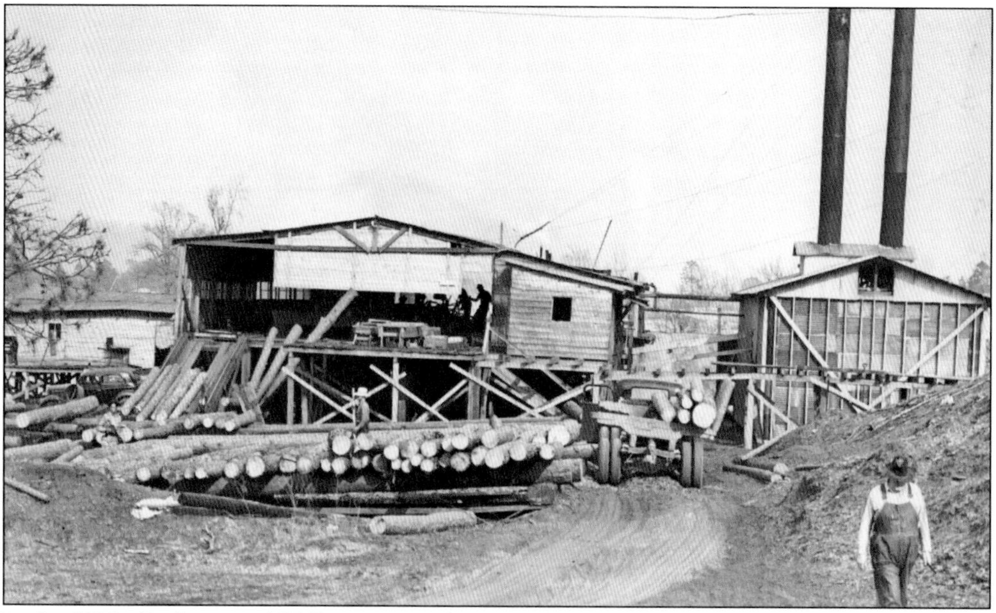

In the 1930s, Dedman and Williams opened a sawmill on South Montgomery Street, which they operated until 1942, when they sold out to Raymond and Roy Snider. After World War II, the Snider brothers sold the property to John Edward Dean, and the mill remains in the hands of the Dean family to this day. (RHL.)

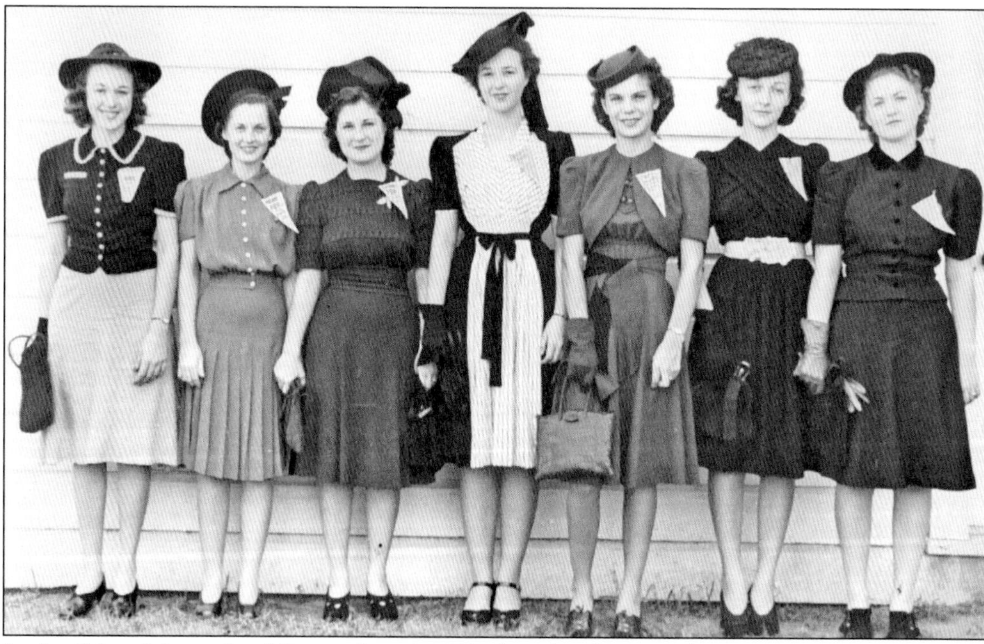

In the *Gilmer Mirror* dated September 19, 1939, these lovely young ladies in their hats and gloves were ready to leave for college. From left to right are Mary Marie Hogg, Centenary College, Shreveport, Louisiana; Natalie Harrison, Texas State College for Women, Denton; Dorothy McPhail, Southwestern University; Marjorie Mullinix, Texas State College for Women; Sarah Jo Williams, Stephens College, Columbia, Missouri; and LuElla Futrell and Earnestine Dedman, Baylor University, Waco. Dedman was the fourth queen of the Yamboree. (GM.)

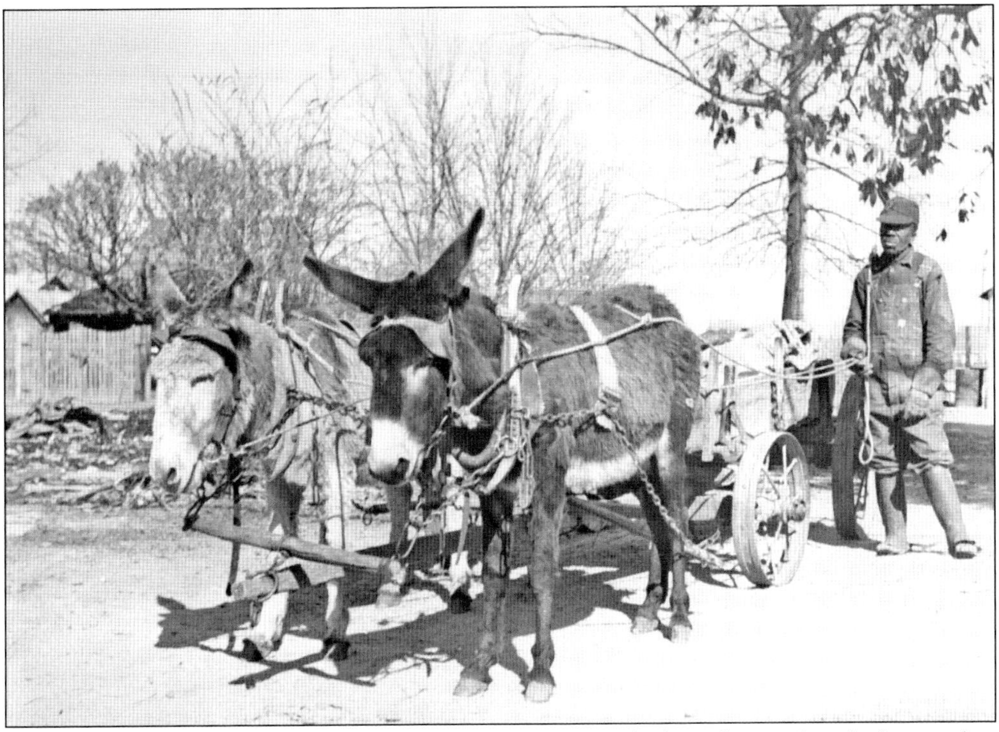

A familiar sight in Gilmer was John Bowin and his mules as he brought wood to the homes that still used woodstoves either to cook or to heat their homes. After he had finished picking cotton, Bowin supplemented his family's income by delivering wood. (RHL.)

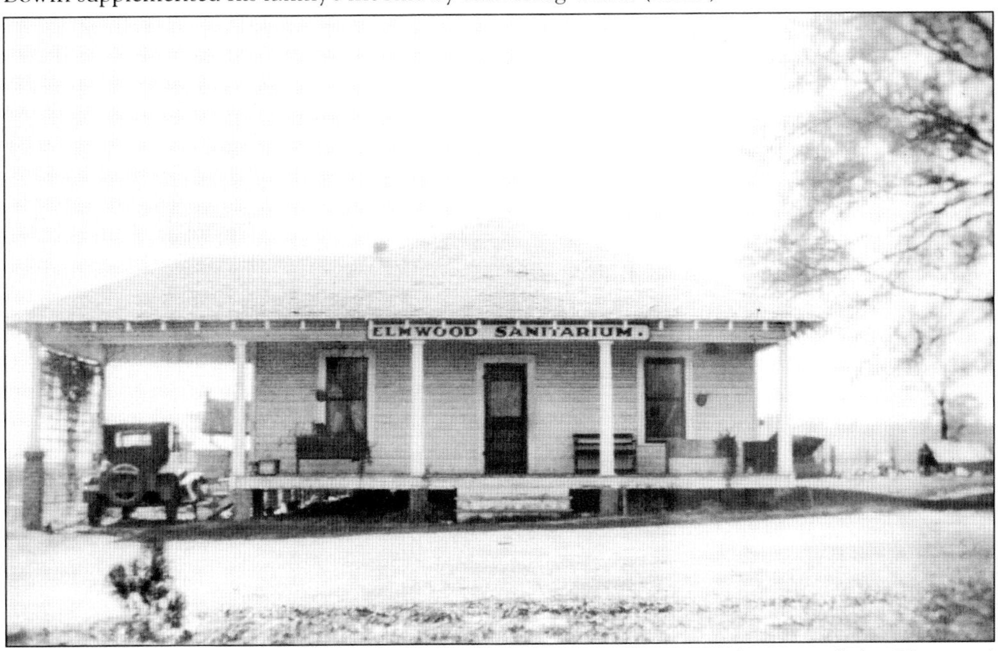

Dr. James C. Winn moved to town from Simpsonville in 1922 and operated the Elmwood Sanitarium on North Titus Street from 1927 until his death in 1942. The Glaze Chiropractic Office is at that location today. (HUM.)

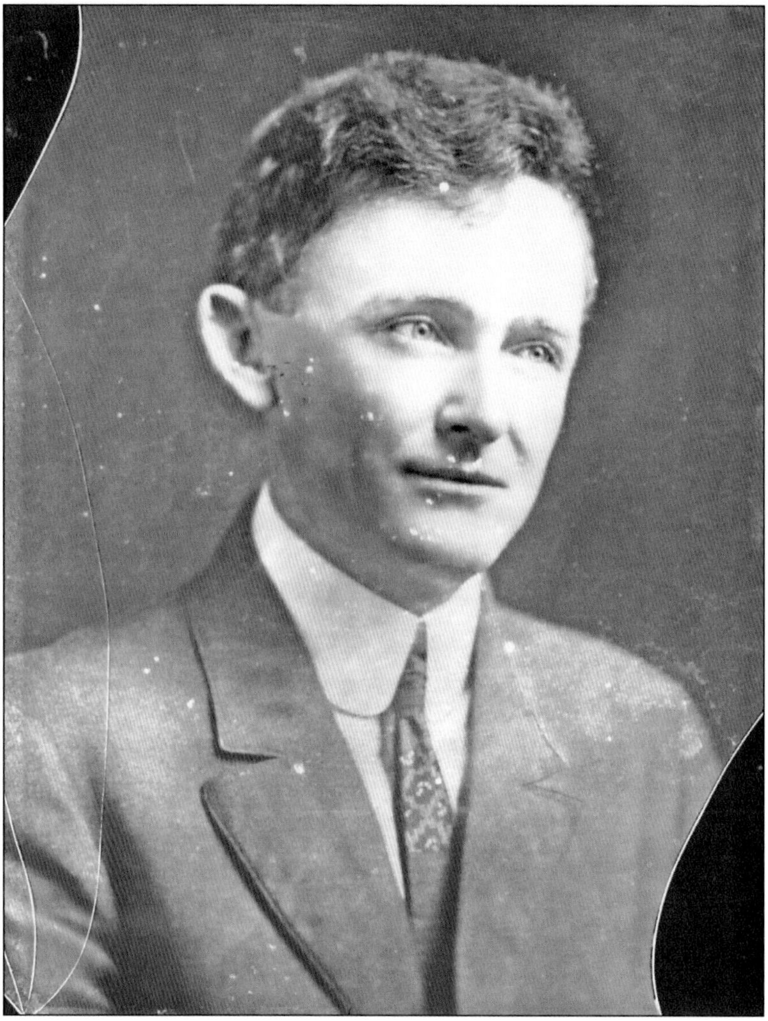

Dr. H. J. Childress opened the first hospital in Gilmer and was joined in his practice by Dr. Tom E. Marshall in 1935. In addition to his extensive medical practice, he served on the Selective Service Board and was active in Republican Party politics. (HUM.)

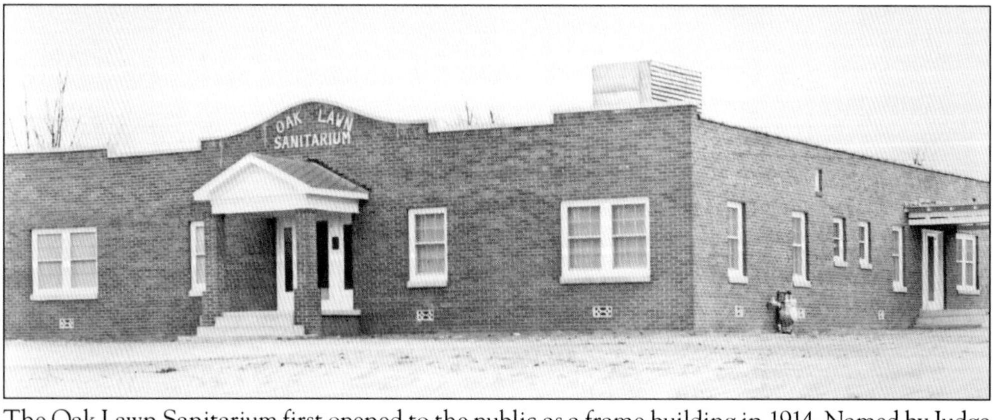

The Oak Lawn Sanitarium first opened to the public as a frame building in 1914. Named by Judge Tom Briggs because of the oak trees on the property, the first hospital served as a family residence as well as a hospital. The redbrick structure, which opened in January 1939, was fully air-conditioned, one of the first businesses in Gilmer to offer cooling comfort in the summer. (GM.)

Clemmie "Bip" Mathis was a familiar figure in the 1930s when he would join his father and brother in creating barbeque pits, goldfish ponds, and other structures of native stone. Seen here painting the home of R. H. Laschinger, Mathis departed with his wife, Mildred, in 1940 for California. After stops in south Texas and New Mexico to earn more funds, by 1943, he had a place in San Francisco where he could raise his children. (RHL.)

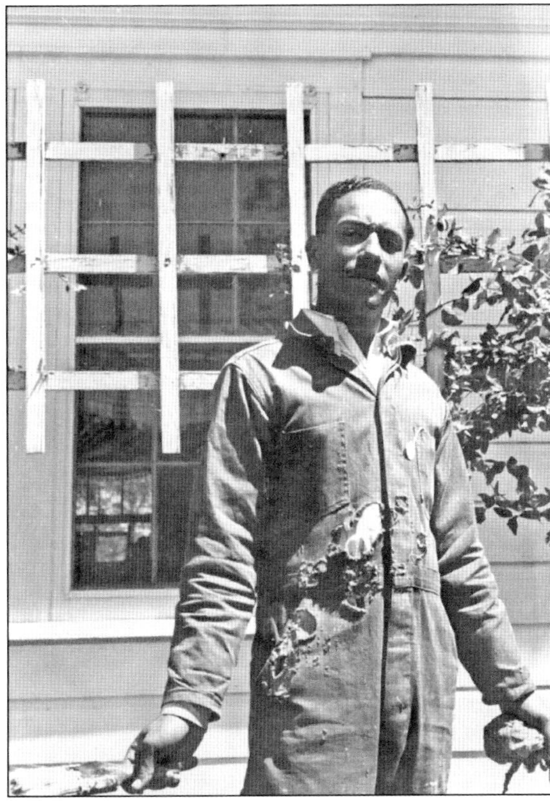

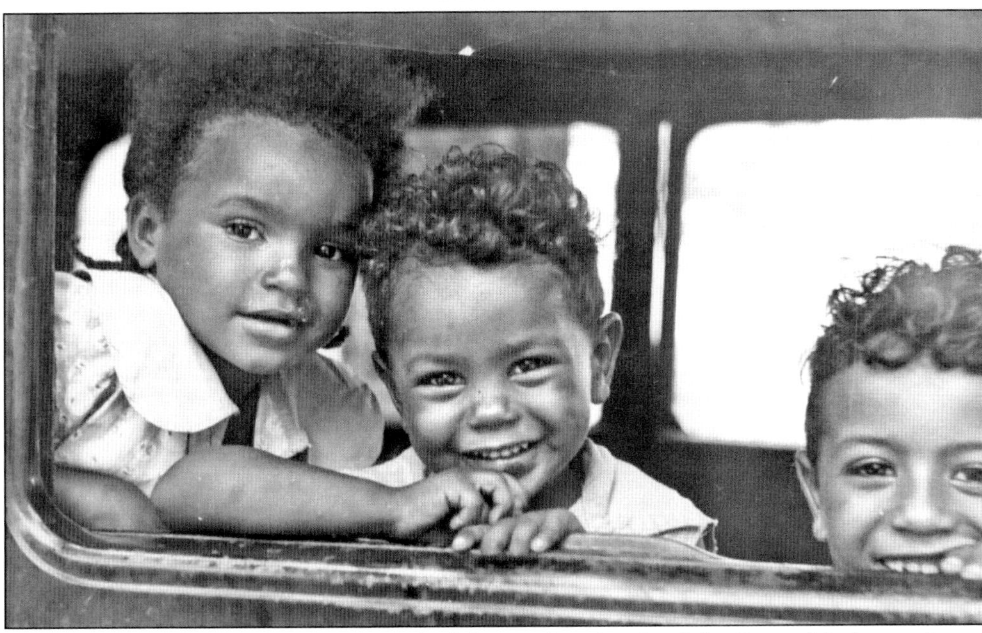

Elizabeth Anne (left) and Clemmie Jr. (right) join their brother John Royce Mathis in the car as they prepare for a ride home. As Johnny Mathis, the singer of romantic ballads, the fourth child of "Bip" and Mildred Mathis would have a successful career lasting more than a half century. (RHL.)

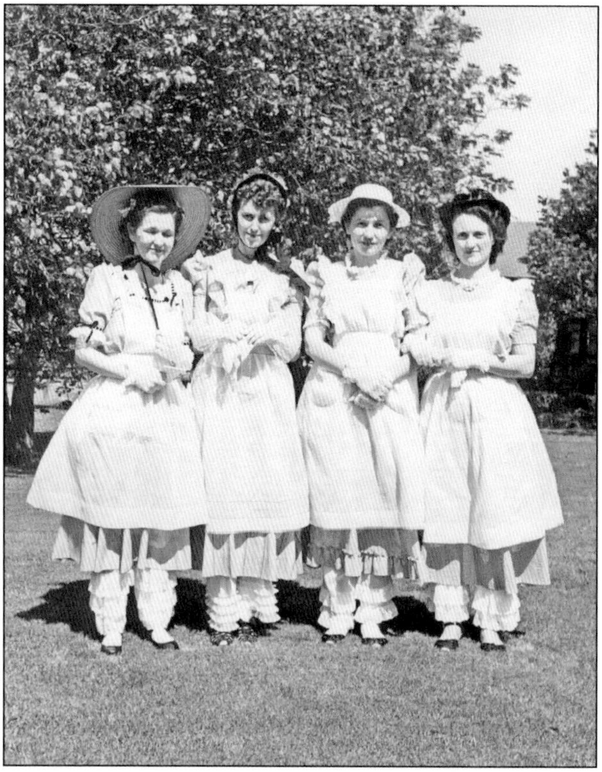

These ladies of the Twentieth Century Club—(from left to right) Elizabeth Marshall Ragland, Rae Thelma Hogg, Virginia Marshall, and Lois Marshall—portrayed *Little Women* when club members dressed as their favorite character in a book for their spring luncheon. (RHL.)

"Miss Lib" Ragland, Dr. Madison Ragland, and their first two children, James Madison "Buzzy" and Mary Anne, moved into this white two-story home on South Montgomery Street in 1940. The spindly live oak tree that is barely visible on the recently landscaped lawn grew to such a size that the house is almost hidden from view. (RHL.)

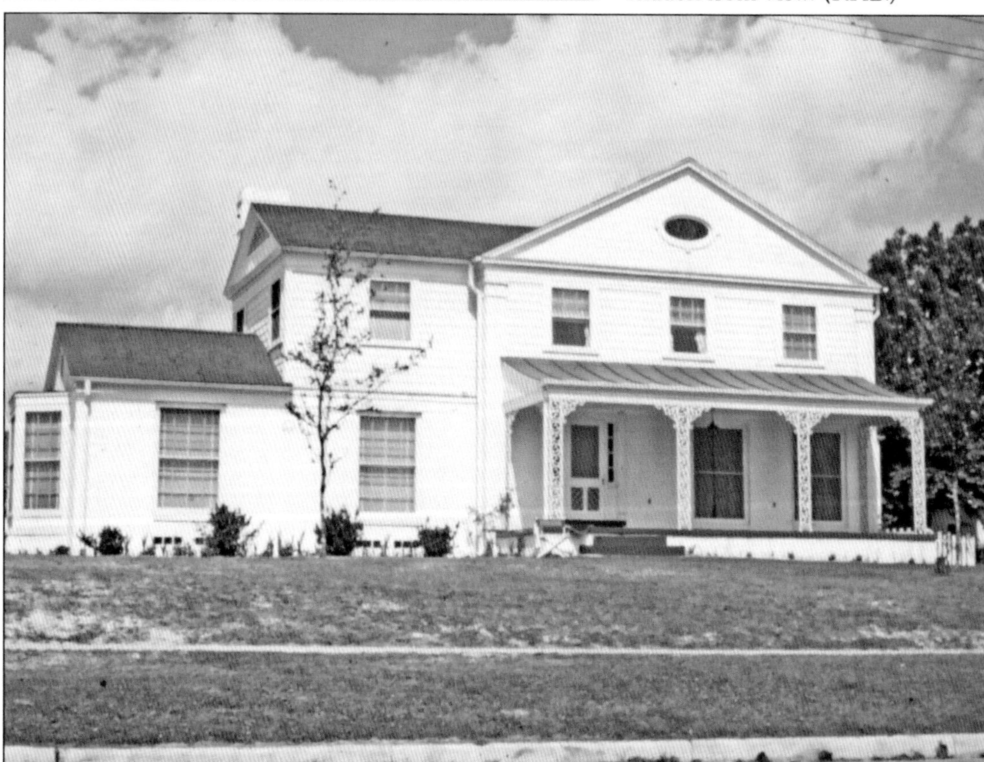

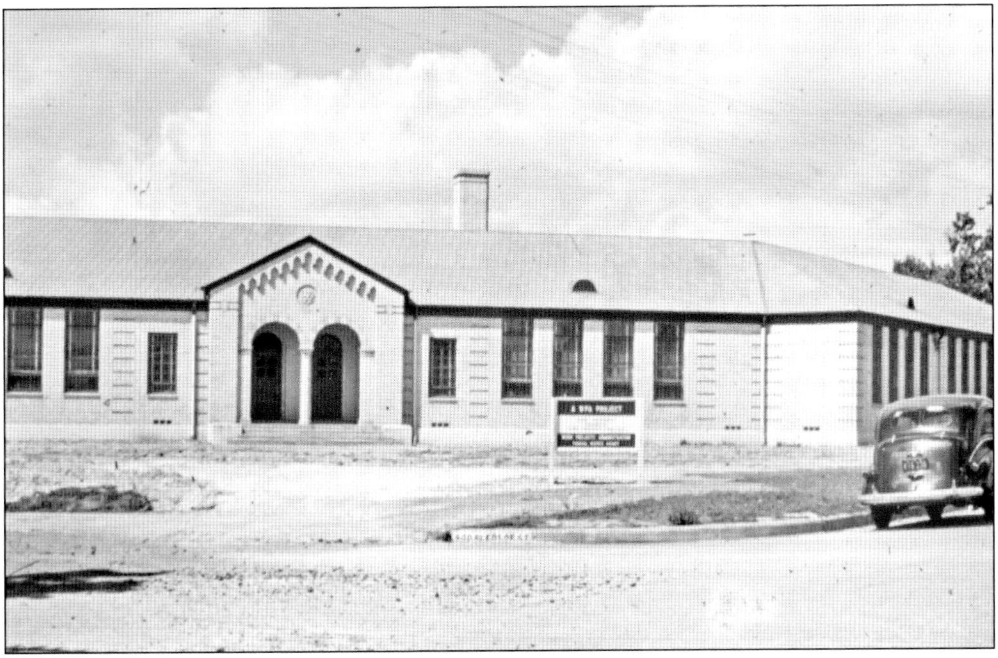

With an increase in population as a result of the oil boom and with compulsory education laws, the Gilmer enrollment had grown from 75 students in 1916 to 350 in 1941. Built with funds from the Public Works Administration (PWA), with landscaping by the Works Progress Administration, the Gilmer Elementary School was completed in 1939 to serve Gilmer children for 67 years. (RHL.)

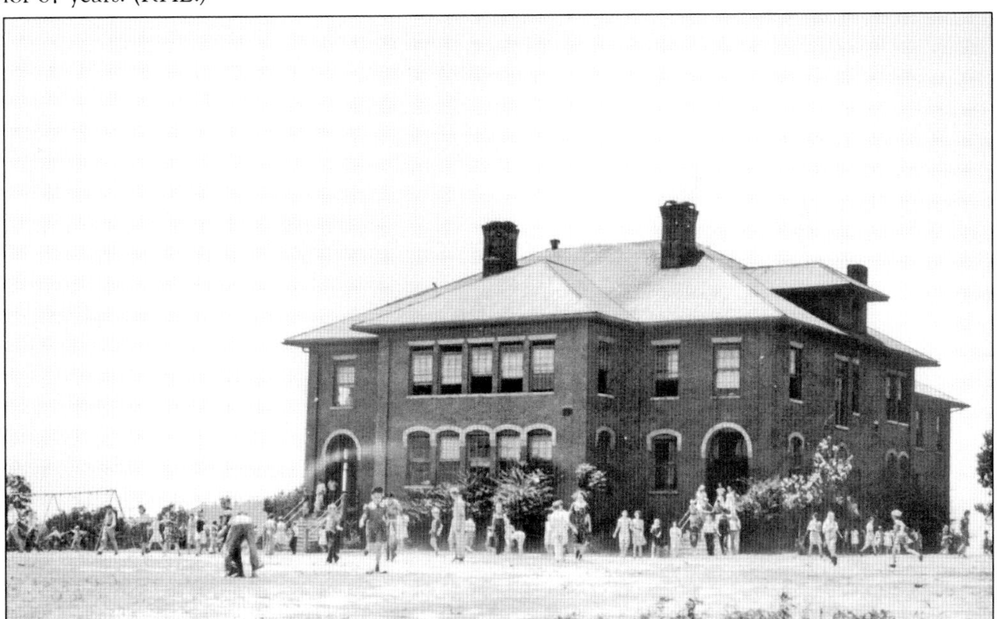

Children were enjoying recess when the photographer captured this image of the old Gilmer Ward School before the new PWA building was constructed. After its demolition, the bricks from the 1905 building went into the new Bruce School campus south of town near Gilgal Baptist Church. (RHL.)

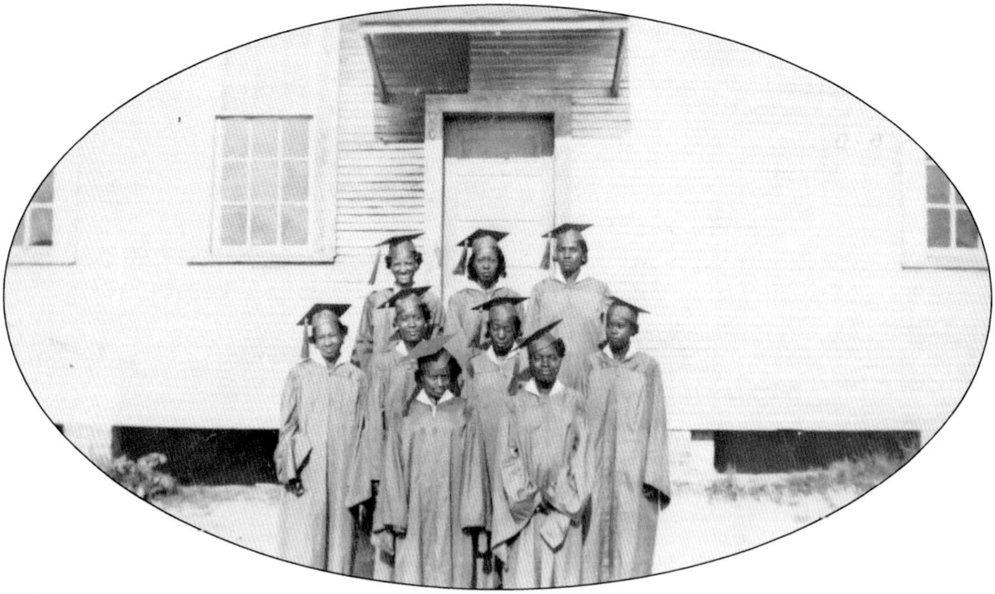

When Frankie Lindley (far left) graduated from the Bruce School, she and her friends gathered outside the white frame structure on Roberts Street near the Moses Chapel Colored Methodist Episcopal Church. This image is the only known view at the first location. (Frankie Lindley.)

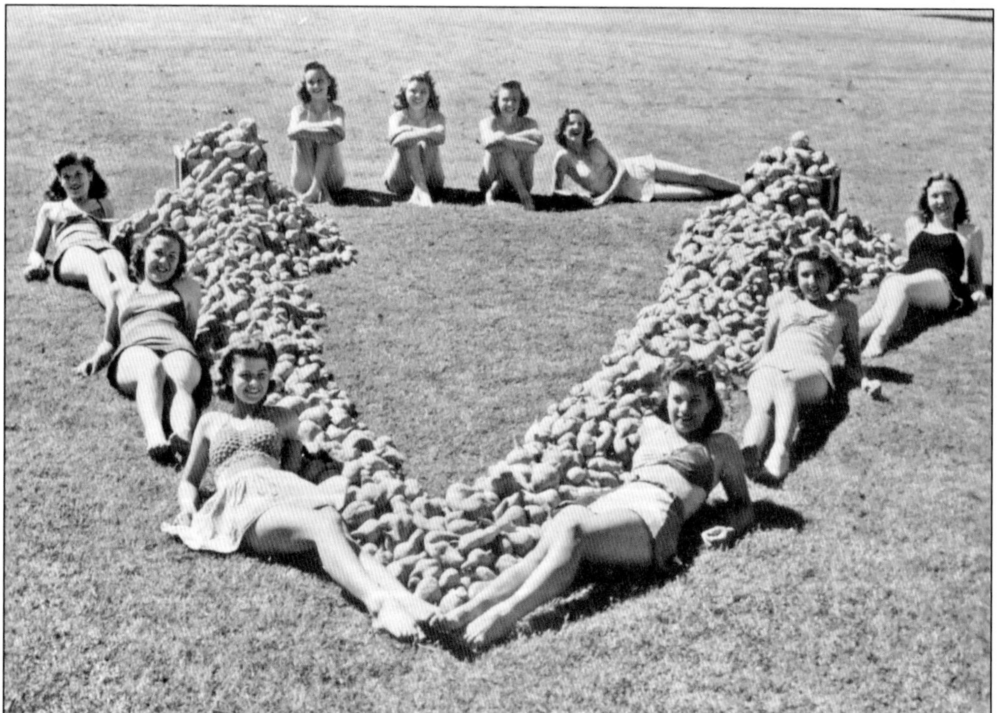

With the "Phony War" occurring in Europe and the Japanese in China, local people nervously made preparations for the 1940 Yamboree with this celebration of the sweet potato and pretty girls. Although the Yamboree never had a swimsuit competition, the planners had no problems with using a scantily clad young lady to promote the sweet potato crop. (RHL.)

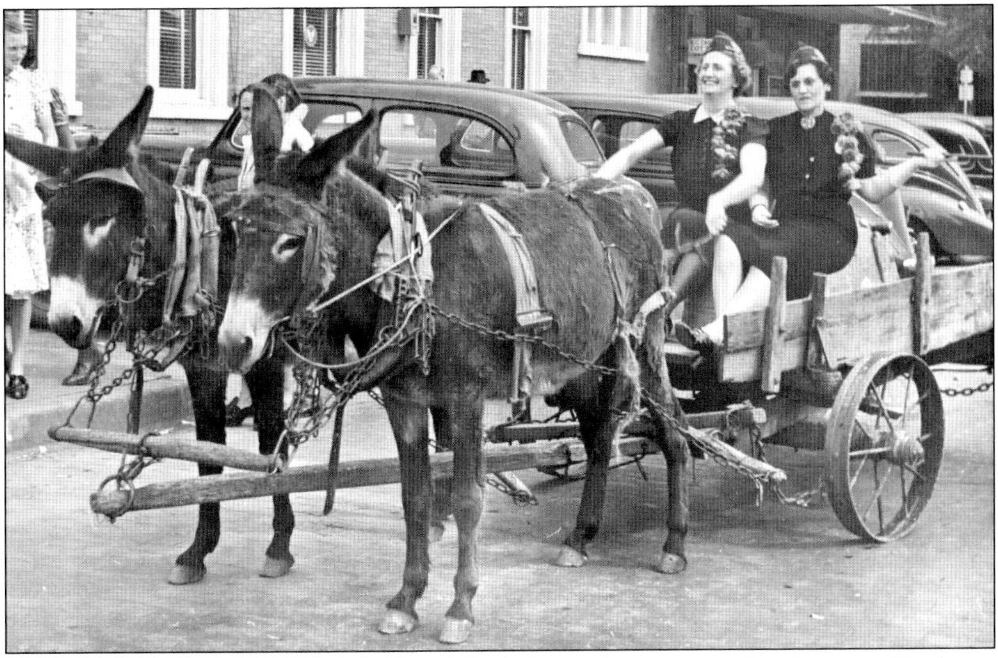

All in good fun, Manie Stephens (left) and Stella Prater drive a team of mules in the Yamboree Queen's Parade. A few years earlier, Stephens had joined with Cecile Ragland in stopping a train because the parade was crossing the railroad tracks and had to proceed. Since then, the parade has always remained on the east side of the tracks. (RHL.)

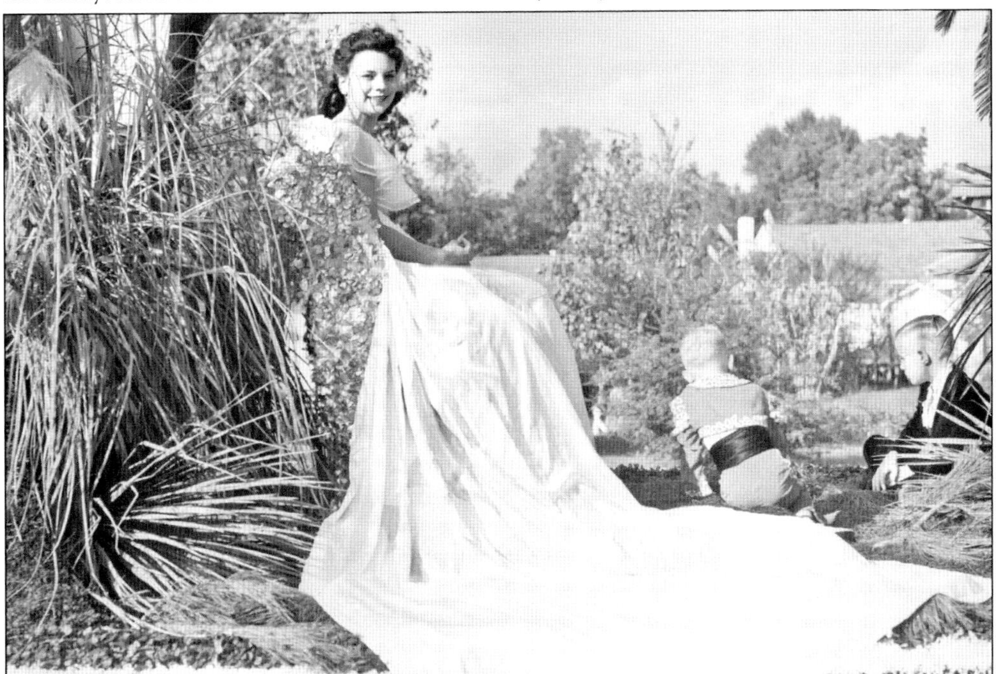

Genice Graves rides in beautiful weather on her day to be the seventh queen of the East Texas Yamboree in 1941. Graves won over Marceile Marr of East Mountain, Dorothy Smith, and Lila Blanche Stephens. (GM.)

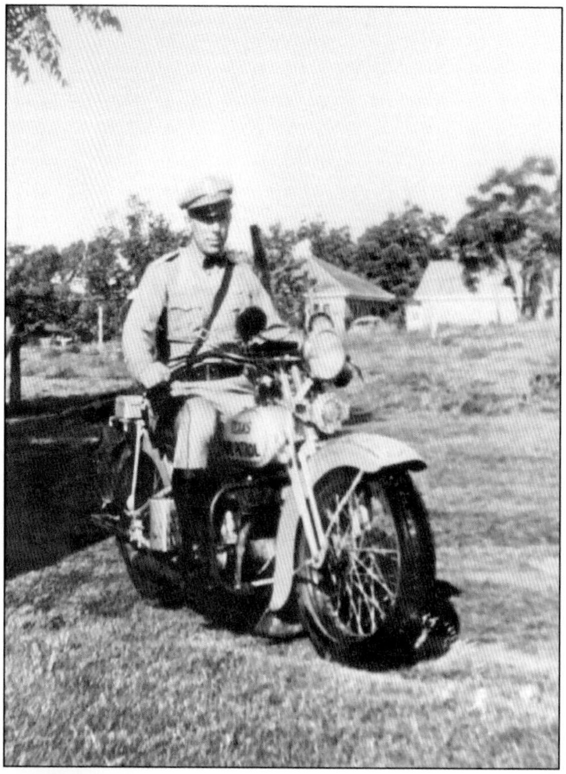

After graduating Gilmer High as the valedictorian and serving as the first principal at Harmony High School, Wilson F. "Pat" Speir joined the Highway Patrol of the Texas Department of Public Safety as a trooper in 1941. After rising through the ranks, Speir served as the director from 1968 to 1980, during which time he oversaw the reorganization of the Texas Rangers. (GM.)

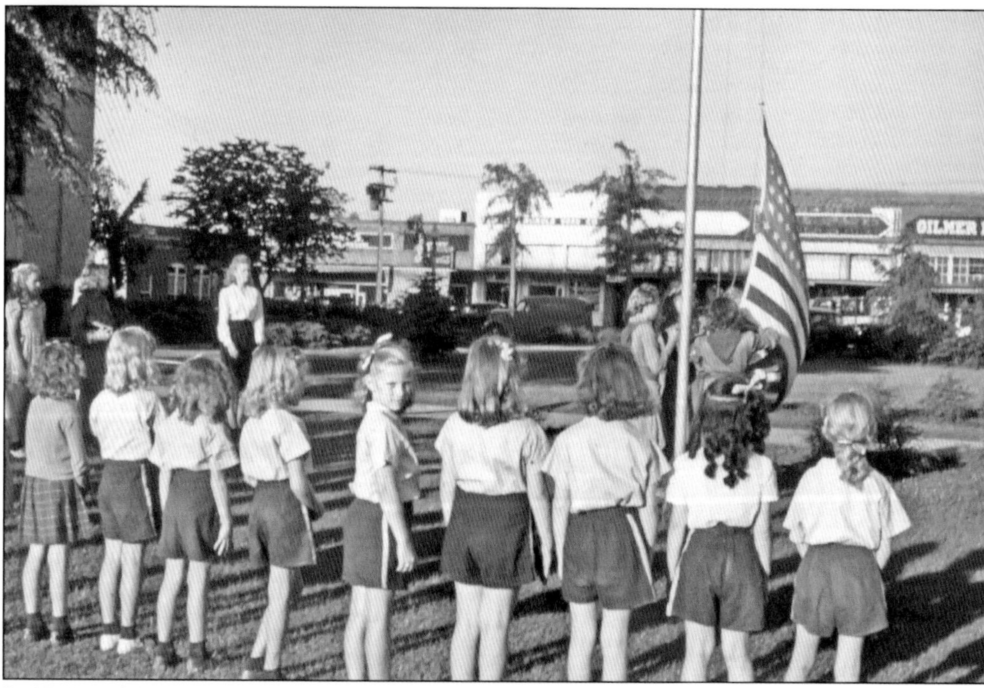

In 1941, with Virginia Laschinger as the leader of the Girl Scouts in Gilmer, the girls gathered for a ceremonial raising of the flag. Many girls in the community joined in Scouting for the activities and the fellowship. During the uneasy peace that summer, patriotism ran high at home. (RHL.)

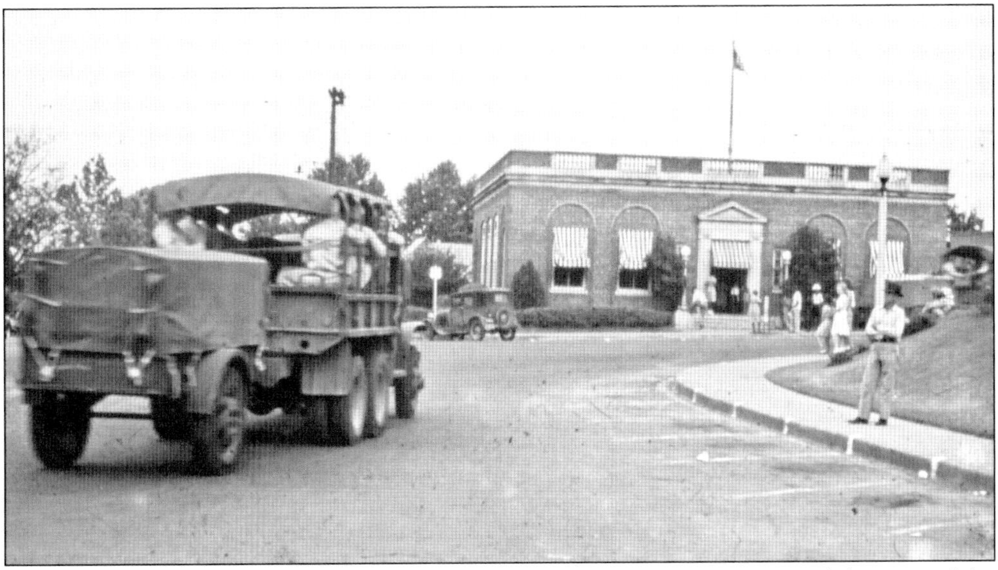

With almost breathless excitement, the *Gilmer Mirror* described the capture of elements of the Red Army scouts in the Jefferson Hotel by members of the Blue Army, who were plotting an "invasion" of Shreveport, where the Red Army was located. The Blue Army drove through the town on maneuvers on U.S. Highway 271 "at a fast clip between 7:00 and 8:30 o'clock . . . up from the south and turned eastward on Highway 154." The Red Army was the 1st Armored Division from Fort Knox, Kentucky, while the Blue Army was the 2nd Division from Fort Benning, Georgia. (RHL.)

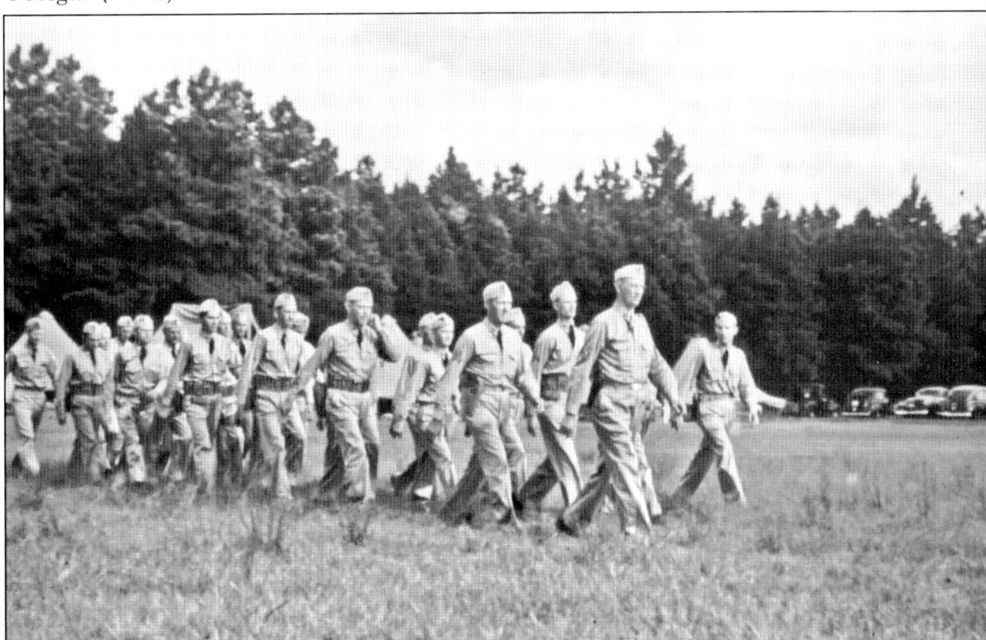

Coach Henry McClelland calls cadence as members of the Texas Home Defense Guard, Company C, 32nd Battalion, march on maneuvers in September 1942. Starting fifth from right and continuing left, Home Guard members include Jimmie Marshall, John Mack Brooks, Woodrow Roark, and H. M. "Ickie" Prater. (RHL.)

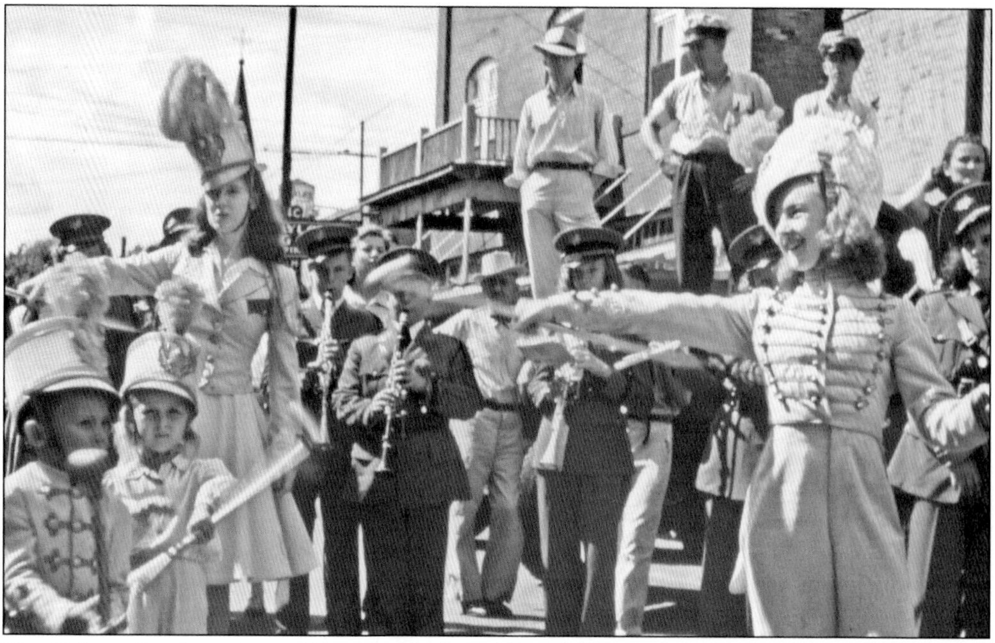

The Gilmer Band, majorette Betty Jo Black (left), and drum major Pat Warren performed with mascots Bobby Warrick and Shirley Ann Gunn in Jefferson on a booster trip. Traveling to promote the East Texas Yamboree, the booster trip consisted of a caravan of business leaders, singers, and the Buckeye Band. They would travel a circuit of neighboring towns to encourage attendance at Gilmer's annual celebration of the sweet potato. (RHL.)

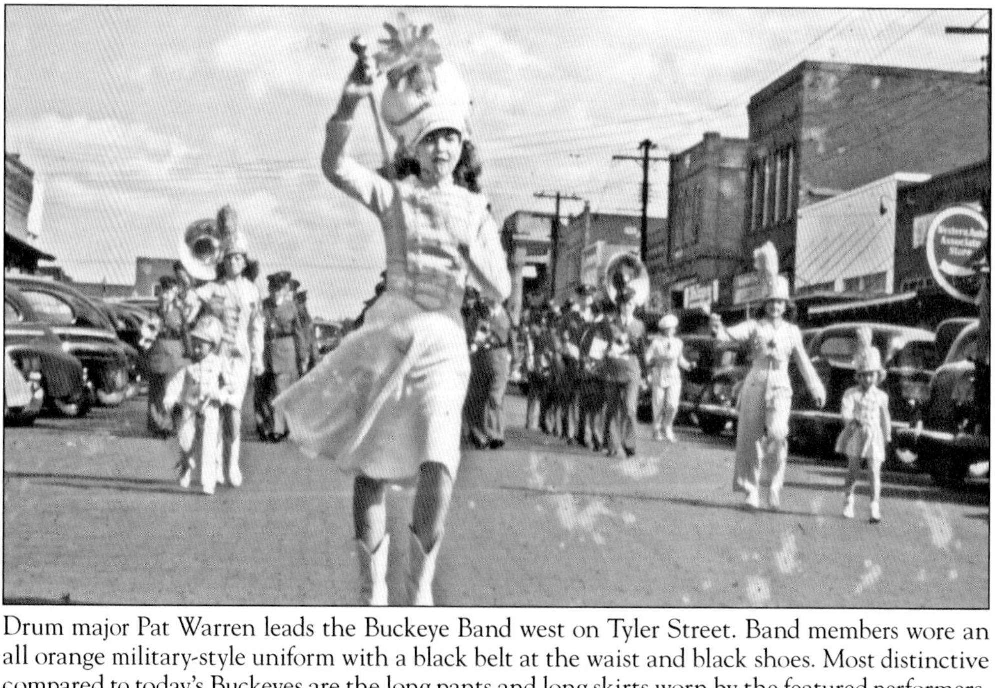

Drum major Pat Warren leads the Buckeye Band west on Tyler Street. Band members wore an all orange military-style uniform with a black belt at the waist and black shoes. Most distinctive compared to today's Buckeyes are the long pants and long skirts worn by the featured performers. Members of the band had worked for several years, begging funds from local businesses and raising money, to get these new uniforms. (RHL.)

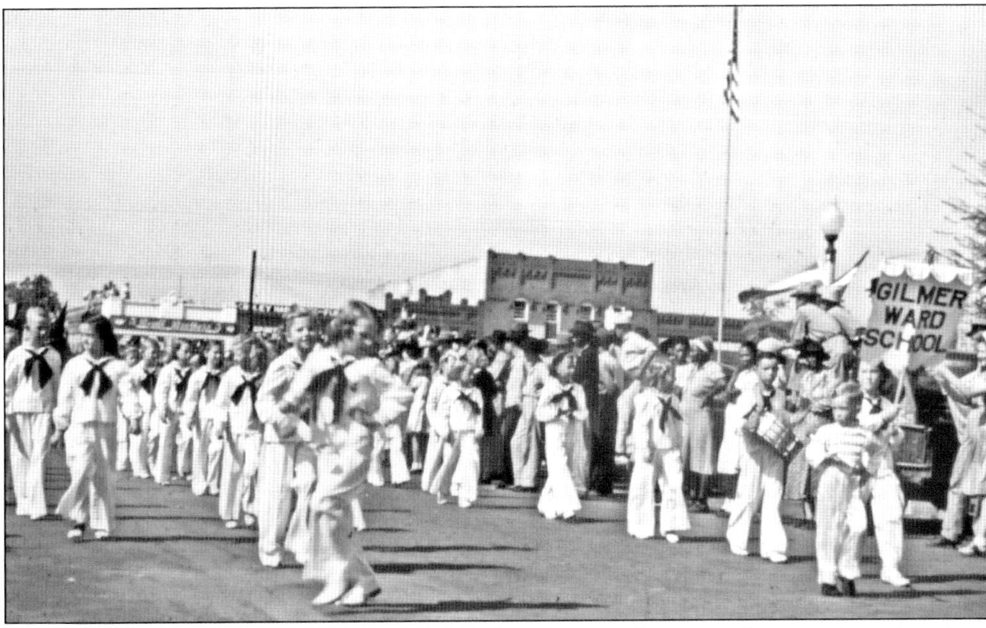

Gilmer Ward School students wear matching white shirts and pants as they march in the school parade in 1941. Even after World War II, parents would sew a costume that fit the theme their child's school was portraying so that hundreds of Upshur County children could march in the parade. (RHL.)

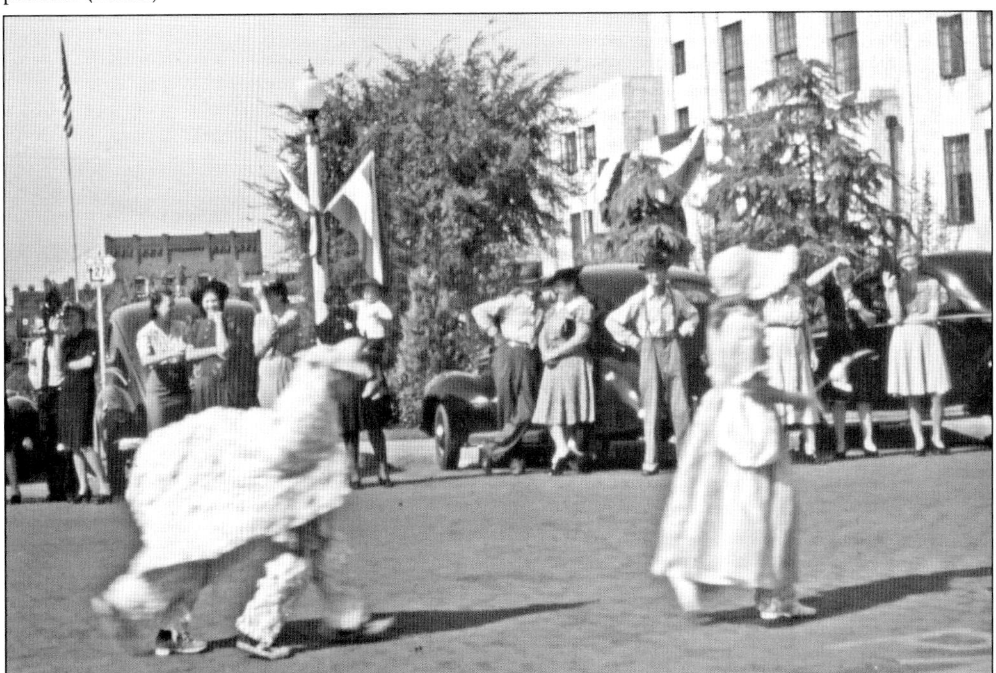

With the theme for the year nursery rhymes, Bo Peep marches past the new courthouse with her sheep following behind her. Courthouse workers and friends pile out on the second-story roof of the eastern wing of the building to get a better view. Women, black and white alike, wear hats and sometimes gloves to attend the parade, an unthinkable sight today. (RHL.)

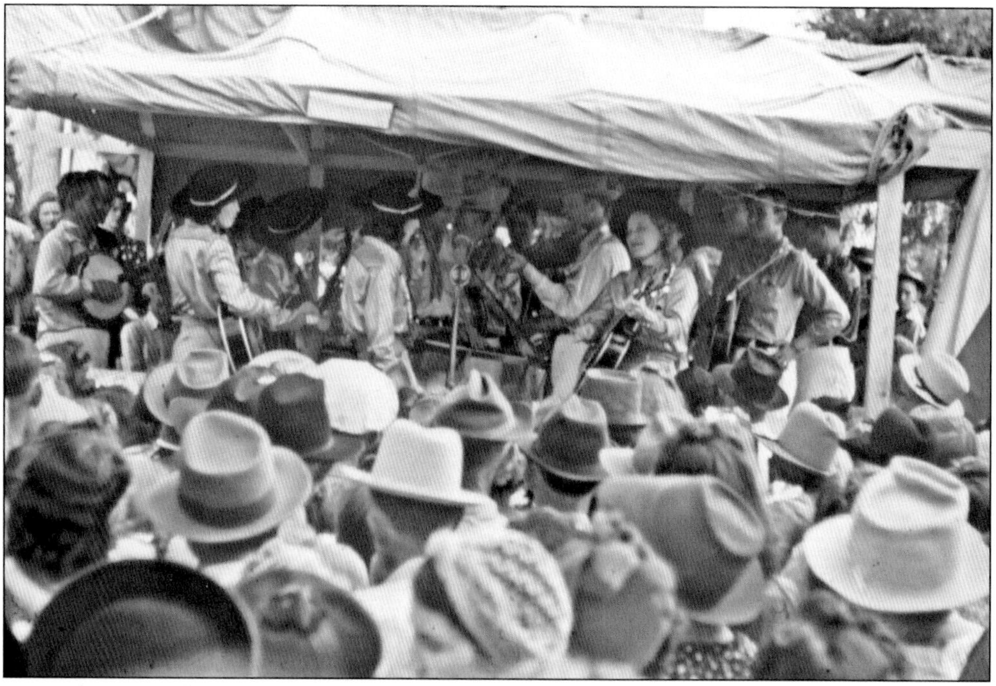

Cowgirls in matching gold satin shirts perform their song on guitar and fiddle, while another "hillbilly" band of guys in blue shirts await their turn at the bandstand at the Yamboree. The fiddle contest is the one event of the East Texas Yamboree that not only has continued from the first year, but also met and competed during the war years. (RHL.)

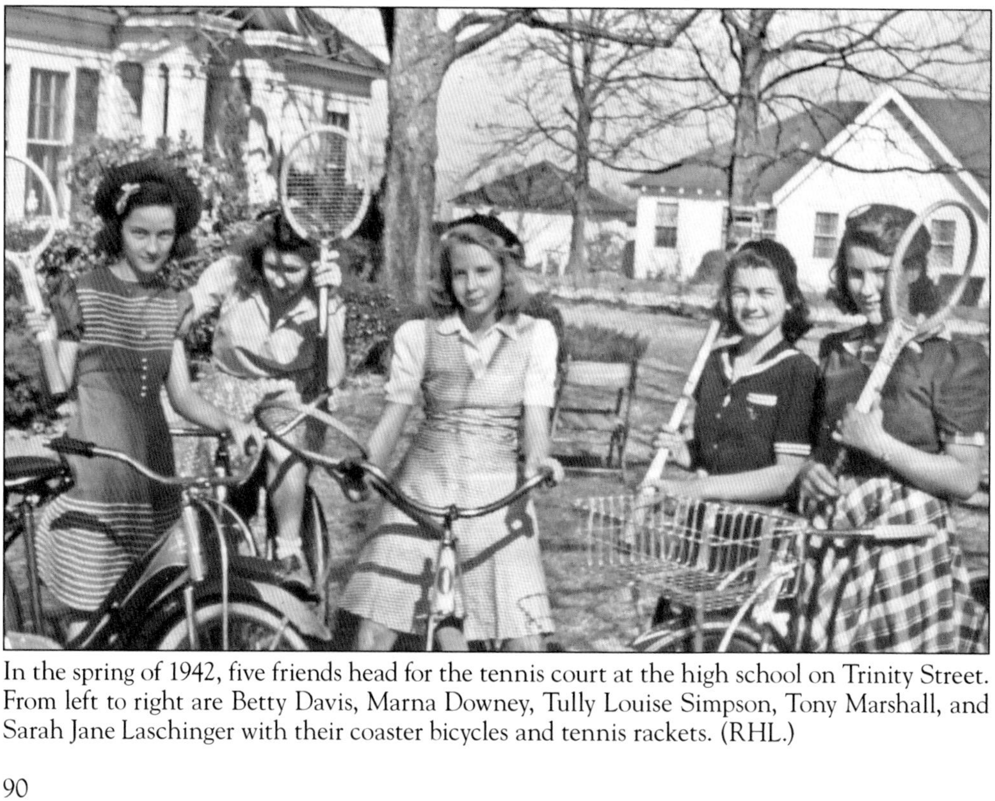

In the spring of 1942, five friends head for the tennis court at the high school on Trinity Street. From left to right are Betty Davis, Marna Downey, Tully Louise Simpson, Tony Marshall, and Sarah Jane Laschinger with their coaster bicycles and tennis rackets. (RHL.)

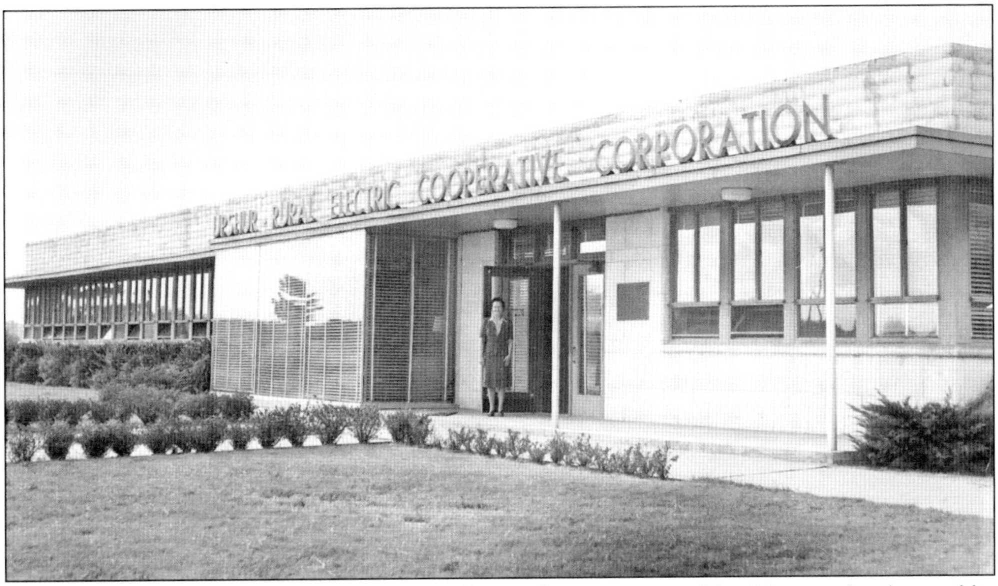

Construction started on April 21, 1941, on the southwest corner of the 26-acre plot donated by the City of Gilmer and Upshur County. The headquarters of Upshur Rural Electric was the result. Using the efforts of 100 members of the National Youth Administration (NYA) on what was probably their first job, Upshur Rural took advantage of a $1.7-million grant to build the facility, including the kitchen and auditorium still in use today. Delta Scales, the second executive director, stands at the door of the newly completed facility. (Rural Electric Administration.)

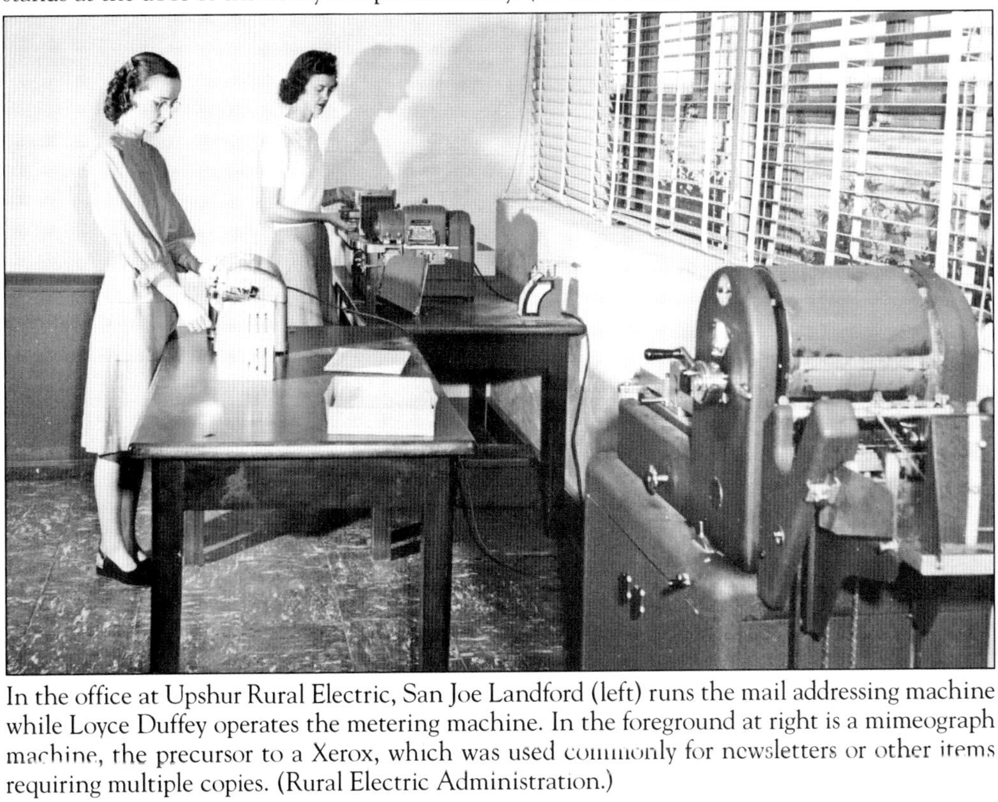

In the office at Upshur Rural Electric, San Joe Landford (left) runs the mail addressing machine while Loyce Duffey operates the metering machine. In the foreground at right is a mimeograph machine, the precursor to a Xerox, which was used commonly for newsletters or other items requiring multiple copies. (Rural Electric Administration.)

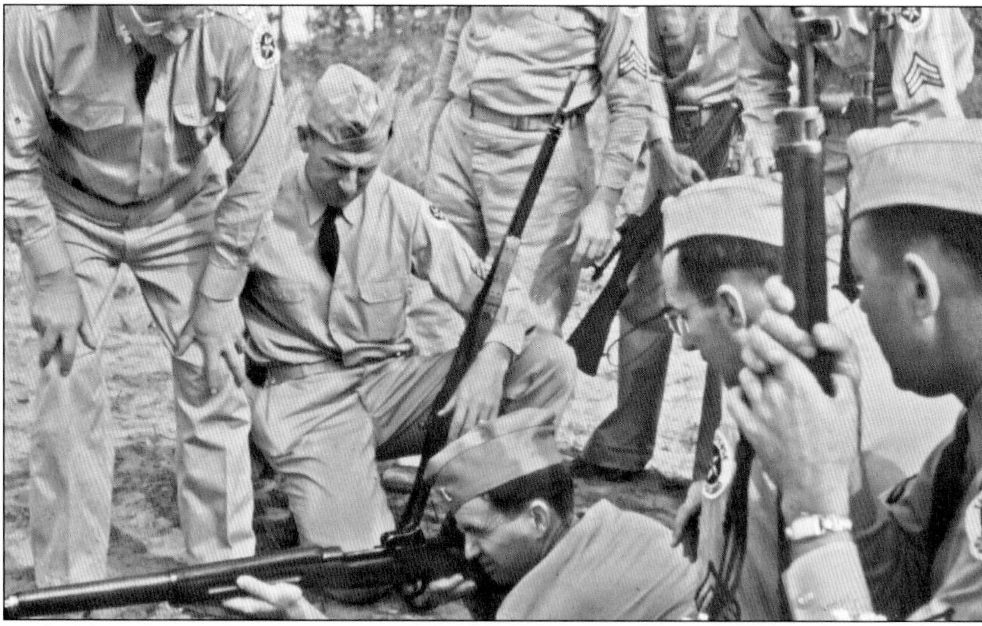

A World War I veteran and county superintendent during the week, Frank Smith (upper left) leans over the demonstration on how to fire one's rifle. Smith served as the captain of Company C, 32nd Battalion, Texas Home Defense Guard. Cecil Sorrells (kneeling to Smith's left) and Paul Williams are the two sergeants next to Smith. (RHL.)

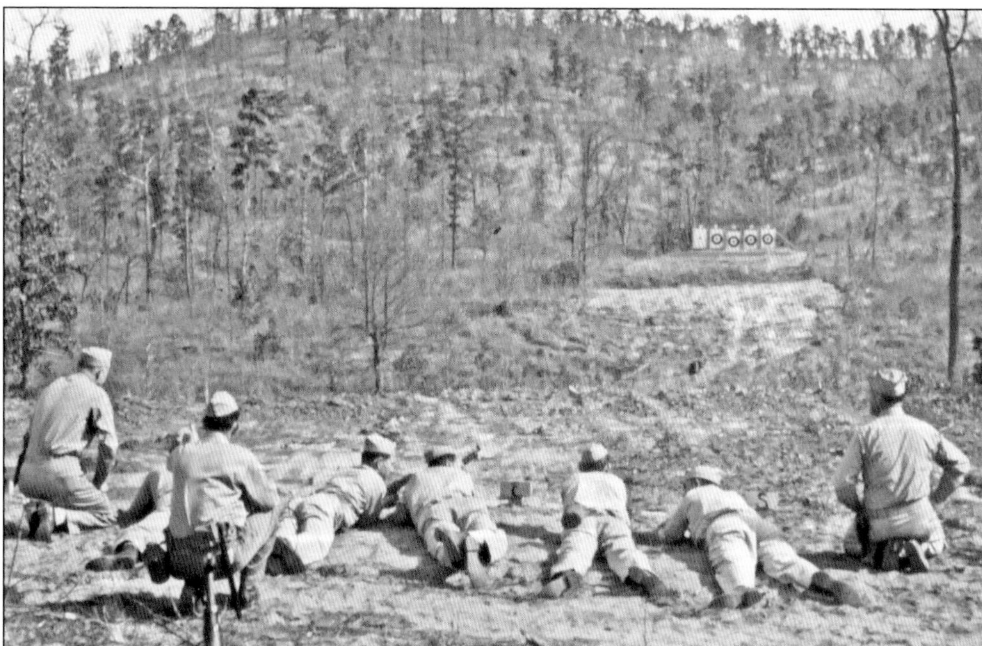

Learning how to fire their weapons, members of the Texas Home Reserve Guard spread out at the firing range east of town. The Texas National Guard had already been mobilized when the Home Guard started recruiting in January 1941. While the United States was talking peace, businessmen in Gilmer were busy preparing for whatever emergency they might have to face. (RHL.)

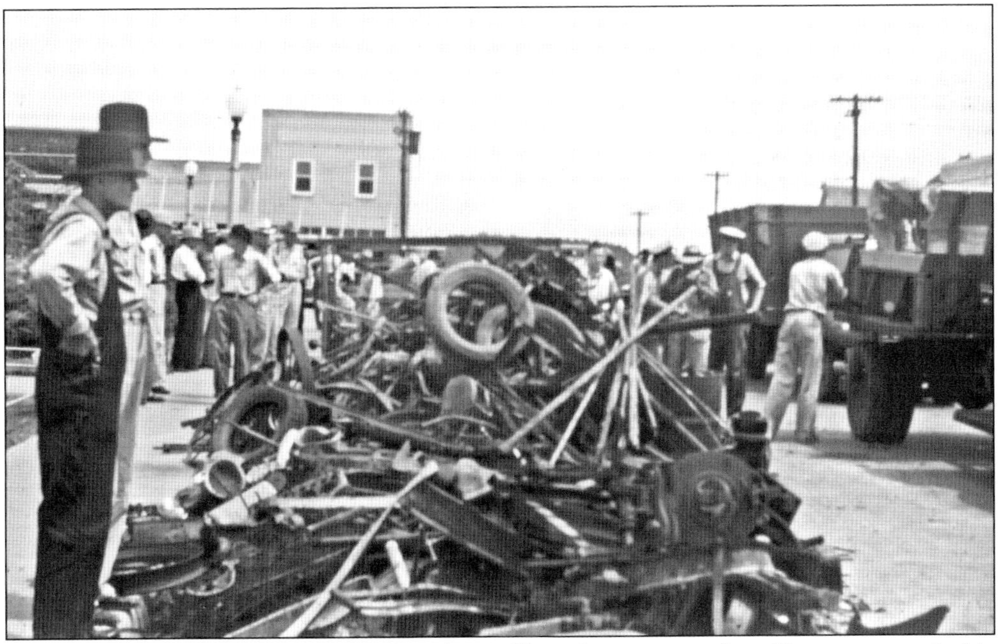

Once war was declared, scare materials such as rubber, aluminum, and steel became too valuable to throw away. Instead, scrap material drives were held, allowing children to contribute their rusty old bicycles, old pipes, tires, boilers, even steel cans, to turn rusty iron into the weapons of victory. (RHL.)

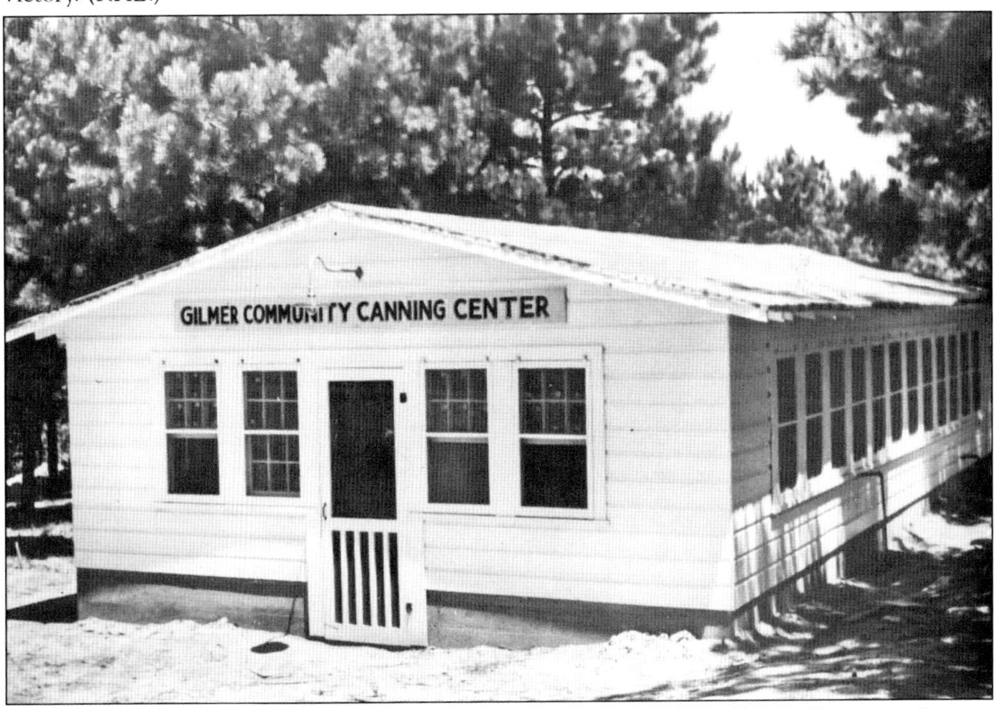

The Gilmer Community Canning Center was one of several established by the Extension Service throughout the county. Methods of canning and brining pickles were taught, and in the communal facilities, larger canning equipment was available for joint use. (Upshur Rural Electric.)

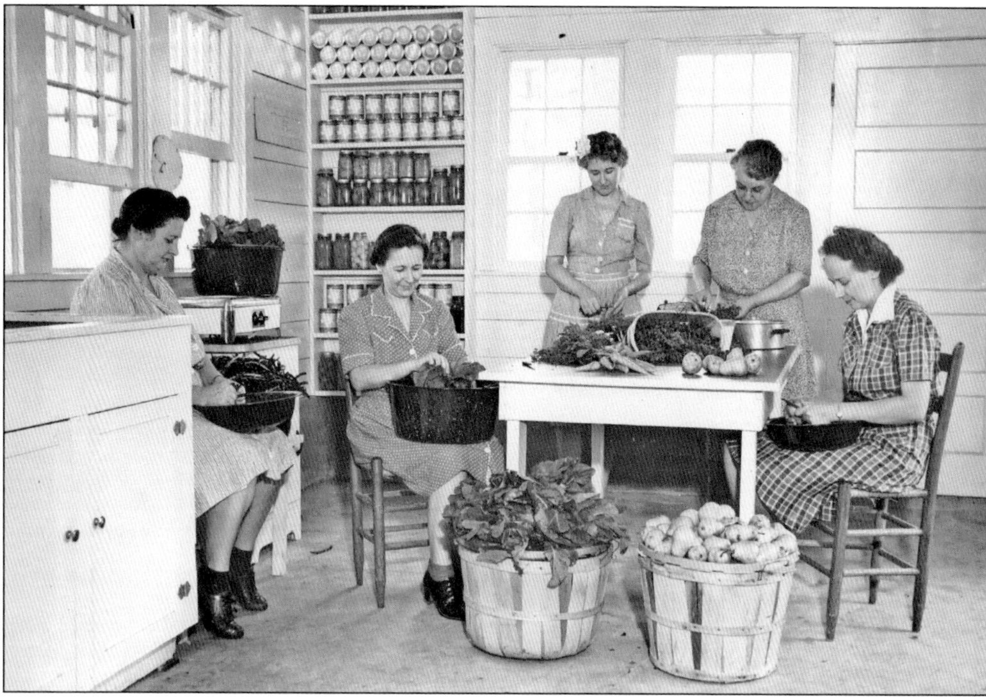

As a contribution to the war effort, every family was encouraged to grow and preserve as much food as they could in order to free up the farm-raised food for export to the troops and refugees. Working together to prepare the produce for canning made the work more enjoyable. (Upshur Rural Electric.)

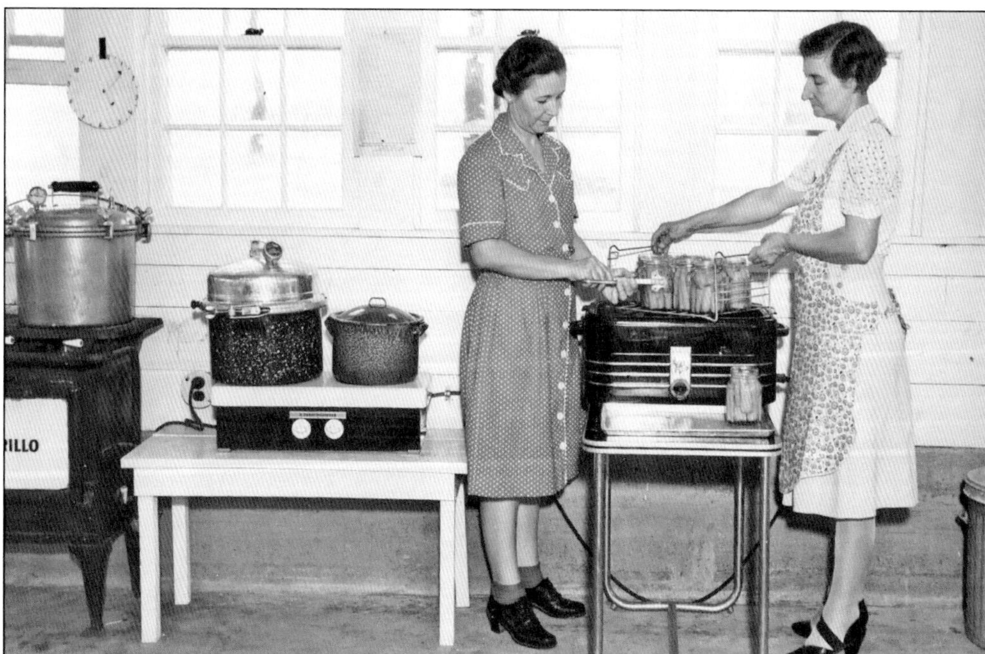

Ella L. (Mrs. Willis) Arnold (left) and Madge Singleton (Mrs. P. B.) Lindsey prepare fruit in glass jars for immersion in a hot water bath to seal the jars with a vacuum seal. (Upshur Rural Electric.)

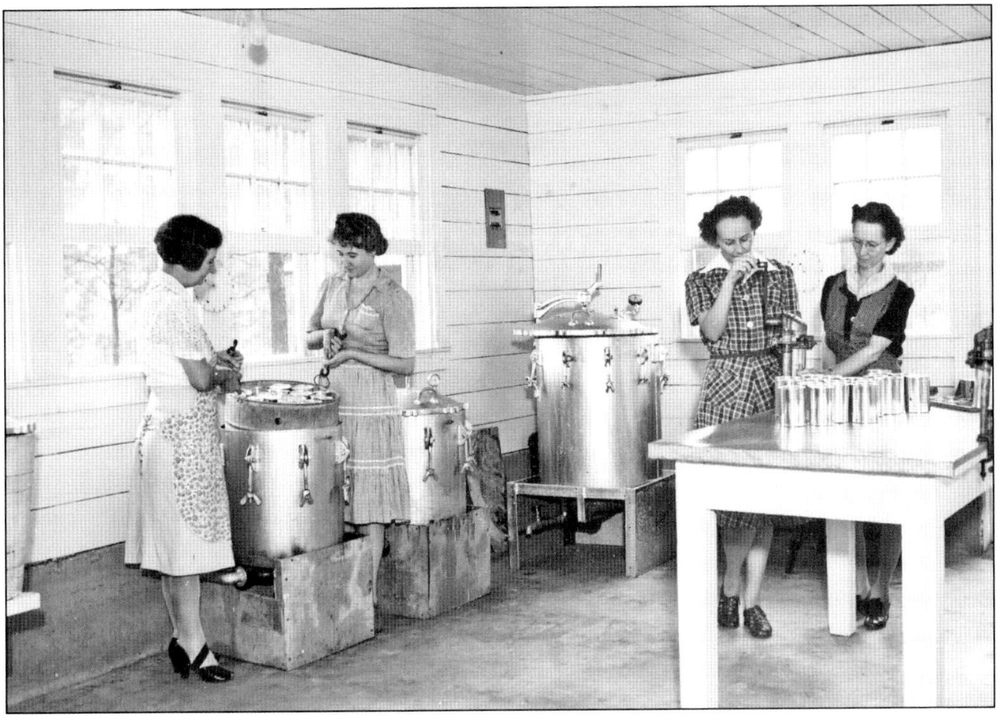

Madge Singleton (Mrs. P. B.) Lindsey (far left) and her companion lift the sealed cans out of the pressure cooker, while Alice Billingsley (third from left) and another lady do the preliminary sealing of the cans. All cans were twice sealed to ensure a better seal. (Upshur Rural Electric.)

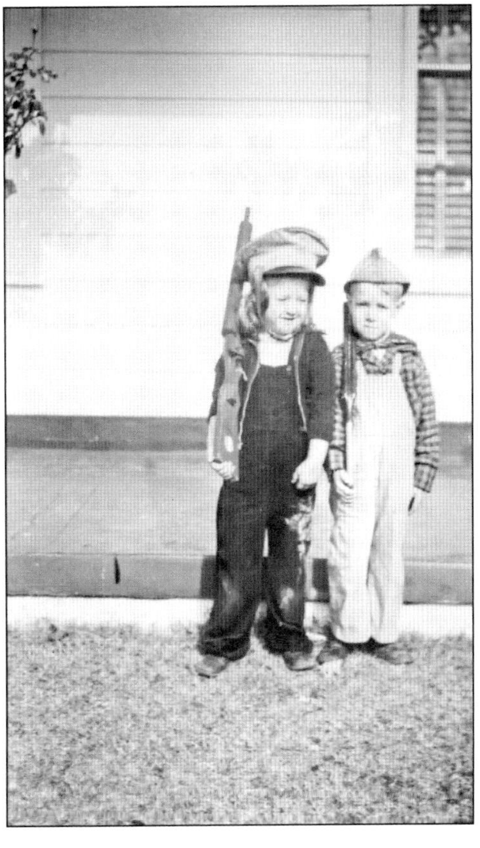

Even children got involved in helping with the war effort. Some fed chickens and others picked vegetables, while Sarah Ragland (left) and Charlie Hogg shouldered their wooden weapons as they prepared to defeat the Nazis and the other enemies of America. Charlie Hogg would like "playing soldier" so much that he graduated from West Point and served in the U.S. Army. (Center for East Texas Studies, Stephen F. Austin State University, Marshall Collection.)

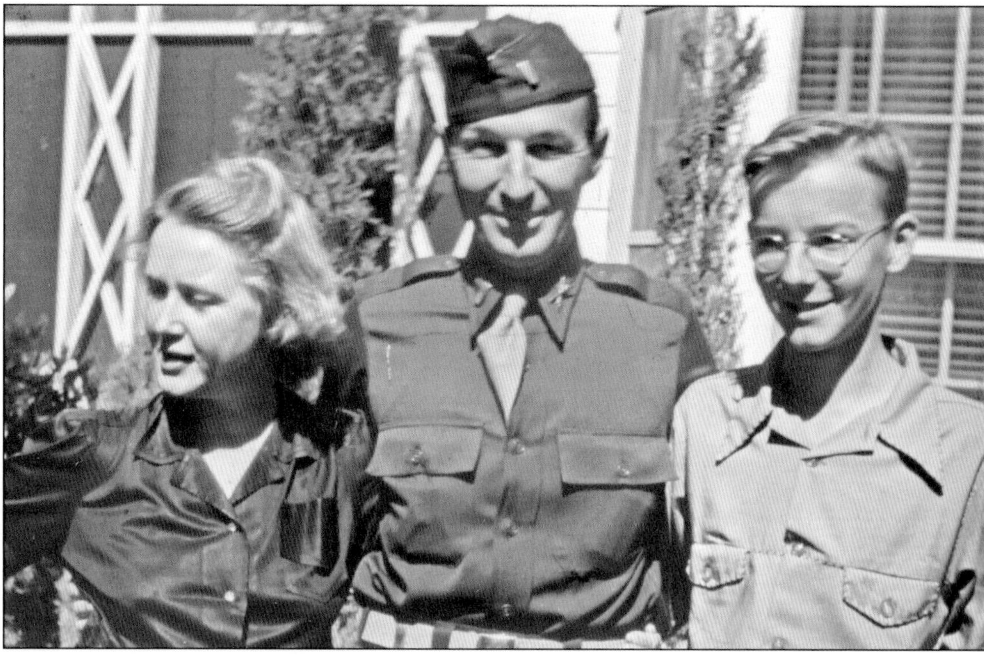

Older men such as superintendent of Gilmer Schools Henry McClelland served in positions stateside so that younger men could go overseas. Elfie McClelland (left) and Bill (right) joined with Lieutenant McClelland before he left for Camp Maxey in Paris, Texas. (RHL.)

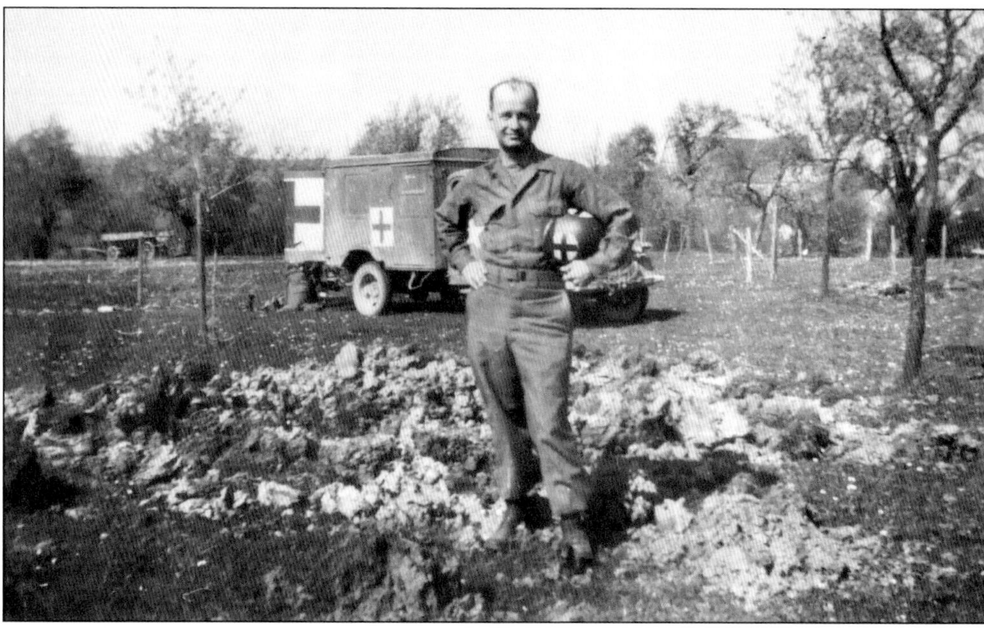

Jimmie Marshall was another member of the Texas Home Defense Guard who was called into active duty. Marshall joined the 4th Division, the Ivy. He thought he was assigned to the medical corps because his brother-in-law was a doctor. Seen in this image in France, Marshall arrived on "D Day+4" or June 10, 1944. He saw the liberation of Paris and the Battle of the Bulge before returning home to Marshall's dry-goods store. (Center for East Texas Studies, Stephen F. Austin State University, Marshall Collection.)

Five

Baby Boom, New Industries, and New Challenges 1947–1972

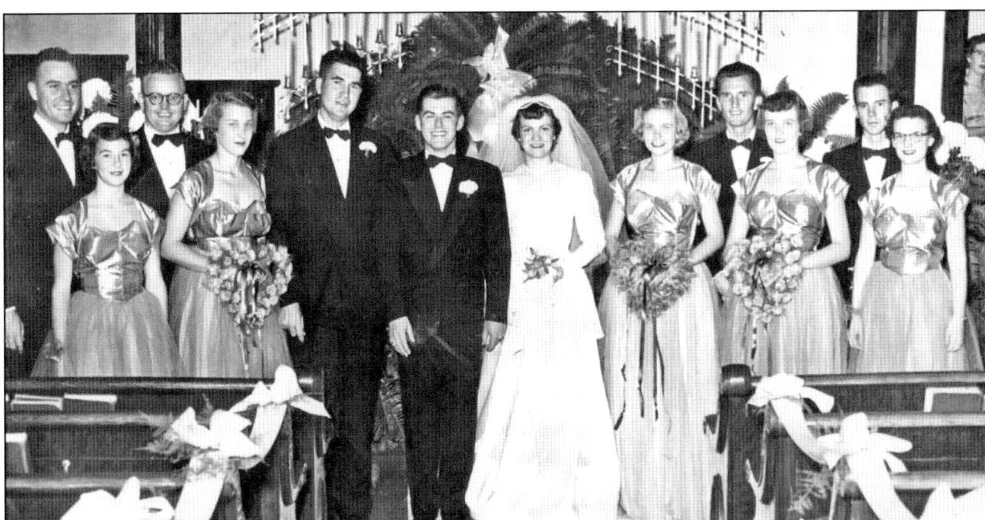

With victory of the Axis powers, the veterans came home ready to study under the GI Bill and to start a family. Gene Ray Faires was a fortunate veteran. A graduate of the Gilmer High class of 1946, he served in the army and then attended Southern Methodist University on the GI Bill. Then he married his sweetheart, Jeanine Wallace, in a ceremony at the First Methodist Church in 1950. Here are, from left to right, Mark Arnold, Martha Faires, James Croley, Sarah Laschinger, Steve Castloo, Gene Ray Faires, Jeanine Faires, Kathryn Rantzel, John Wheeler, Lou Ethel Ramey, Bill Nelms, and two unidentified. (MLK.)

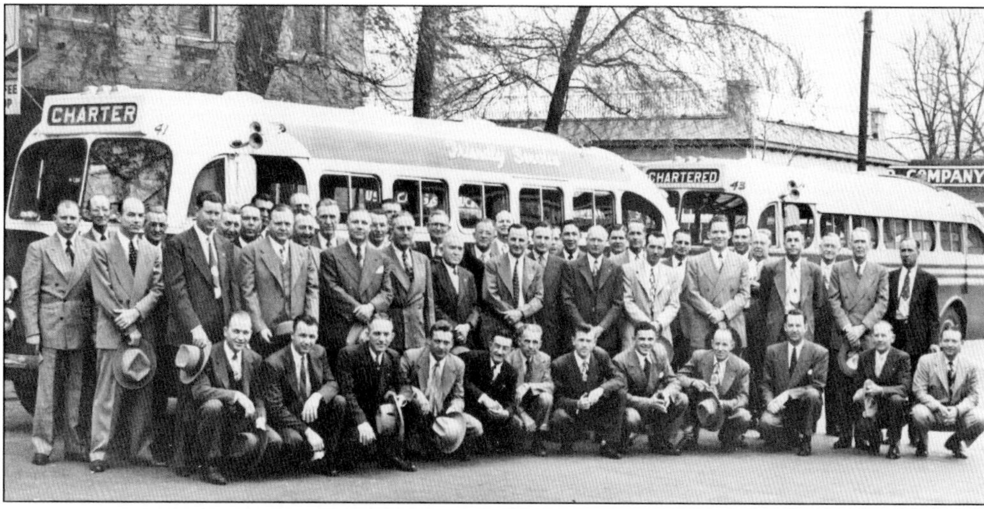

Rotarians were all present and accounted for when they road buses to Dallas to hear Angus S. Mitchell of Australia speak to 1,200 Rotarians from the district. Gilmer was the only chapter with 100 percent in attendance. From left to right are (first row) Dr. Douglas Daniels, Geddy Mathis, Truman Jones, Don Williams, R. H. Laschinger, E. F. Aldredge, Joe Harper, Harry Aldredge, Royce Hogg, Wayne McCleskey, John Brogoitti, and Cranfill Cox Jr.; (second row) Gene Gatlin, Thomas Arch Marshall, J. L. Johns, Fred Odom, Aubrey Foster, Paul Williams, Fred Hamm, Jake Long, Temple Ingram, Jimmy Shepperd, Bill Farmer, Ralph Michael, Romie Bishop, and Bryan Floyd; (third row) Nolan Coe, B. E. Porter Jr., Henry Stropp, C. T. Crosby Jr., Leonard Pickitt, Hollis Arnold, Horace Webb, John Mack Brooks, Henry McClelland, Ed Gooch, Horace Davis, Frank Smith, Hugh Knowles, Bill Buie, Malcolm Smith, Royce Hudgins, Childress Quinn, Jake Dupree, Bob Parsons, Wayne Fennell, W. H. Lake, and Cranfill Cox Sr. (Hill Studio/GM.)

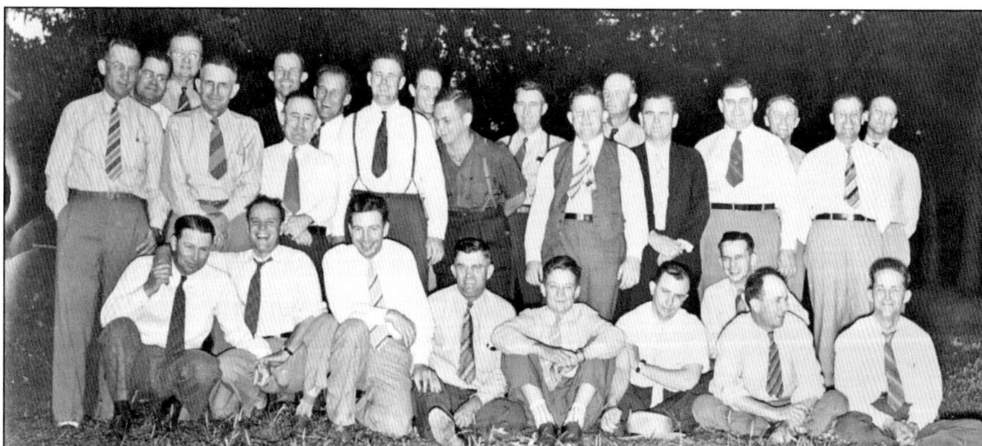

Trips to interesting places such as Cross Lake in Louisiana and the camaraderie that developed among the Masons was another factor that contributed to their success. Among those who went to Cross Lake were, from left to right, (seated) Freddy Arnold, S. E. Nolley, George Smith, Oscar Darnell, Don Williams, Harold Trammell, Ralph Mahan, Tommy Mitchell, and Jake Dupree; (standing) John D. Goolsby, Joe Steed, H. M. Prater, W. F. Gipson, Homer Mings, Leo Hart, A. E. Acternach of Waskom, Roy Hair, Clark Wolcott, John B. King (dark shirt), John Mack Brooks, Lee L. Johnson, Frog Haralson, Steve Castloo, Leo Presnell, Oreb Owen, Hub Owen, and Gilbert Warrick. (RHL.)

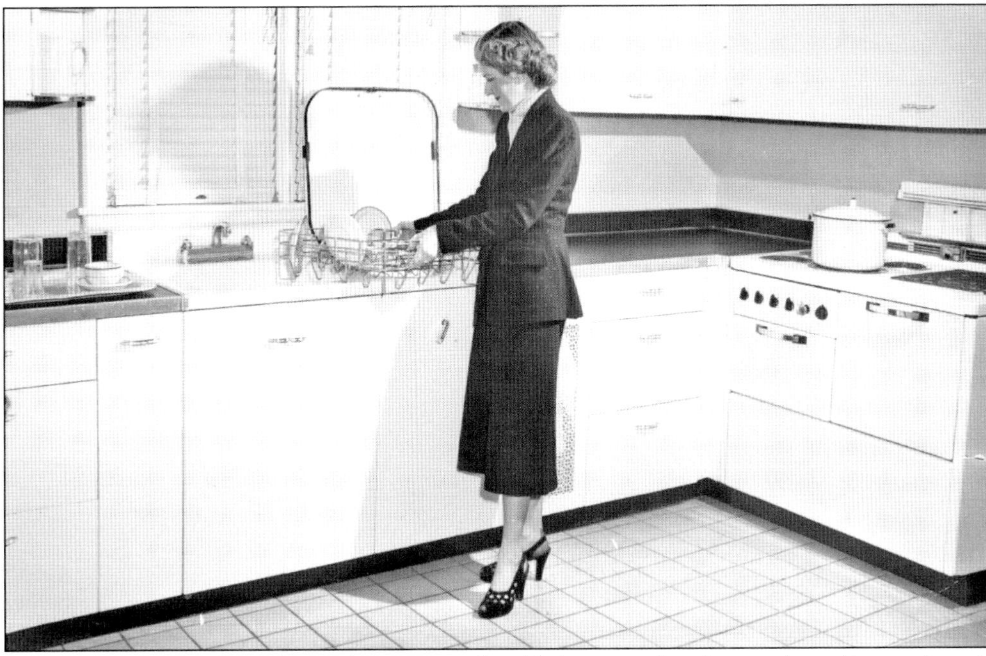

At Upshur Rural Electric, the employees not only sold electricity, but they explained how to benefit from the service. Next to the auditorium, the architect installed a kitchen with sleek, modern white metal cabinets, the latest in home design. Business office employee Myrtis Herring loaded the dishwasher as a demonstration of electrical appliances. (Upshur Rural Electric.)

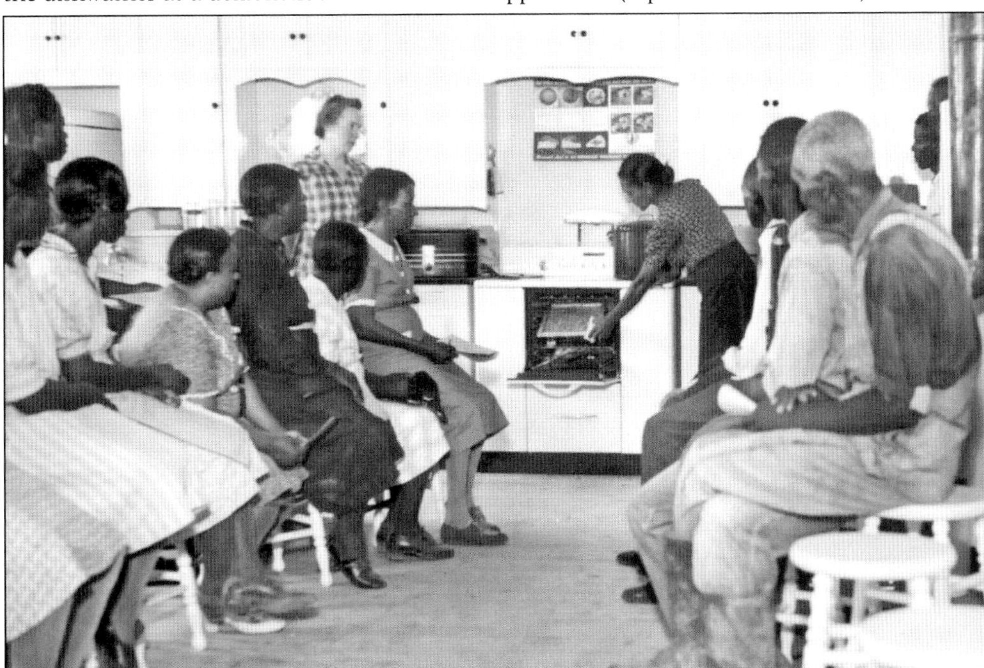

In addition to opening the auditorium to civic and extension clubs, Upshur Rural Electric trained blacks and whites in separate classes, helping the rural user make the transition from kerosene lantern and wood cook fire to electrical lighting and other conveniences. (Upshur Rural Electric.)

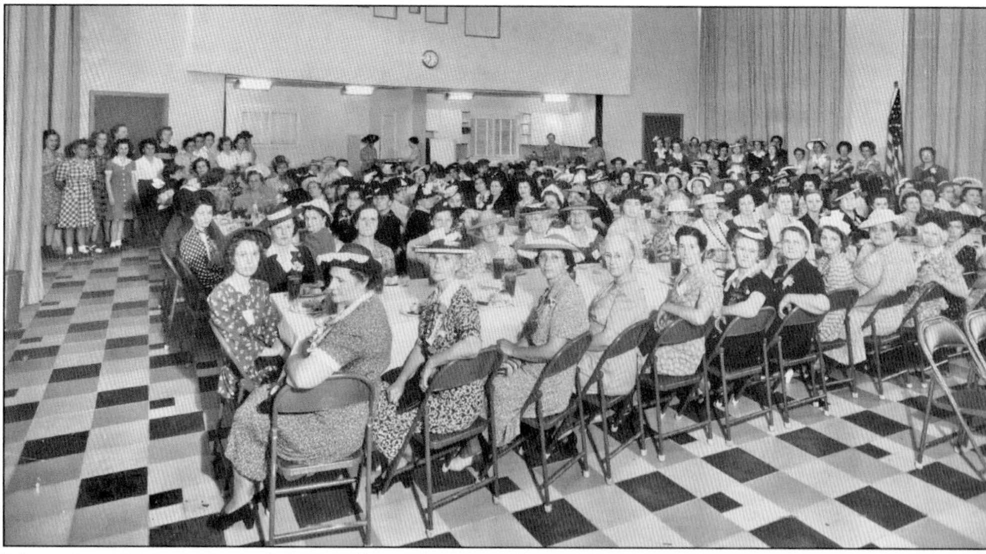

More than 400 women piled into the auditorium for a meeting of the District Five, Texas Home Demonstration Association on April 5, 1949. Every woman was properly attired with her hat, gloves, and purse. (Upshur Rural Electric.)

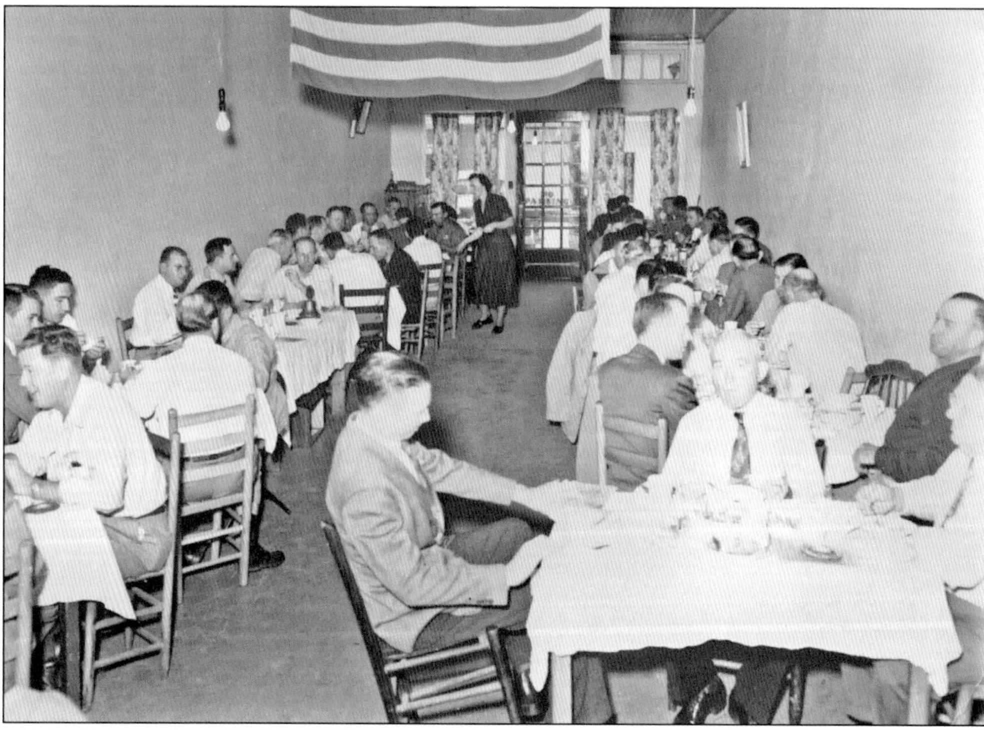

The Rotary Club and other groups met for many years in the long, lean room off the Coffee Shop at the Jefferson Hotel. Standing in the back, Lila Maud Sharp, owner of the Coffee Shop, served the Rotarians. George Smith, the Pontiac dealer (front left), along with Dr. Harris Daniels, Fred Hamm, and Leon Hudgins (seated at the table to the right), attended regularly. Robert Gates and Royce Hogg were seated at the head table the day this image was made. (Randlyn Sharp Holmes.)

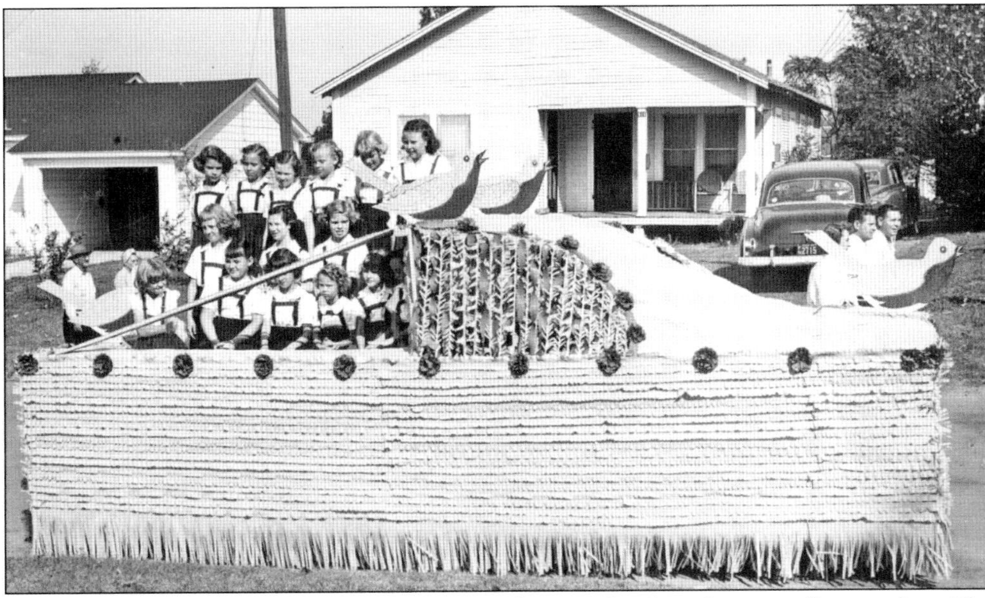

After World War II, Camp Fire Girls came to Gilmer, and girls enthusiastically joined up. The youngest girls belong to the Blue Birds, and in 1950, they filled the "nest" in the back of a pickup truck for the Yamboree Queen's Parade. With Blue Birds painted by Herschel Wallace, and in a truck decorated with light and dark blue crepe paper, the girls rode around the square. After several drivers lost consciousness from heat or exhaust fumes, people abandoned enclosing the vehicles in the float decorations. (Hill Studio/MLK.)

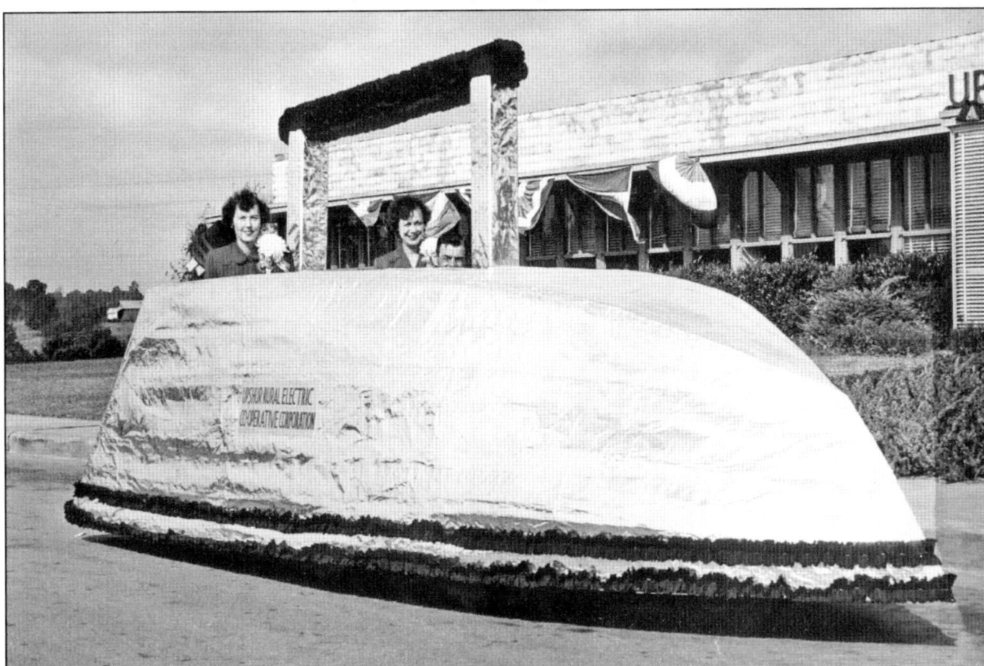

Upshur Rural Electric joined in the festivities at the Yamboree. About 1950, Sabra Whatley (left), Marie Stout, and Cody Yocom went to the Queen's Parade riding in an electric steam iron. (Hill Studio/Upshur Rural Electric.)

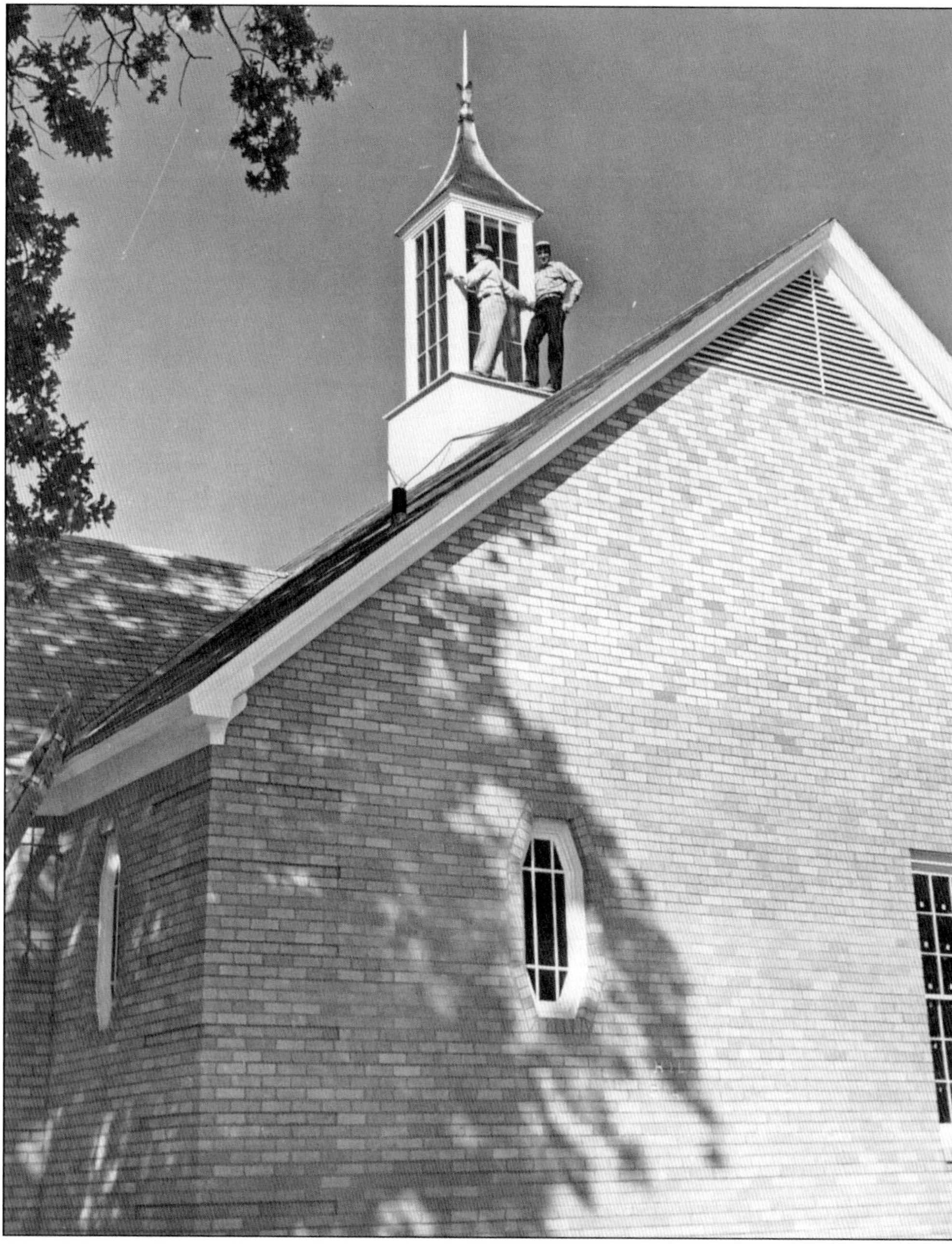

After John and James Edgar settled in Kelsey in the late 19th century, the Church of Jesus Christ of Latter-day Saints became well established in Upshur County. In 1941, the Mormons started the Gilmer Branch in a house on South Trinity Street opposite the Trinity Street Gymnasium. In preparation for the dedication of the Gilmer Chapel on November 11, 1951, Joe Lindsey (left) and Merrill Denton applied finishing touches to the brick building at the corner of Tyler and Bledsoe Streets. (Hill Studio/Genice Bryant.)

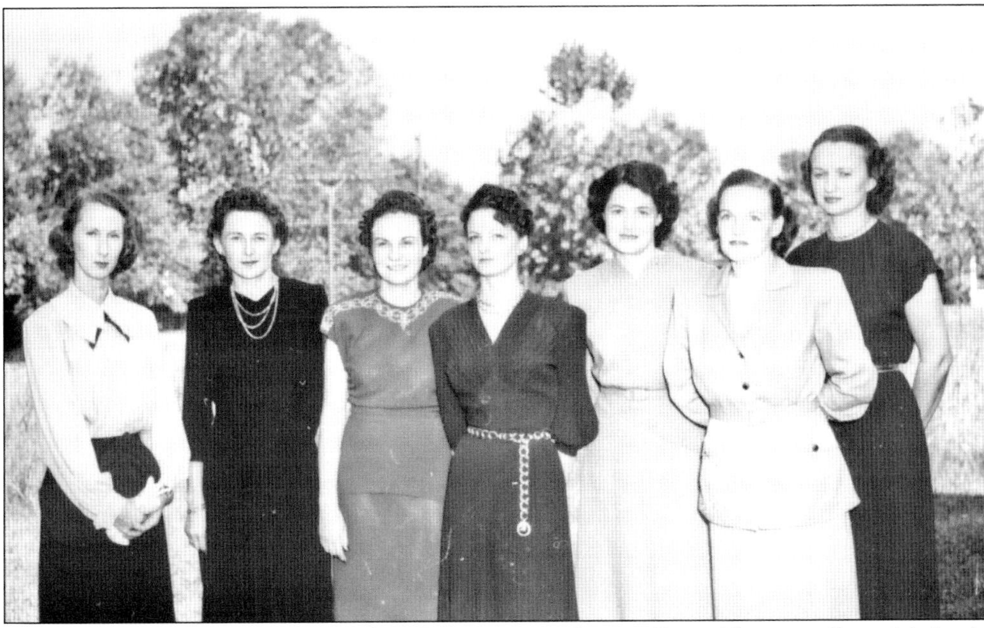

From left to right, Ruth Gates, Pauline Byman, Loise Graves, Doris Clements, Betty Michaels, unidentified, and Sara Lou Cook gathered about 1949. All were members of the Bluebonnet Club, a second women's civic club established in 1946 with the help of the Twentieth Century Club. (RHL.)

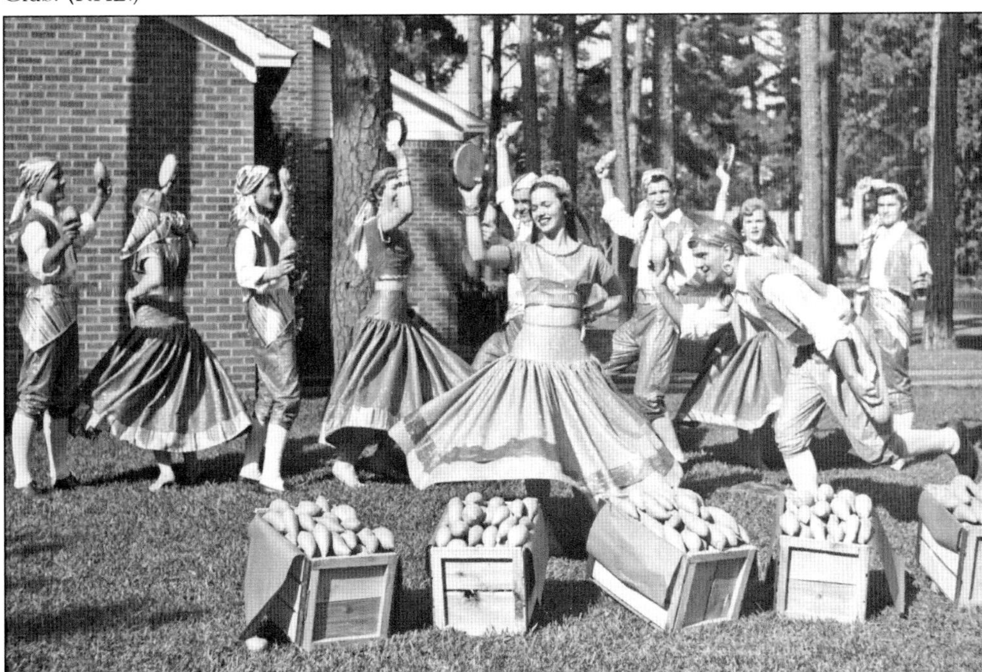

When Yamboree coronation dancers gathered for a publicity photograph, a yard in the new section of the Mitchell addition between Park and North Streets was selected. Nestled under stately pine trees, the new residences between North Montgomery and Bradford Streets quickly filled the empty lots. (*Progressive Farmer, Gilmer Mirror.*)

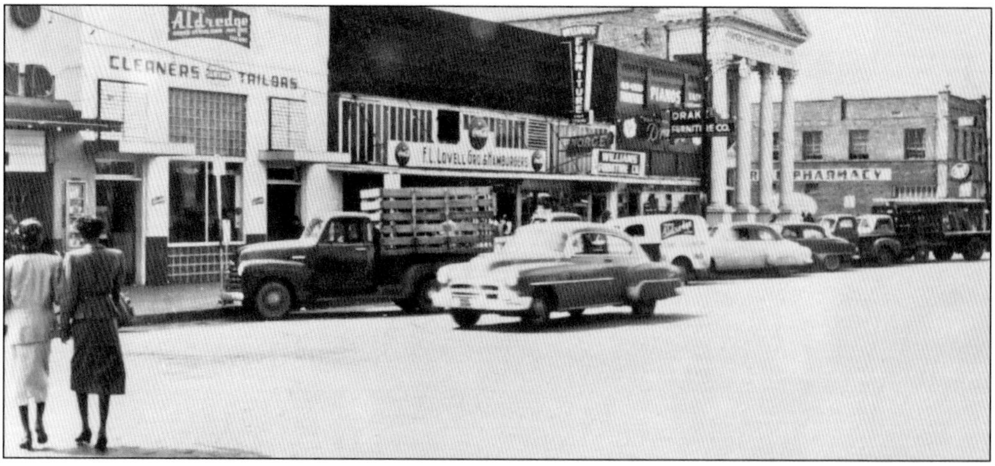

From a picture postcard from 1953, the transition in Gilmer businesses can be determined. The Farmers and Merchants Bank was still in its stately, two-story building, and the Strand anchored the block on the left. Lovell's was perhaps the most popular spot for a hamburger, and Williams Furniture had become a fixture. At the corner of Henderson and Tyler Streets, the Gates-Reed Drug Store was under the offices of Dr. H. J. Childress and Dr. Tom Marshall. (HUM.)

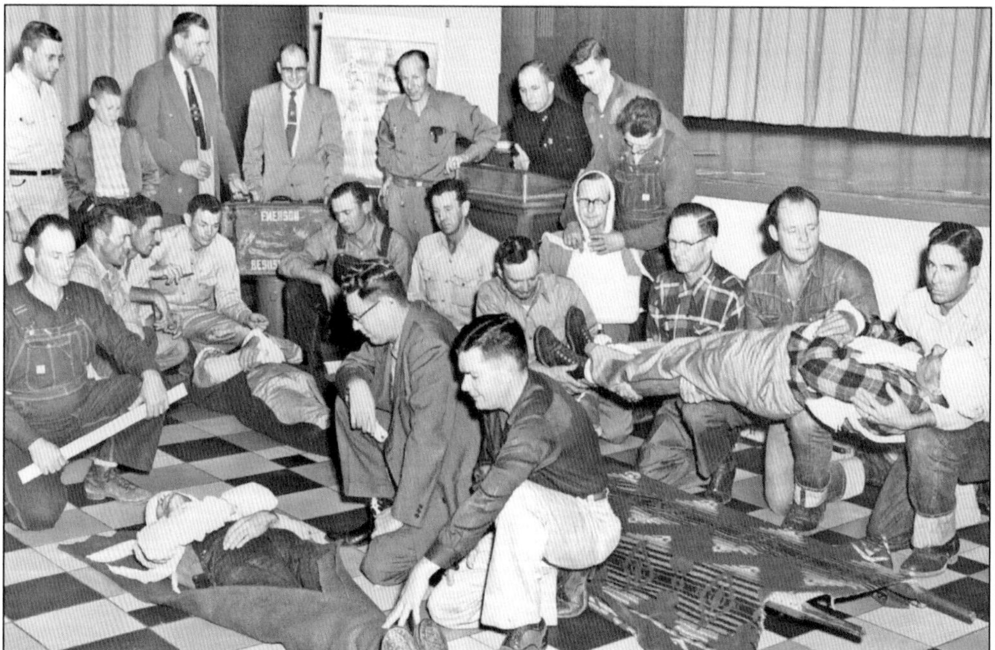

Protecting employees and keeping them well trained in case of emergencies has always been a policy at Upshur Rural Electric. Special training in first aid was the order of the day when, standing from left to right, Wiley Cook, Richard Yocom, Sheriff Orear Watson, city manager Gene Gatlin, fire chief and instructor Royce Hogg, city police officer Henry Fink, instructor L. Monk, and Lester Ballard gathered. Giving treatment to the injured were Ellie Johnson; Raymond Jones; Joe Brasher; Cody Yocom, line foreman; Gerald Vick; W. T. Simpson; Carson Bates; W. A. Jones, engineer; Charles Kibbe; and Jay Moon. Kneeling were Newman Robertson; J. L. Johns, co-op manager; and C. A. Harris. The patients were Ernest Fink, Hubert Whatley, and B. A. Floyd. (Upshur Rural Electric.)

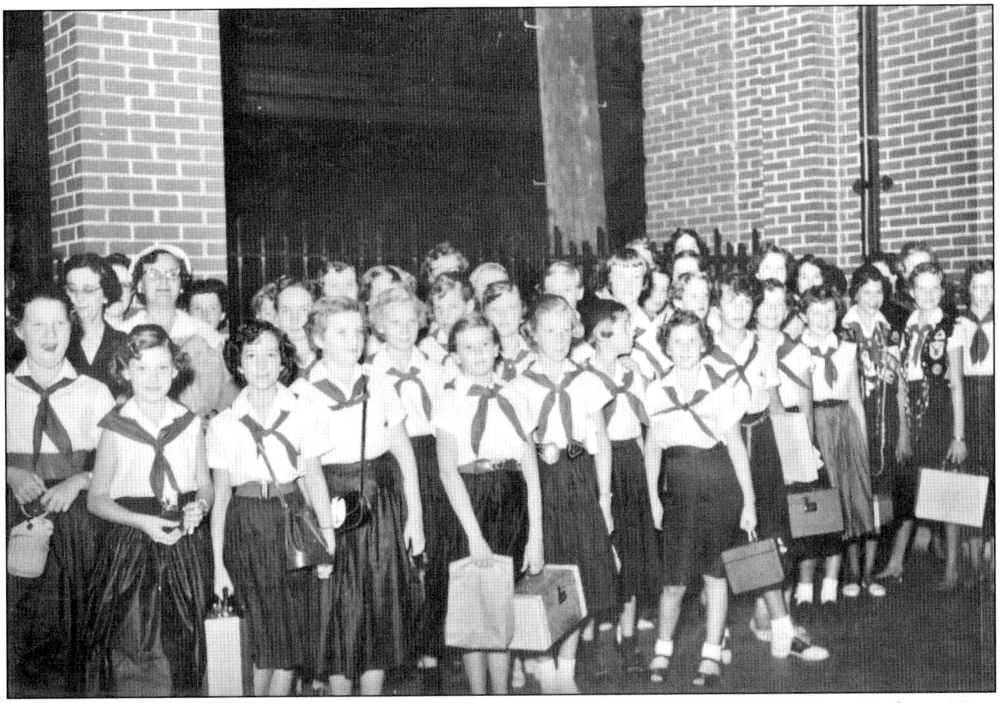

On August 17, 1954, dozens of Camp Fire Girls prepared to board the *Louisiana Eagle* to New Orlean, where they spent a day enjoying the Big Easy. The next year, in the East Texas Council, more than 500 girls, including some from Gilmer, traveled to Dallas. (RHG.)

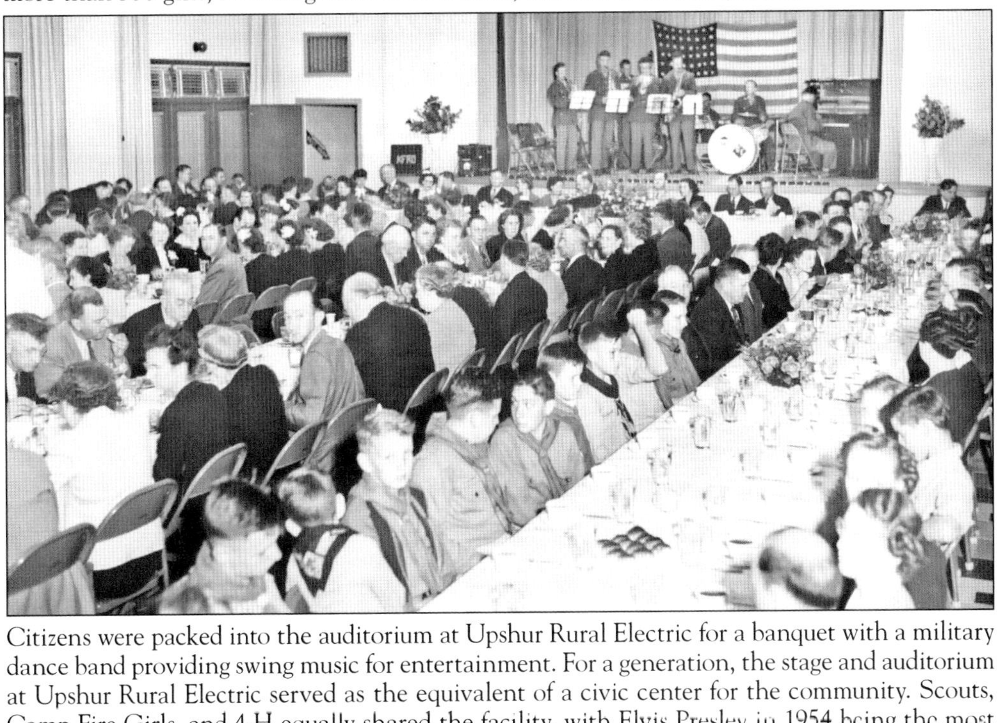

Citizens were packed into the auditorium at Upshur Rural Electric for a banquet with a military dance band providing swing music for entertainment. For a generation, the stage and auditorium at Upshur Rural Electric served as the equivalent of a civic center for the community. Scouts, Camp Fire Girls, and 4-H equally shared the facility, with Elvis Presley in 1954 being the most famous performer to use this stage. (Upshur Rural Electric.)

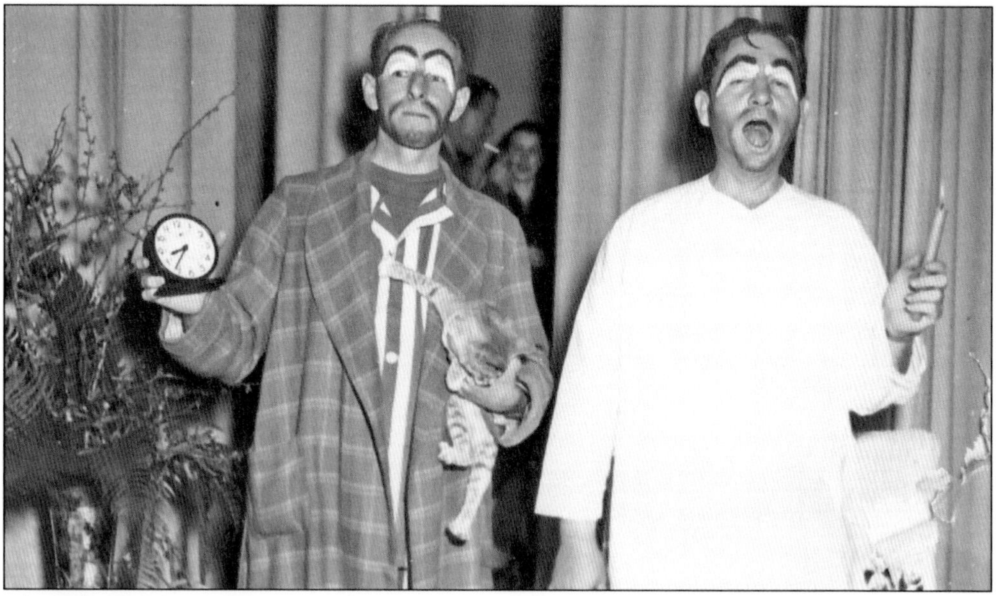

The Gilmer Volunteer Fire Department held a minstrel show each year to raise funds to purchase equipment for the department. Fire chief Royce Hogg (left) and Cranfill Cox Jr. dressed as clowns for this routine, which delighted the audience. (GM.)

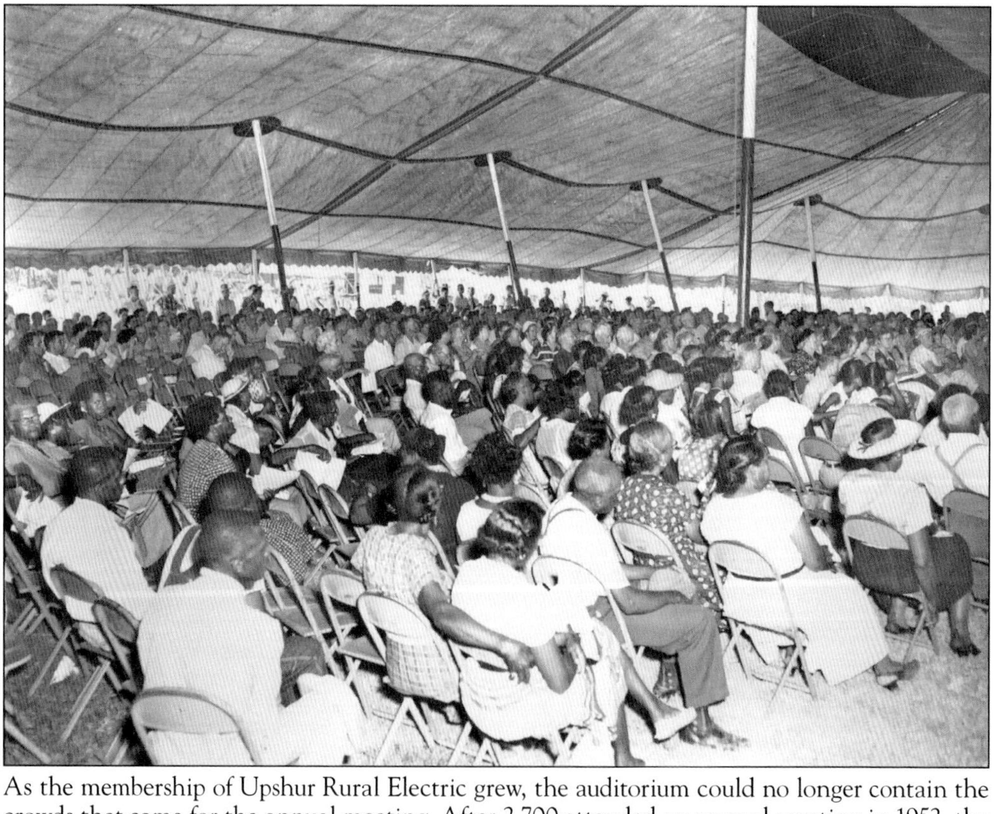

As the membership of Upshur Rural Electric grew, the auditorium could no longer contain the crowds that came for the annual meeting. After 2,700 attended an annual meeting in 1952, the cooperative began erecting tents on the grounds to house the crowd. (Upshur Rural Electric.)

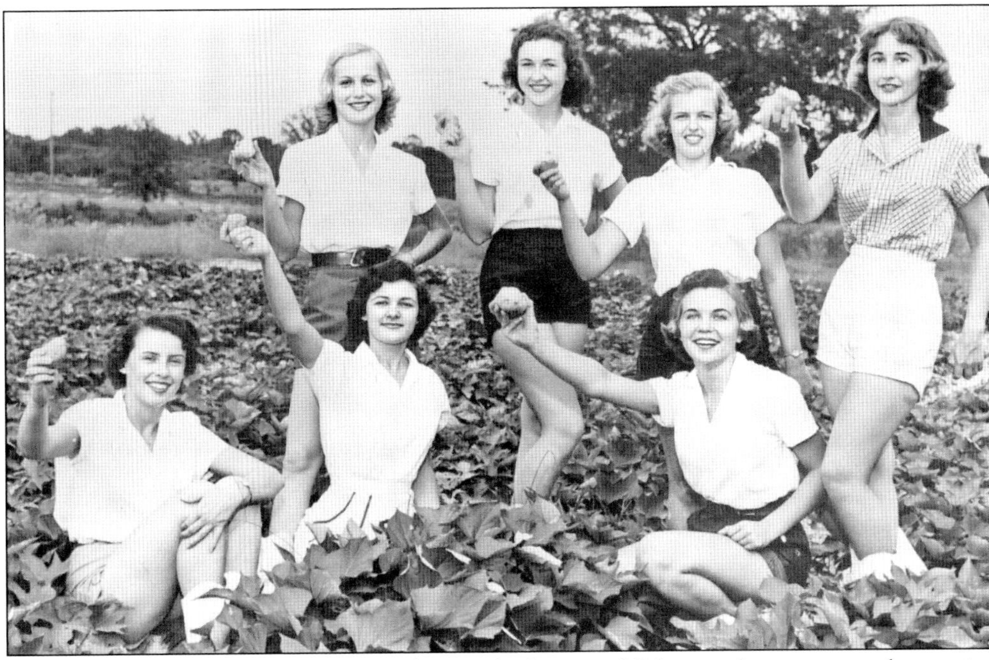

The Yamboree Association still enjoyed using the beauty of Gilmer girls to promote the coming festival. From left to right are (seated) LaJuan Sorrells, June Gunn, and Linda Dalrymple; (standing) Greta Cates, Sarah Sharp, Sandra Petty, and Jane Gaddis, majorettes and the drum major of the Buckeye Band when they gathered in a sweet potato field in September 1955. (GM.)

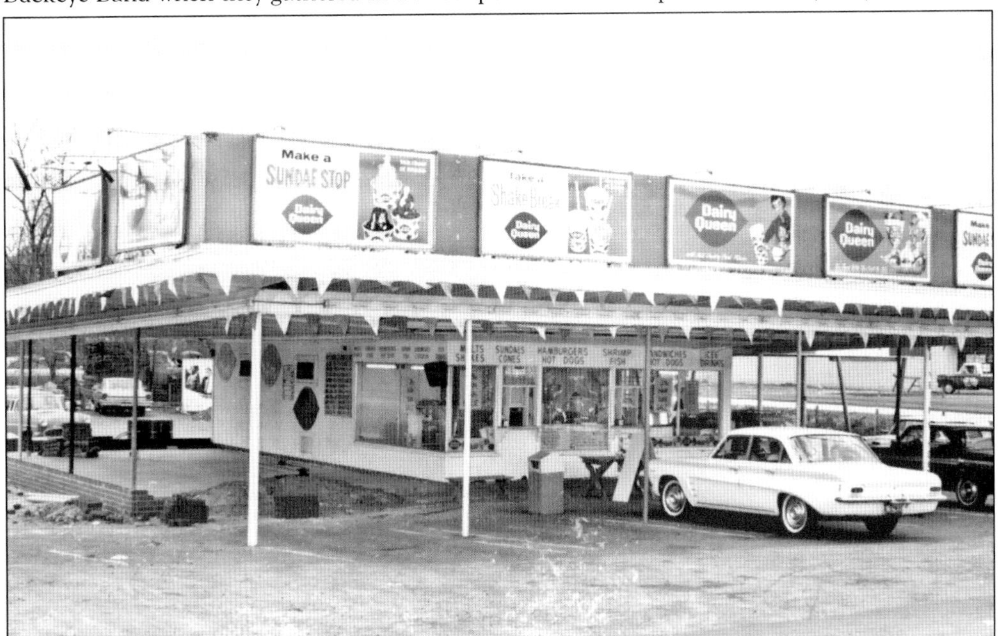

After school, students headed for the Dairy Queen at Scott Street and U.S. 271 to find the rest of their friends "hanging out." The popularity of the "D.Q." among a generation of youth inspired the Cox family to expand into additional outlets. After 1964, the "colored only" window on the north side became a drive-in window for picking up orders. (GM.)

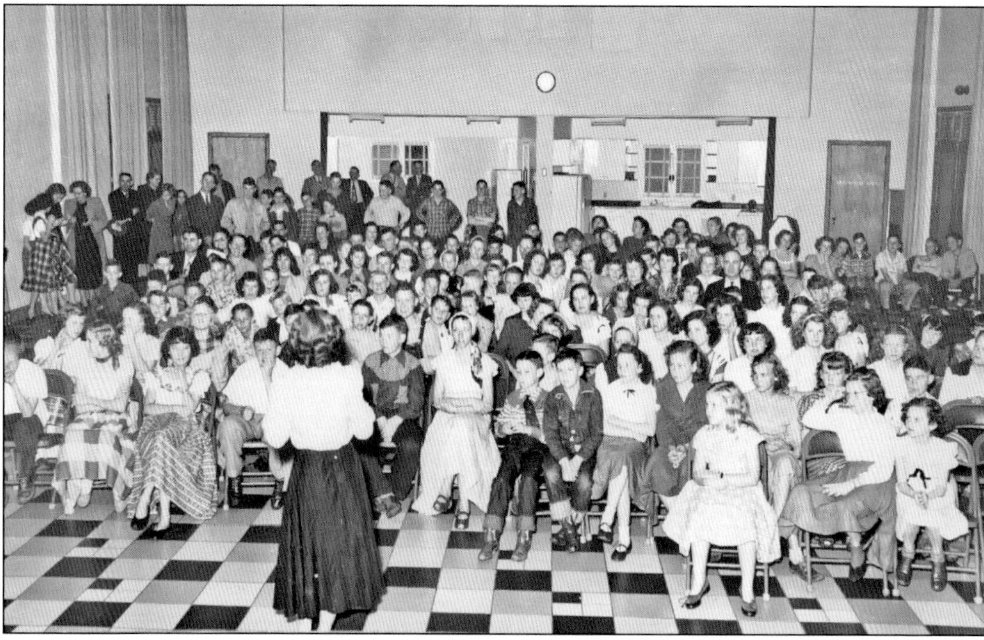

Hundreds of 4-H youth came to the auditorium for training in how to lead their chapters in songs and games at their individual club meetings. The training was held during 4-H week in October 1955. (Upshur Rural Electric.)

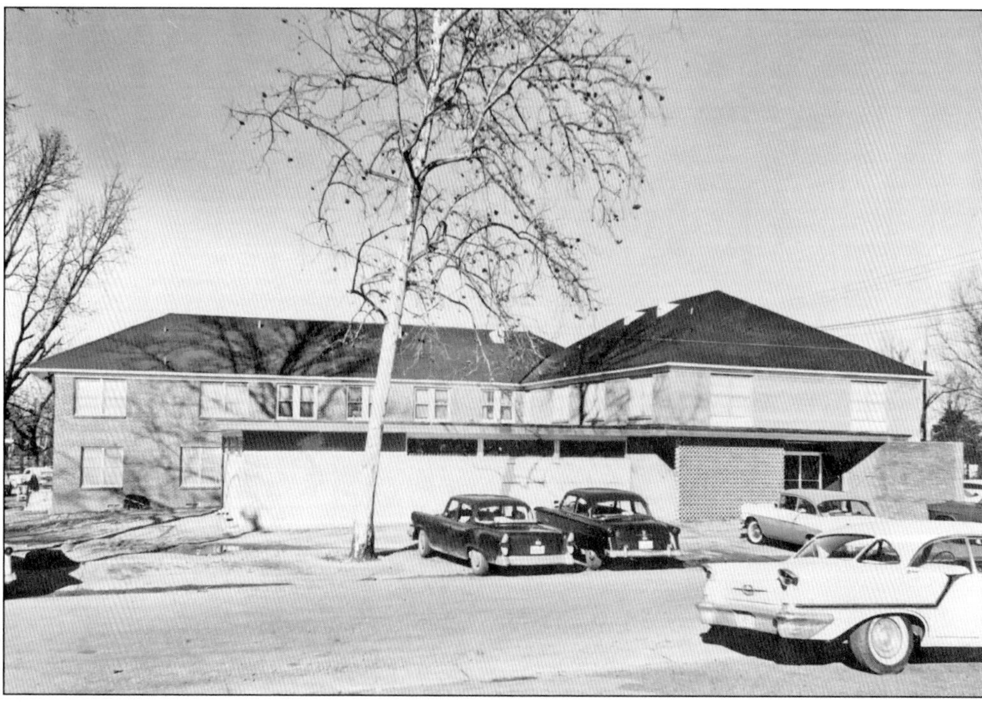

The Ragland-Fenlaw Clinic added an additional examination room with a new wing built in the 1950s. The wing included offices for the doctors: Dr. Madison Ragland, Dr. Hugh Ragland, and Dr. J. Looney Fenlaw. Dr. Tedroe Ford joined the group in 1960 and supervised the construction of a new hospital on U.S. Highway 271. (GM.)

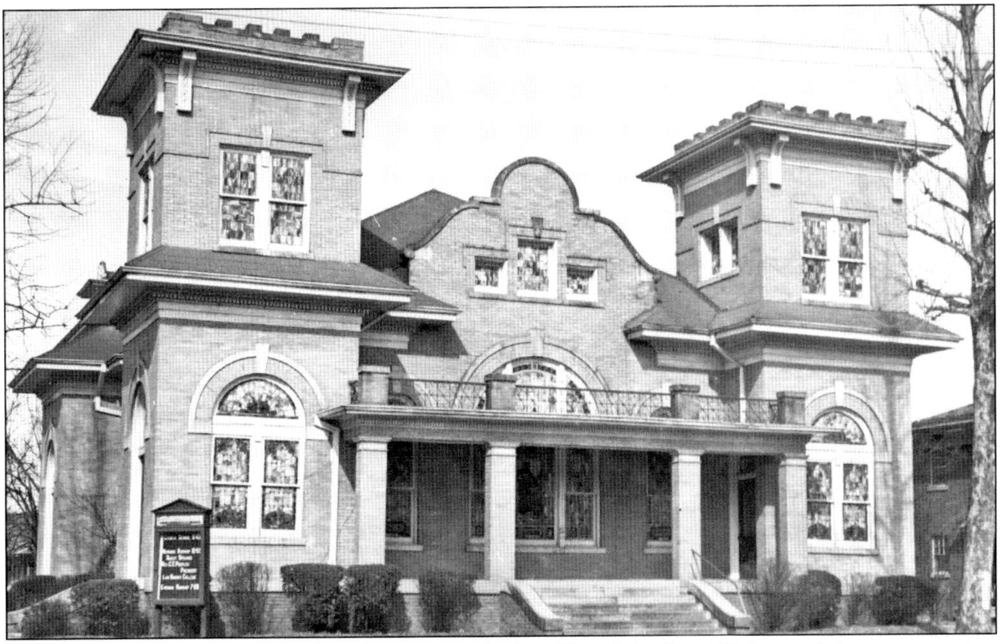

The sanctuary and classrooms that the First Methodist Church built in 1912 served the congregation well for more than 40 years. After adding additional classrooms and the Briggs Room fellowship hall, the church needed still more space, so the sanctuary was torn down in 1955. (RHL.)

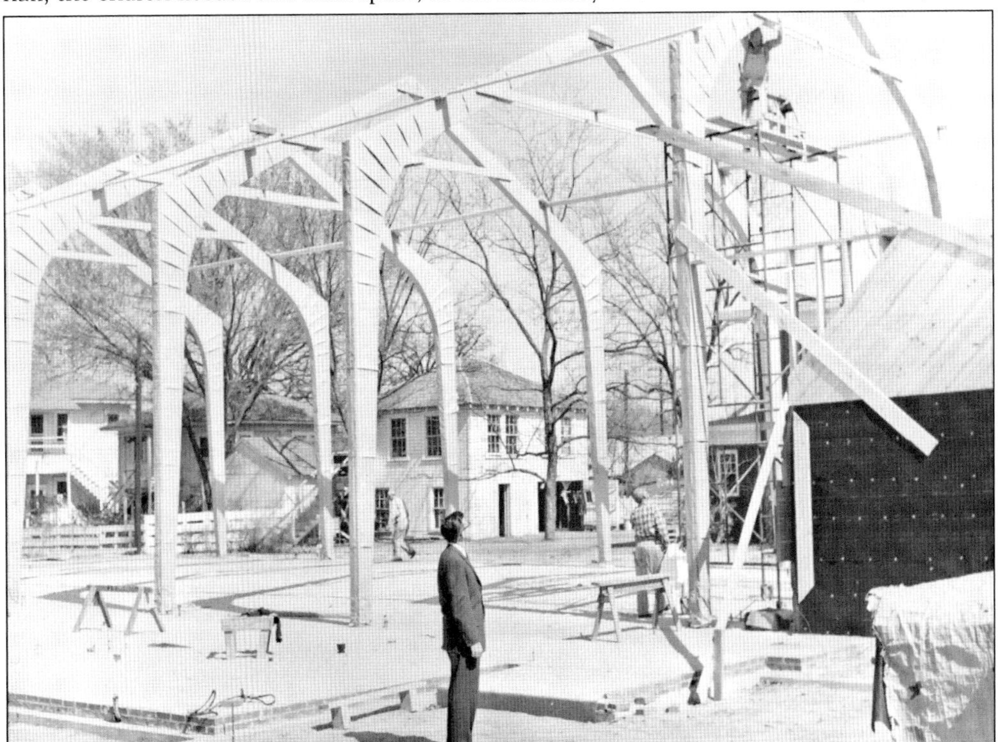

The Reverend James Lee Riley oversaw the construction of the new sanctuary for the First Methodist Church. The new sanctuary was dedicated in September 1956. (GM.)

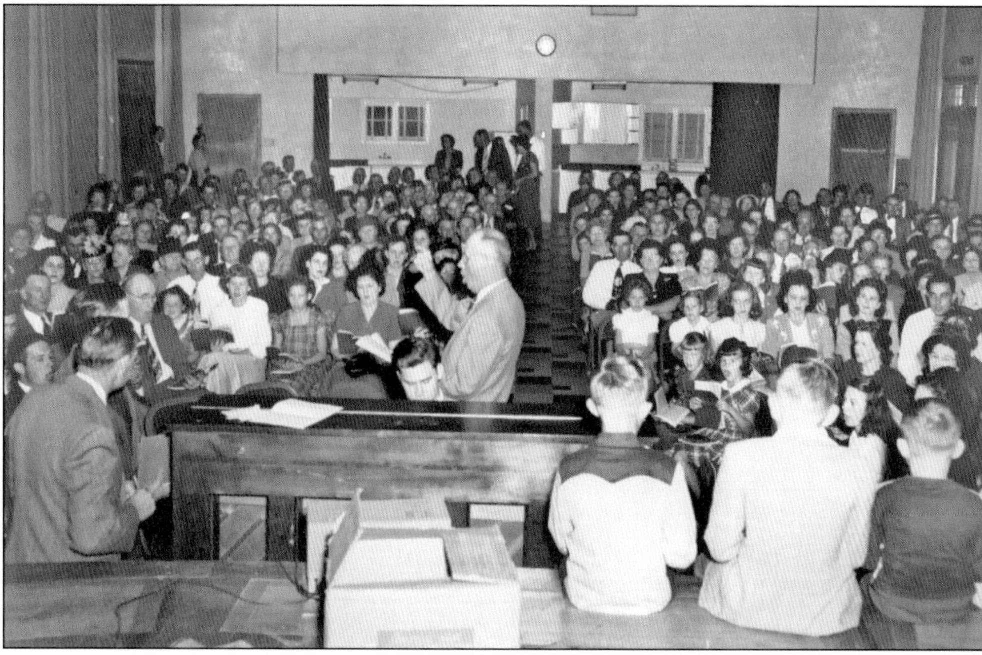

Sundays were for more than worship. For hundreds of faithful singers of gospel music, Sunday was a time to go to the auditorium at Upshur Rural Electric and sing with others. Grady Landsdale led this meeting of the East Texas Singing Convention, the modern refashioning of the "singing bees" held in pioneering times. (Upshur Rural Electric.)

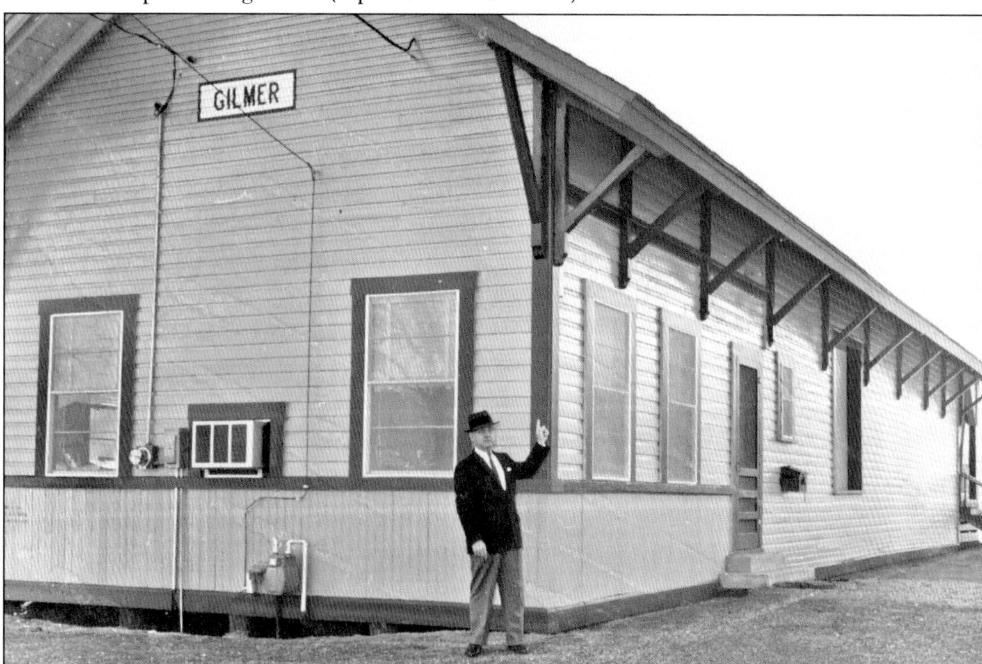

With the 1950s also came the demise of passenger train service in Gilmer. Harry Lucas was the longtime station manager. After he no longer had passenger trains to manage, he became the long-serving mayor of Gilmer. (GM.)

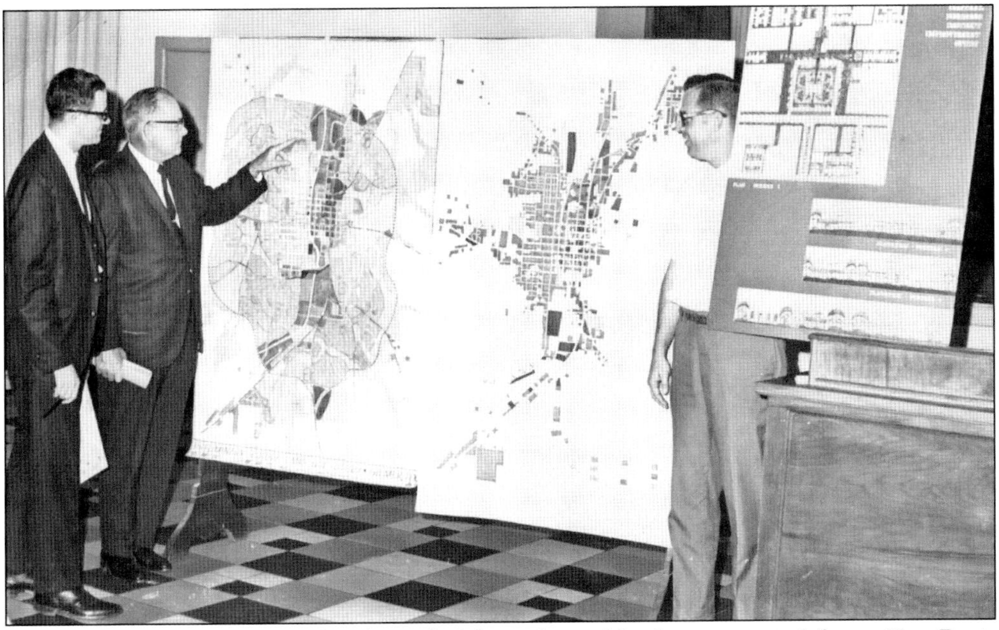

Under the leadership of Fred Odom (center), Gilmer planned for the community's future. Tom Davis (right) joined Odom in examining the plans by consultant Steve Kelly (left) for the development of the downtown long before the Main Street Project of 1998. The $18,000 city planning program was to help prepare for the next 25 years. (GM.)

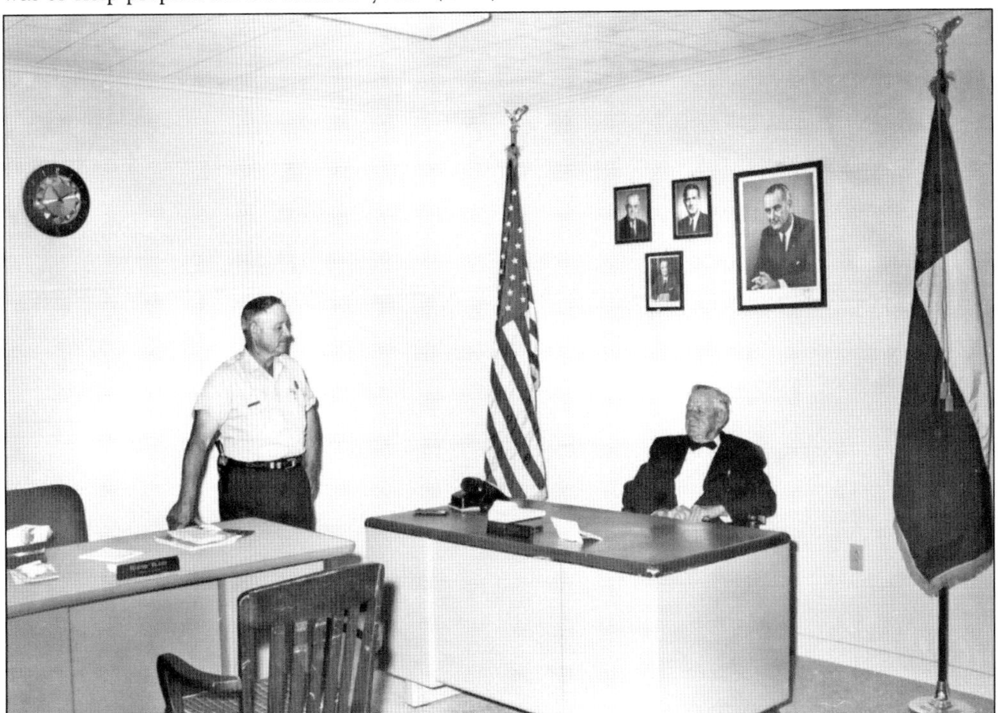

Gilmer police chief Harper Bland (left) and Judge Wes Bryce led the law enforcement and municipal courts during the 1960s for the city of Gilmer. (GM.)

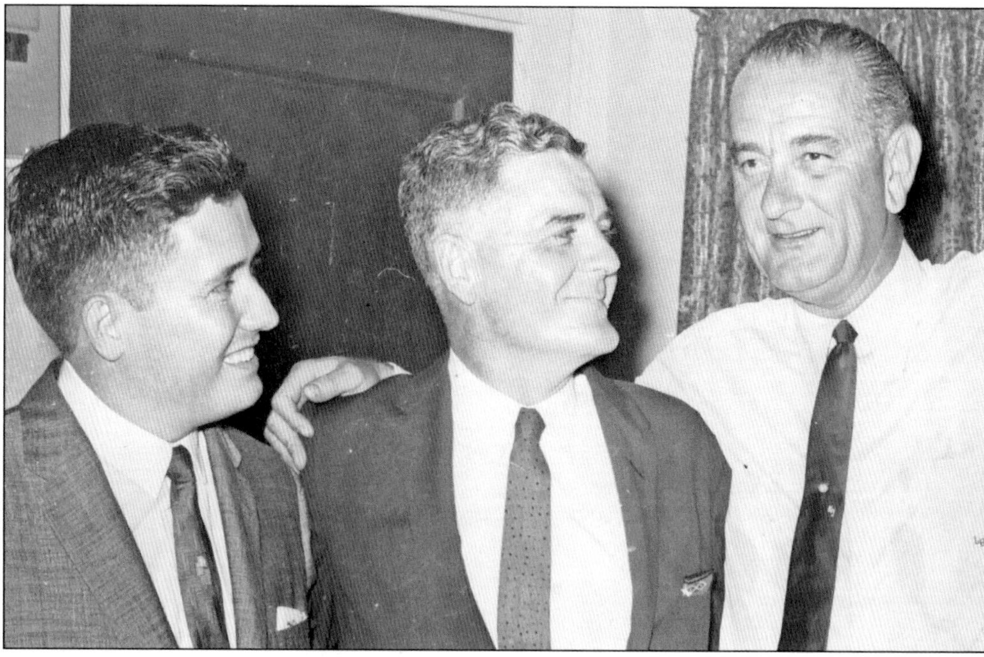

In 1959, a deputation from Gilmer went to hear then-senator Lyndon B. Johnson speak. The times were changing, but most of the residents of Gilmer did not anticipate what lay ahead. The Reverend Eugene Cragg (left), pastor of the First Methodist Church, and Judge Looney Lindsey (center) joined Johnson after his speech. (GM.)

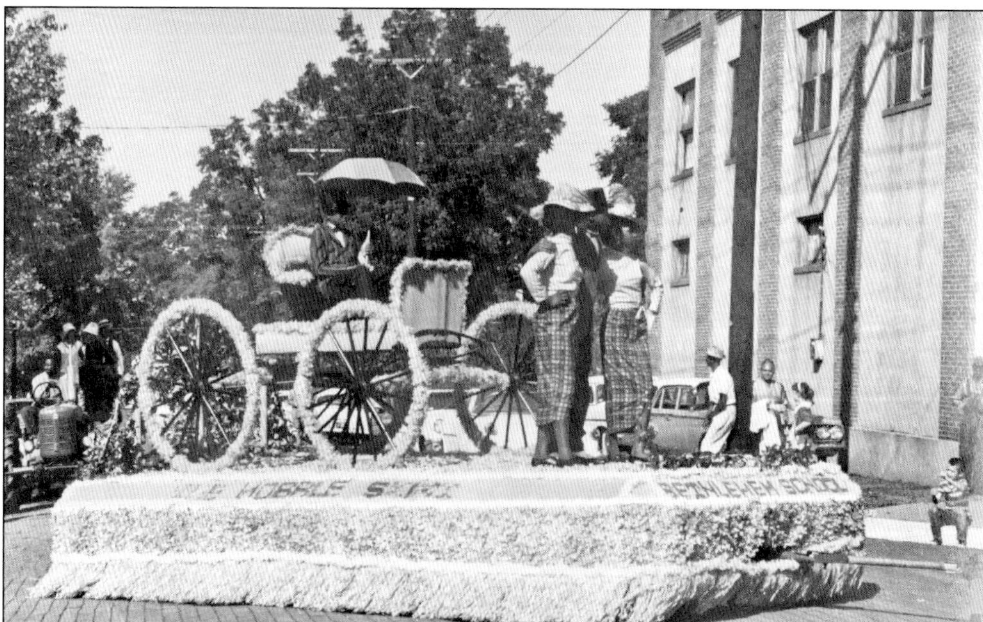

The Yamboree Association had accommodated the wishes of the African American community by allowing a separate Colored School Parade, where their leading schools and civic organizations pooled their efforts in a celebration of their achievements. This prize-winning float was photographed by John Hill in 1960. (Hill Studios/GM.)

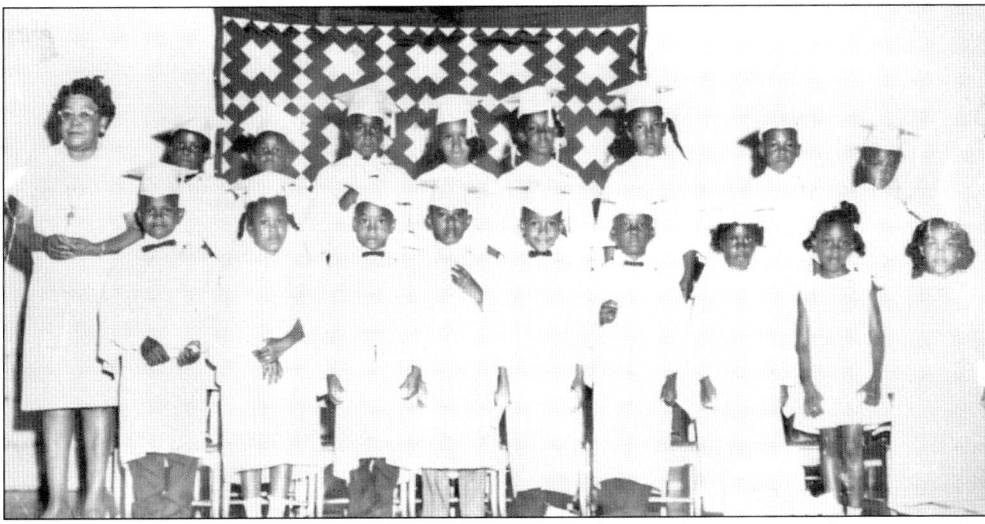

Mary Mathis led a kindergarten for African American students at the same time that young white students went to Beulah Rutledge Bishop's Kiddie Kollege or to Montie Morris's Kindergarten. Many an incorrect telephone call went to either the "white Mary Mathis" or the "colored Mary Mathis" as confused citizens sought answers to questions. (Robinson.)

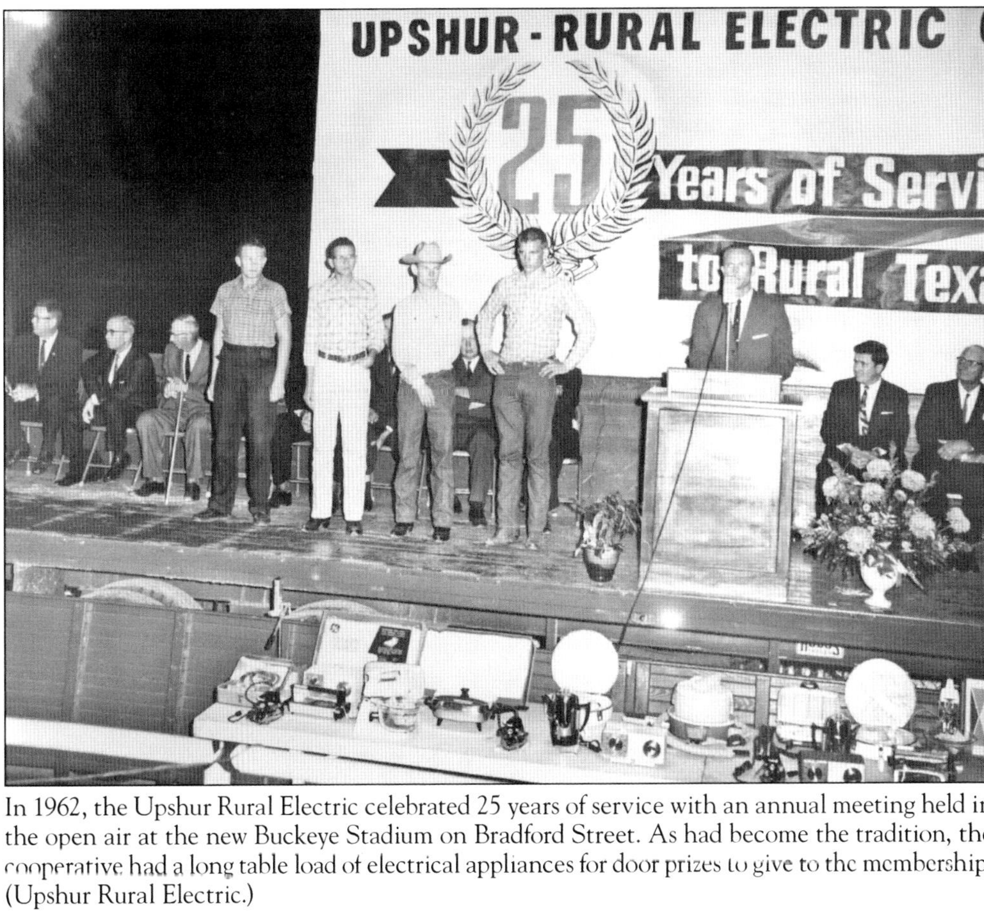

In 1962, the Upshur Rural Electric celebrated 25 years of service with an annual meeting held in the open air at the new Buckeye Stadium on Bradford Street. As had become the tradition, the cooperative had a long table load of electrical appliances for door prizes to give to the membership. (Upshur Rural Electric.)

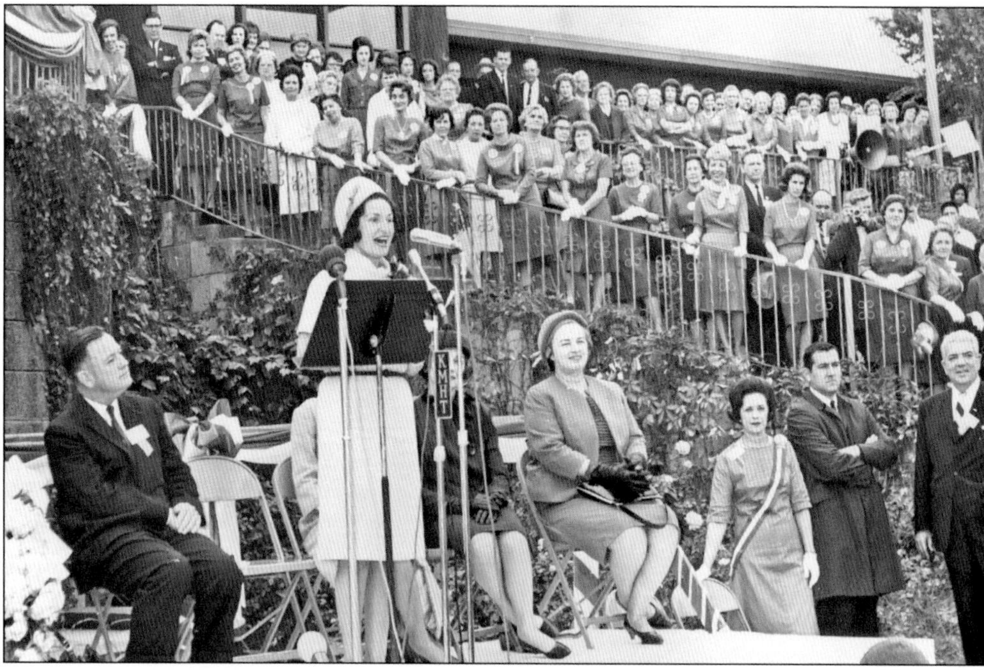

During the presidential election campaign of 1964, Lady Bird Johnson came home to East Texas, where she was welcomed at the Tyler Rose Garden. Georgia Laschinger served as the point person in the planning of the event, and ladies from Gilmer helped line the stairway from the Rose Center to the rose garden where the First Lady spoke. From the top to the bottom of the stairs stood Jeanie Farris, Daisy Potter, Martha Marshall, unidentified, Catherine Parsons, five unidentified, Allis Marshall, and third from the bottom, Lorine "Lo" Bishop. (GM.)

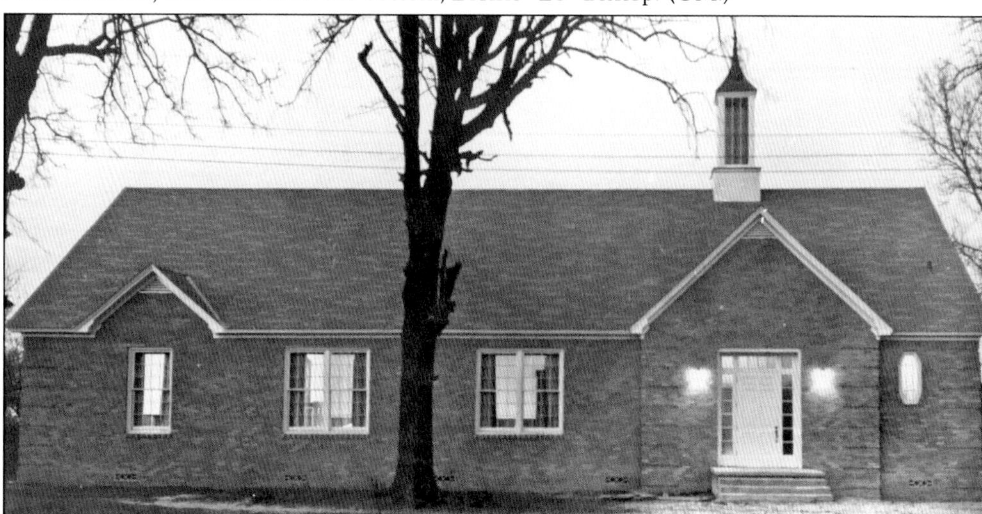

By 1966, when an image of this building graced the cover of a Twentieth Century Club Cook Book, the building that served the Mormon community as the Gilmer Chapel had a new role. The Upshur County Library had moved from its quarters over city hall and now occupied the white brick building. In the 1980s, when a new library building was constructed with a grant from the Reagan Administration, the lights still shone at night when guest speakers and other activities occurred. The building was destroyed by fire in 2003. (Hill Studio/Genice Bryant.)

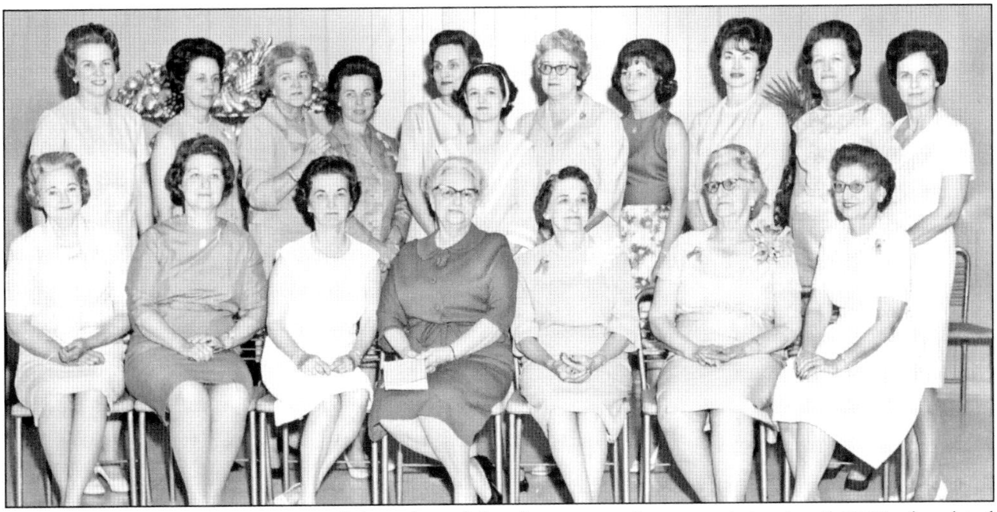

When the Twentieth Century Club gathered for this group photograph in April 1966, the third generation of members was going to the club. In this photograph are (seated) Mrs. J. L. Cartlidge (Amy), Mrs. Harris Daniels (Lucille), Mrs. Madison Ragland (Elizabeth), Mrs. Frank Futrell (Lona), Mrs. Henry Stropp (Mattie), Mrs. V. E. Todd (Ella), and Mrs. Jimmie Marshall (Virginia); (standing) Mrs. Futrell Jones (Virginia), Mrs. Bill Buie (Margaret), Mrs. Jake Long (Mildred), Mrs. Don Williams (Mattie Ruth), Mrs. Robert E. Parsons (Catherine), Mrs. Bill Patterson (Mary Ann), Mrs. Robert Gates (Leone), Mrs. Tommy Marshall (Janet), Mrs. Ted Ford (Margaret), Mrs. Burr Porter Jr. (Kathryn), and Mrs. T. A. Marshall (Martha). Representing the third generation of members, Mary Ann Patterson and Margaret Ford followed the tradition of their relatives, Mrs. T. S. Ragland and Mrs. Madison Ragland.

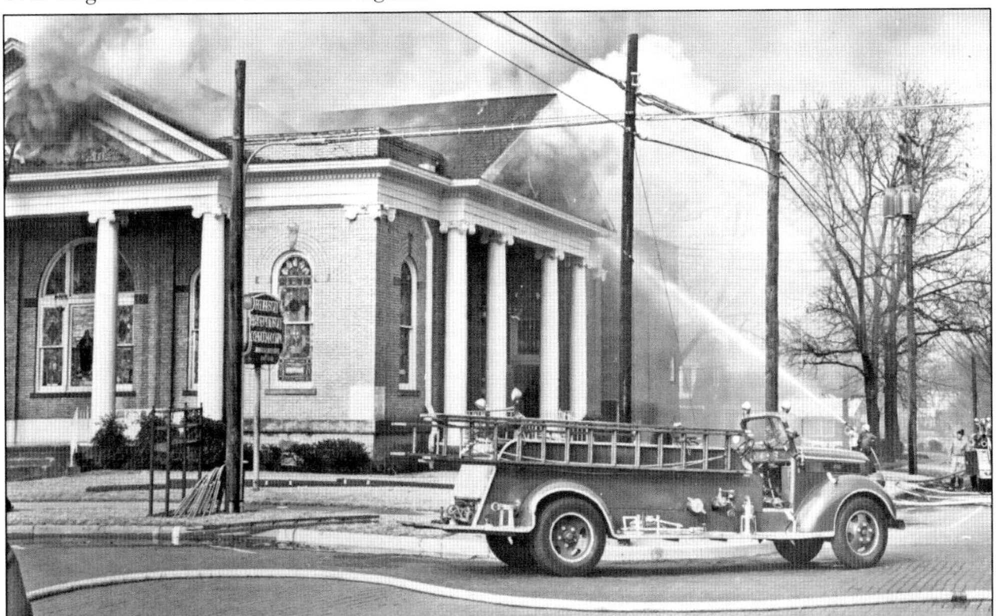

Shortly after members of the First Baptist Church celebrated joyously on Christmas Day in 1966, and after all members had gone home, a neighbor reported smoke coming from the cupola to the Gilmer Fire Department. For the next three hours, the firemen and volunteers fought to save as much as they could from the ravages of the fire. (Hill Studio/GM.)

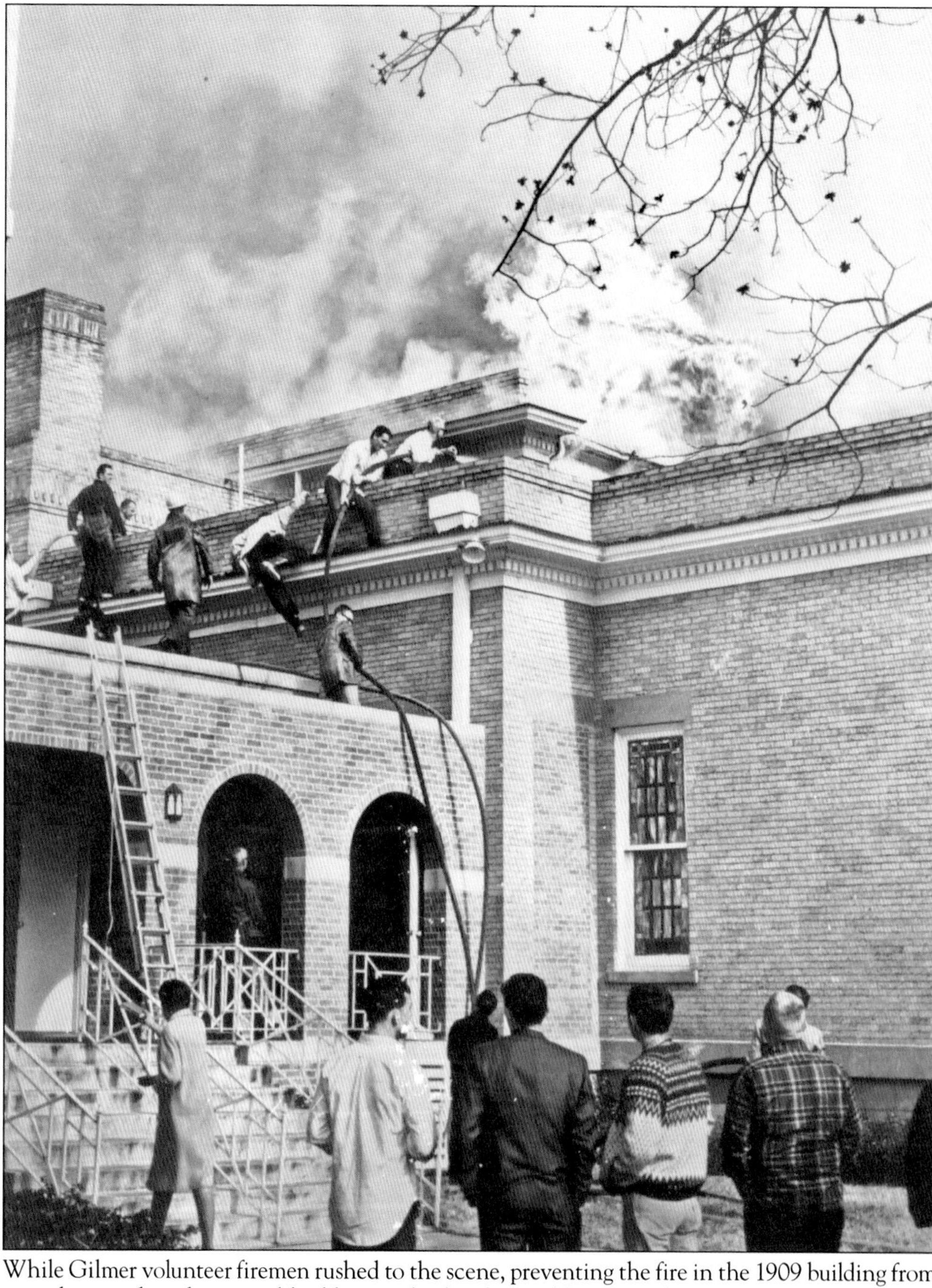

While Gilmer volunteer firemen rushed to the scene, preventing the fire in the 1909 building from spreading to the educational building and other later additions, volunteers rescued the church library, hymnals, choir robes, even the grand piano. Flames soared through the roof of the structure before it was brought under control. The treasured stained-glass window of the baptism of Christ was salvaged to shine another day in the new church, which opened in 1968. (GM.)

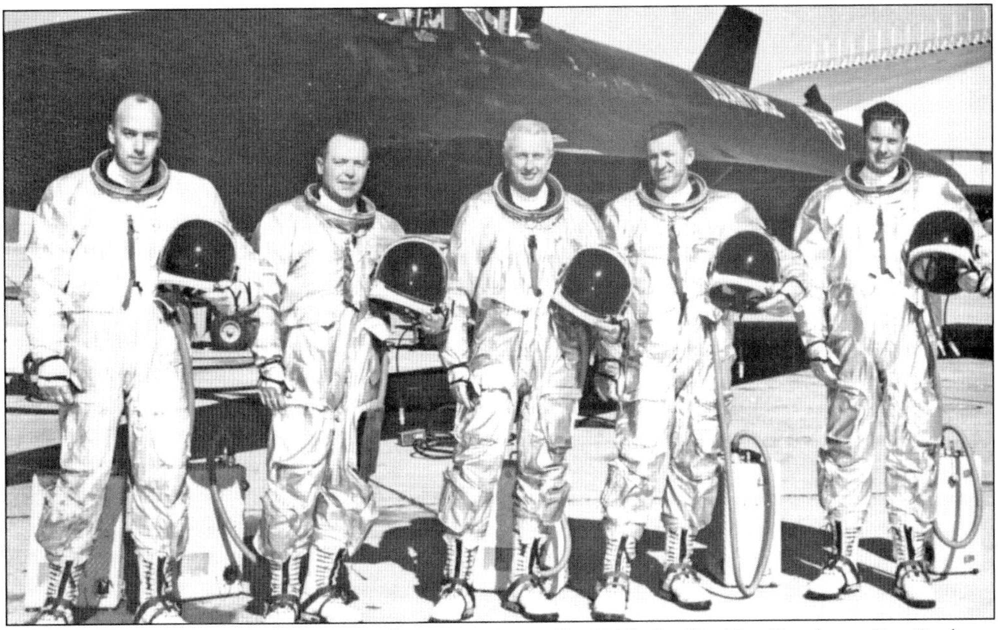

Col. Robert F. "Fox" Stephens came home on June 19, 1966, for "Bobby Stephens Day," where he rode in a parade and joined family and friends in a dinner held in his honor at the Gilmer Country Club. Stephens (center) was the test director of the SR 71/YF 12-A test force at the Air Force Flight Test Center at Edwards Air Force Base and led the team of five test pilots in setting world speed and altitude records. (U.S. Air Force/GM.)

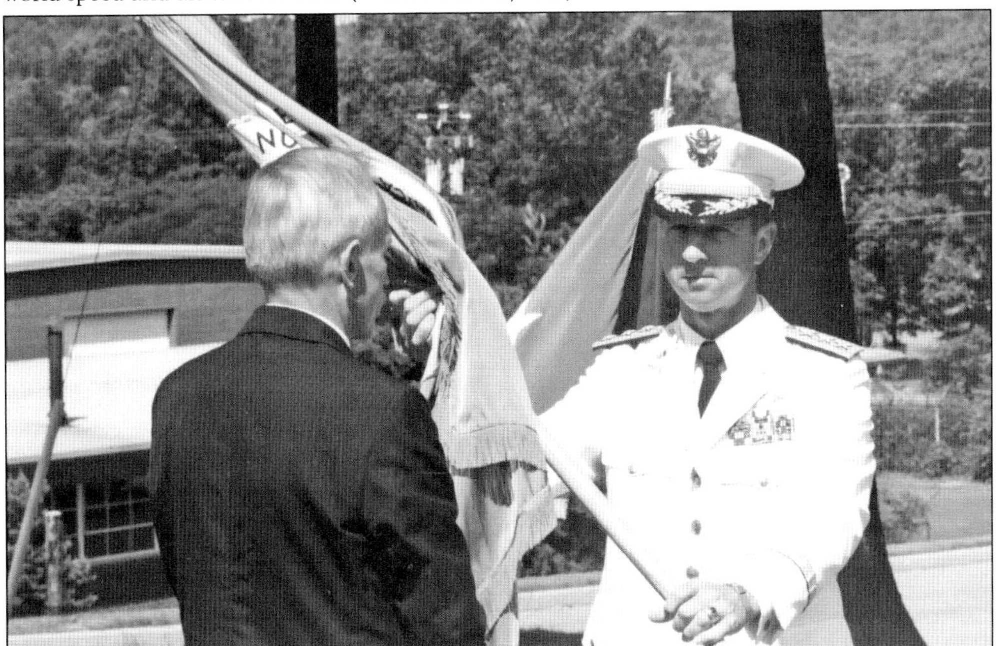

Following the leadership of Bobby Stephens, John Leonard Pickitt attended West Point and went into the U.S. Air Force, where he received the rank of lieutenant general on June 1, 1983. Pickitt was the deputy commander-in-chief United Nations Command and chief of staff of the Republic of Korea before he retired on June 1, 1987. (U.S. Air Force/GM.)

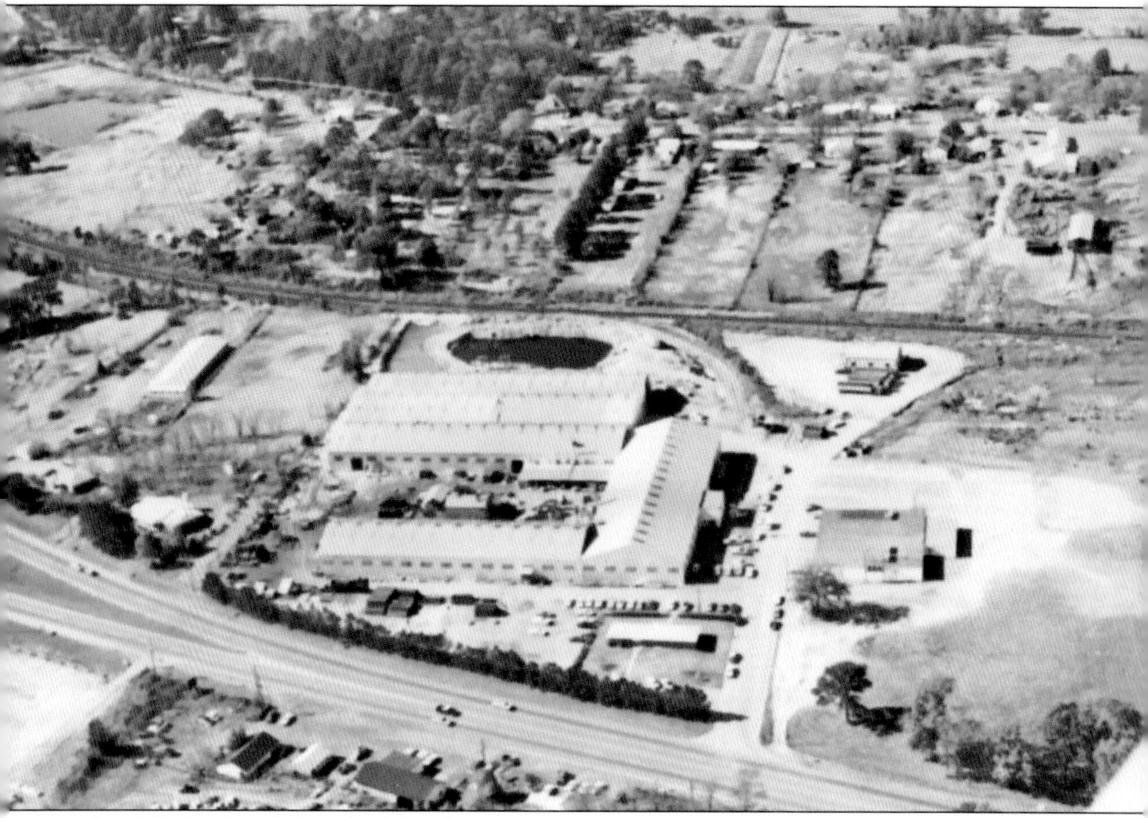

In 1962, Pittsburgh Standard Conduit, now RobRoy Industries, opened a facility south of Gilmer to produce electrical conduit pipe. From the air, the proximity of the plant to the railroad and the highways was clearly visible. Note that as late as the 1960s, there was no road connecting Dean Lumber Company on South Montgomery Street with Highway U.S. 271. (GM.)

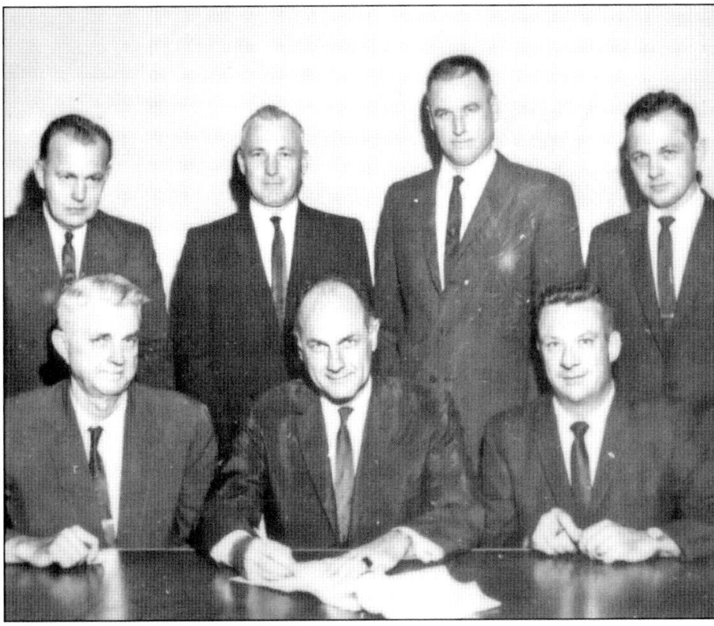

Charter members of Gilmer's Industrial Foundation joined with RobRoy officials when Robert McIlroy signed his commitment to bring his company to Gilmer. From left to right are (first row) D. T. Loyd, McIlroy, and Don Williams; (second row) James Young, W. D. "Bill" Buie, Robert B. Cook, and an unidentified RobRoy official. RobRoy and the Sunny Isle Dress Company were among the businesses recruited to Gilmer. (GM.)

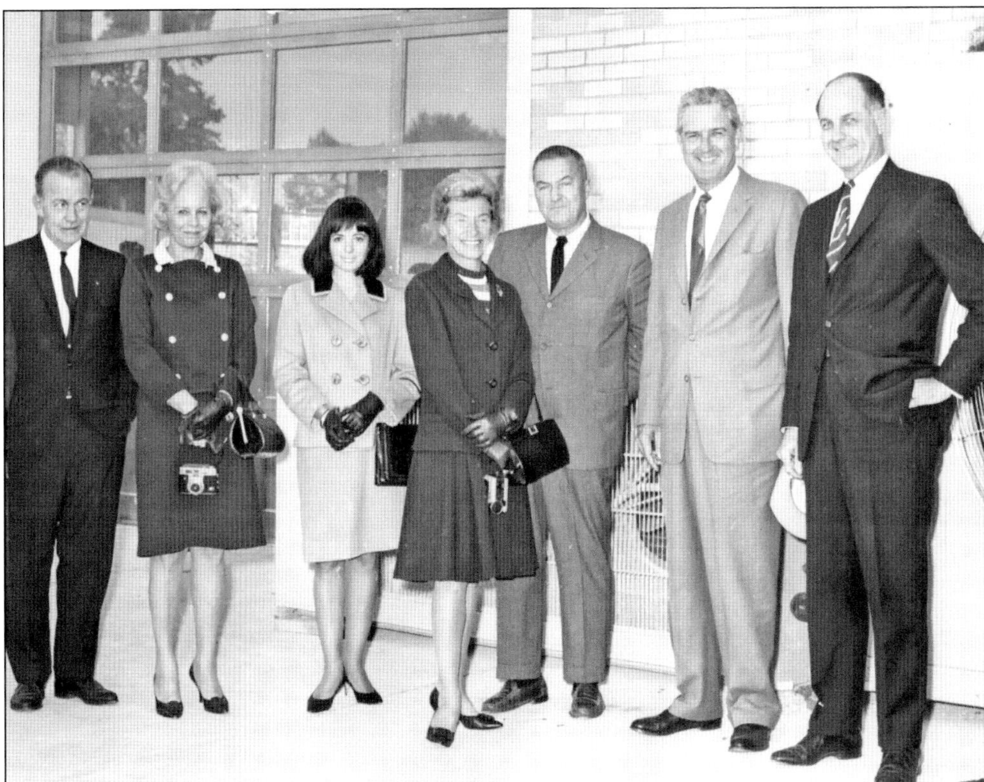

When Gov. John Connally came to Gilmer to dedicate the first area-wide industrial school on October 20, 1966, the RobRoy officials timed the meeting of their board of directors in Gilmer to coincide with the event so they could meet with the governor. Gathering after the dedication were James Young (left), Connally (second from right), and Robert McIlroy (far right). (GM.)

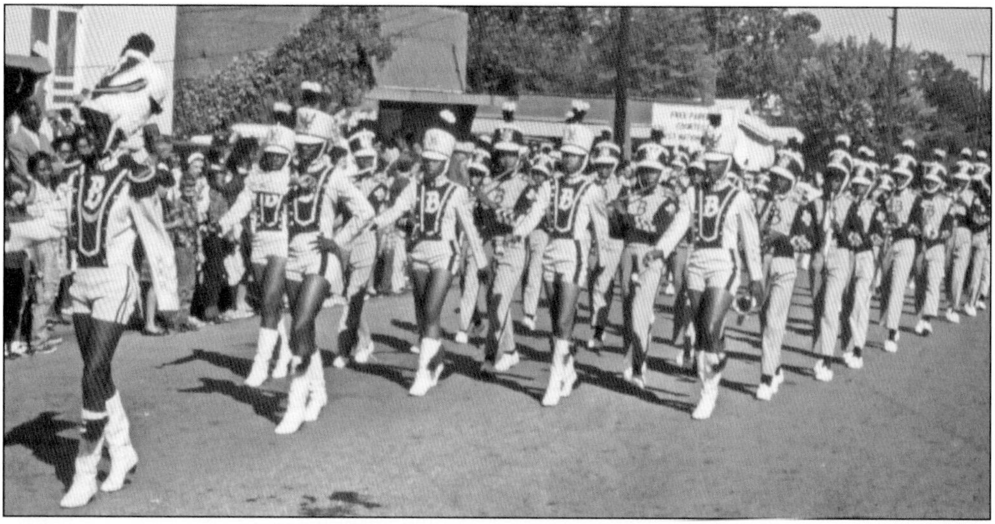

Under the leadership of Harlan Thacker, when he was president of the East Texas Yamboree, the board integrated the school parade, creating one event where schools from across the county could perform together. Parents of the Bruce High School students proudly worked to purchase these new uniforms for their children. It turned out that they were worn just one year before Gilmer integrated classes in 1968, starting with the senior class. (RHL.)

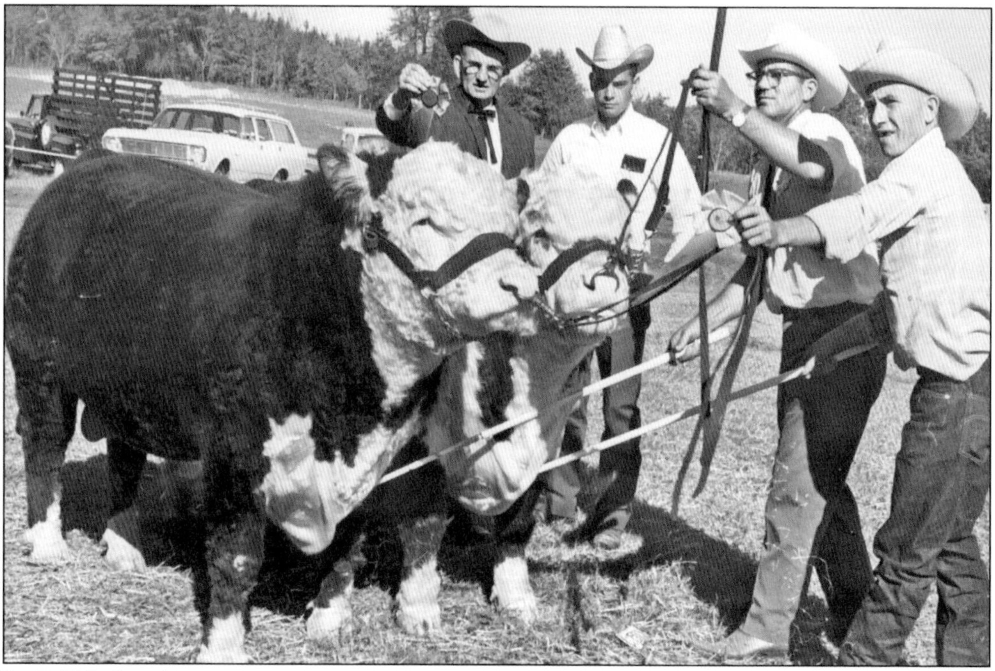

In 1967, before there was a separate steer auction for youth from Upshur County only, the Hereford cattle of the P and R Herford Ranch of Pittsburg dominated the senior class by winning nine of 10 categories. Two of the bulls from Pittsburg were the Reserve and Grand Champions, when (from left to right) Leon Presnell; Harvey Morris of Southern States College, Arkansas; Don Reynolds; and Ray Williams gathered for this photograph. Improved pastures had replaced the cotton fields, and beef and dairy cattle had become a leading source of agricultural income by the late 1960s. (GM.)

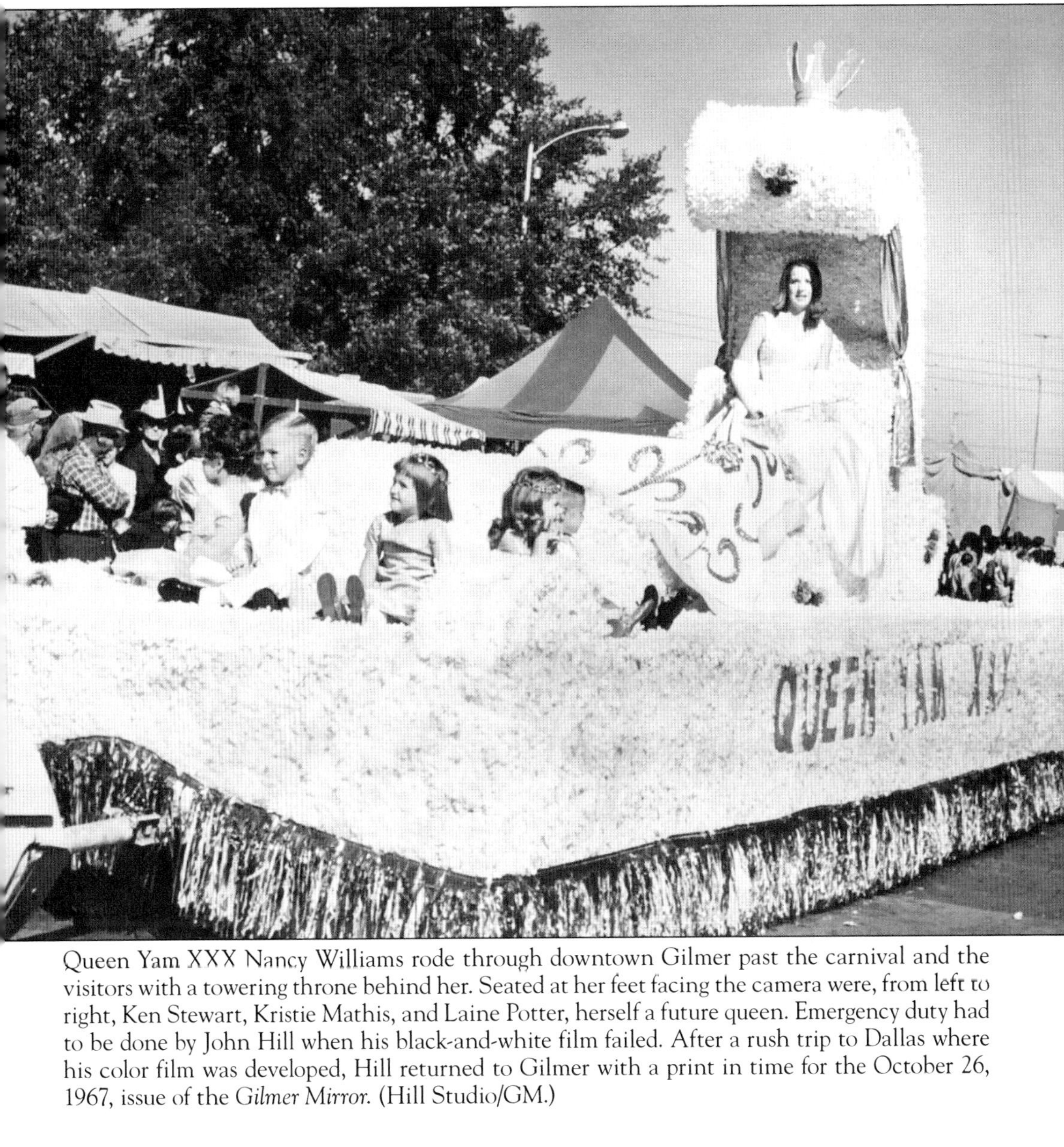

Queen Yam XXX Nancy Williams rode through downtown Gilmer past the carnival and the visitors with a towering throne behind her. Seated at her feet facing the camera were, from left to right, Ken Stewart, Kristie Mathis, and Laine Potter, herself a future queen. Emergency duty had to be done by John Hill when his black-and-white film failed. After a rush trip to Dallas where his color film was developed, Hill returned to Gilmer with a print in time for the October 26, 1967, issue of the *Gilmer Mirror*. (Hill Studio/GM.)

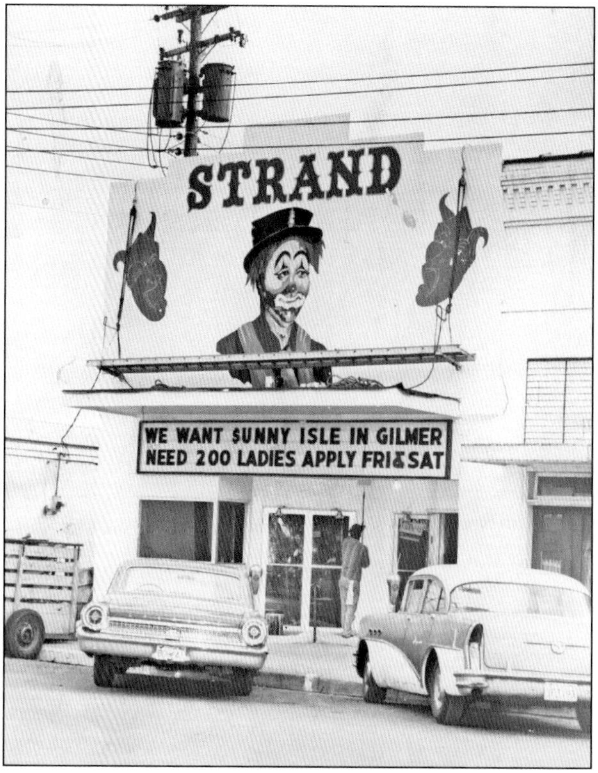

Another fire in Gilmer damaged the Strand Theatre, but Cranfill Cox Jr. was not ready to throw in the towel. It was a festive occasion when the Strand reopened in November 1965, with the face of Cox in his clown persona decorating the remodeled edifice. Soon thereafter, due to a lack of family suitable programming, the Cox family would close the Strand and the Crystal as movie houses. (GM.)

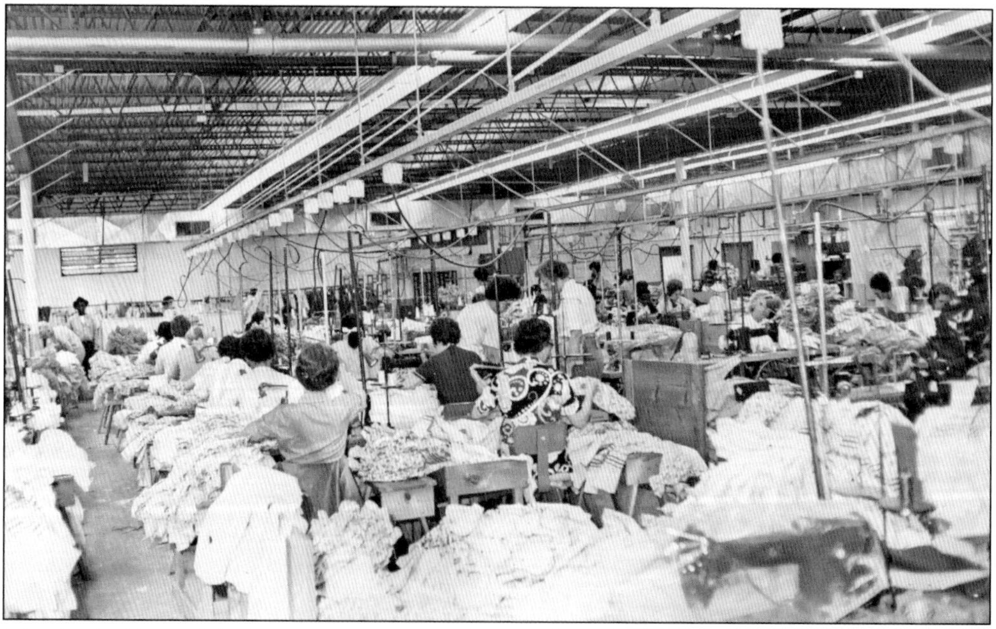

Jobs for the Sunny Isle dress company were advertised on the sign board at the Strand. Located south of town near RobRoy, the dress plant employed women from across the area, creating a steady income for many. At the peak of industrialization for Gilmer, in addition to RobRoy and Sunny Isle, the town had Martin Lumber, Gilmer Potteries, the Gilmer Flooring Mill, and Dean Lumber to generate steady wages for employees. (GM.)

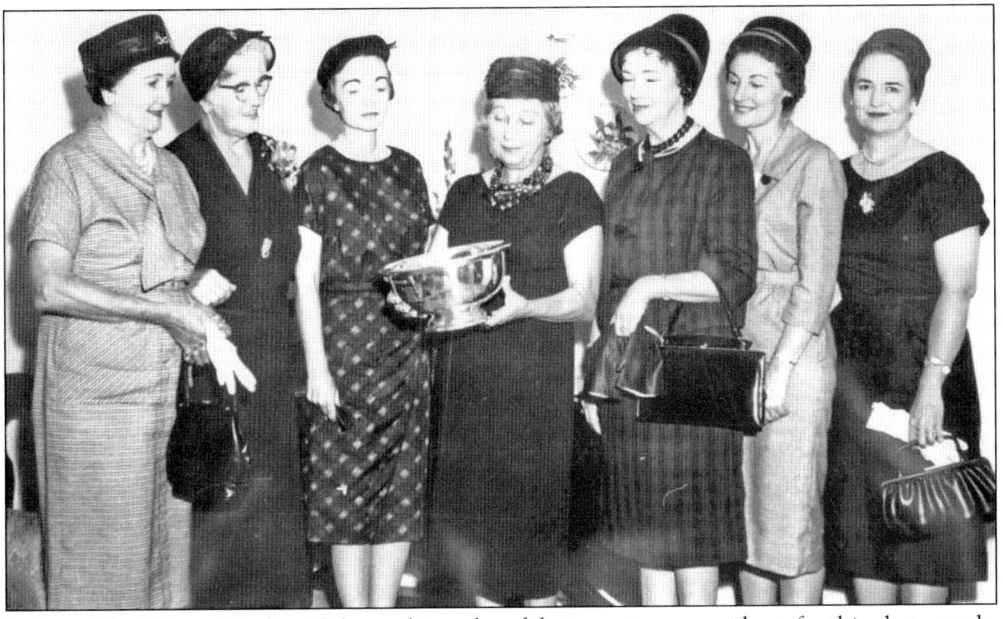

Ladies of the Gilmer Garden Club stood in order of their service as presidents for this photograph. From left to right, Marie Hogg, Bess Harper, Sara Kennedy, Georgia Laschinger, Neva Clark, Johnnie Lou Sorrells, and Alice Odom served between 1951 and 1966. Before the club disbanded, two more ladies would have their names engraved on the bowl now owned by the Historic Upshur Museum. (GM.)

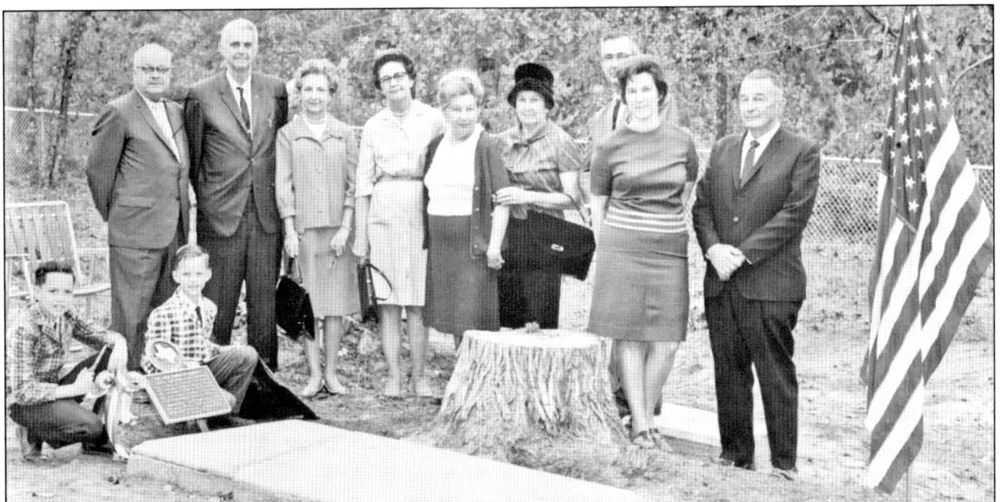

Under the urging of Gov. John Connally, committees sprang up in the counties to survey the historical items in their area and to mark the most significant as a way of attracting tourists to Texas and the Hemisfair in San Antonio. On October 19, 1967, standing from left to right, Robert Cargill of Longview, D. T. Loyd, Mrs. Dan Lester of Jefferson, Mrs. Charles Coppedge of Ore City, chairwoman of the Upshur County Historical Survey Committee Mrs. R. H. Laschinger, and committee members Mrs. Jack Hogg, J. C. Smith, Mrs. Ray Greene, and Henry McClelland gathered at the dedication of the restored Old Coffeeville Cemetery and a marker to John Hamilton McNairy. Kneeling are Jim (left) and John Hogg, relatives of Colonel McNairy who unveiled the marker. (GM.)

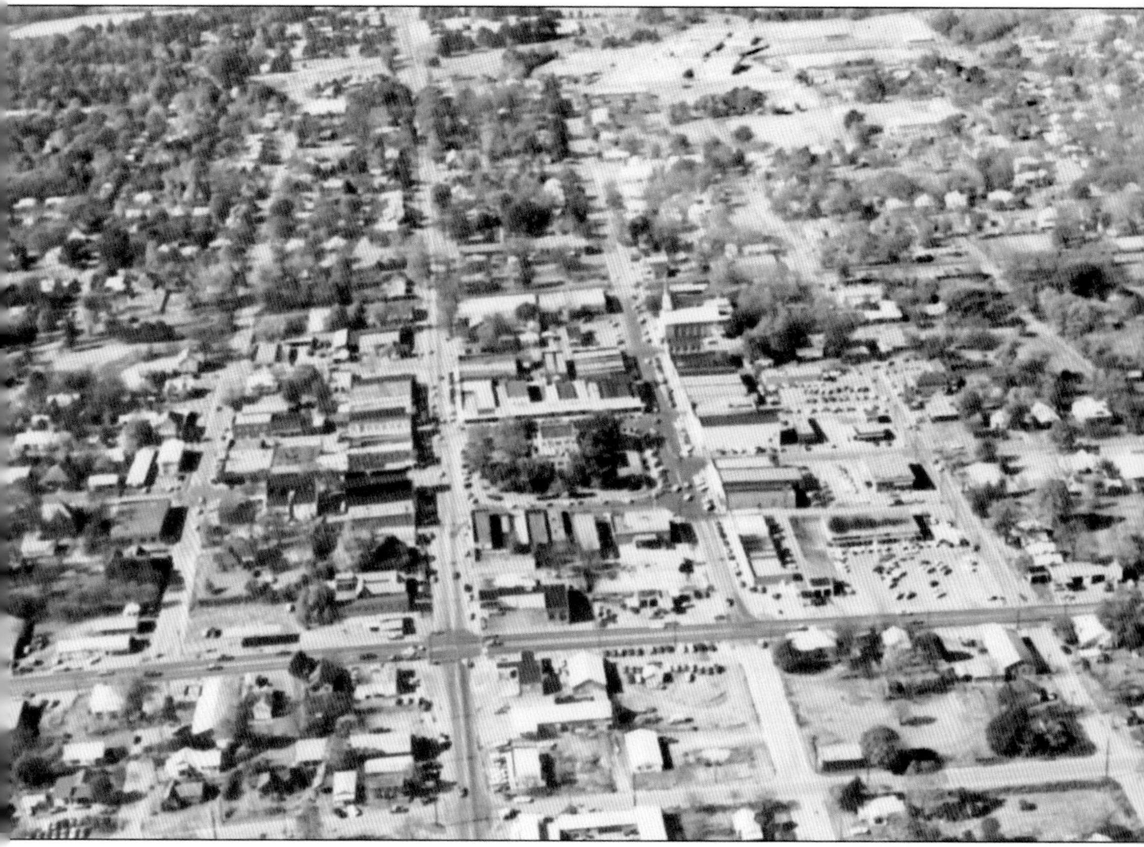

When this aerial photograph of Gilmer was made, the First Baptist Church had completed its new auditorium, and Gilmer High School was a "one-hall" school with the vocational building and Buckeye Stadium on adjoining properties. The Gilmer Elementary School filled another large parcel of northwestern Gilmer in this view, which was made from east of town looking down Texas Highway 154. (GM.)

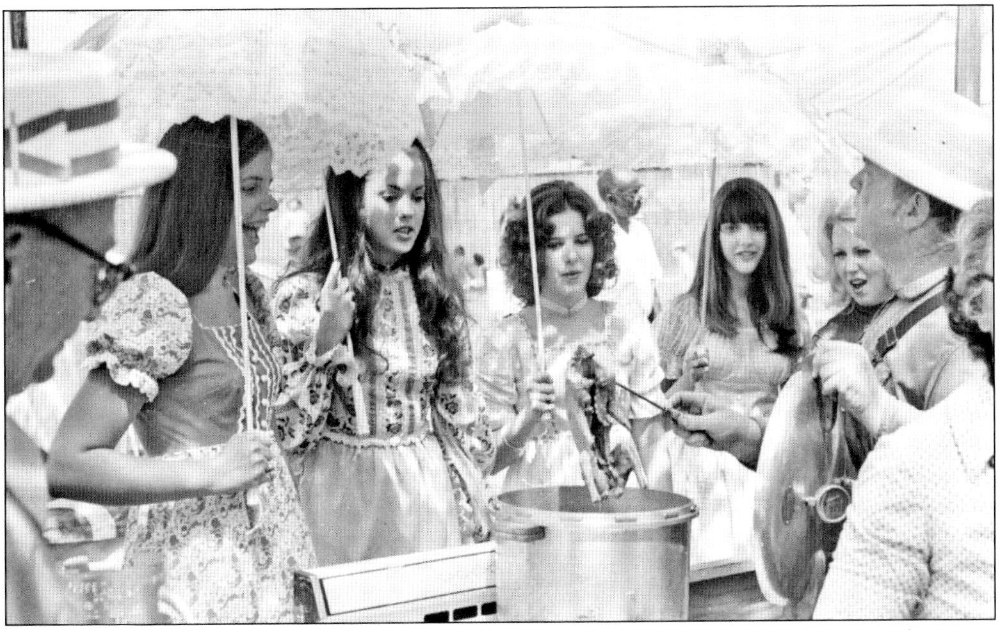

When the Institute of Texan Cultures began celebrating the ethnic diversity of Texas at the Texas Folklife Festival in 1972, the East Texas Yamboree association was there. In their first appearance, all five of the candidates for Queen Yam attended, with Ann Stembridge (far left), Laura Potter, Lesa Jones, Sally Greene, and Sharon Hasten watching Prof. Spot Baird pull a possum out of the pot. (GM.)

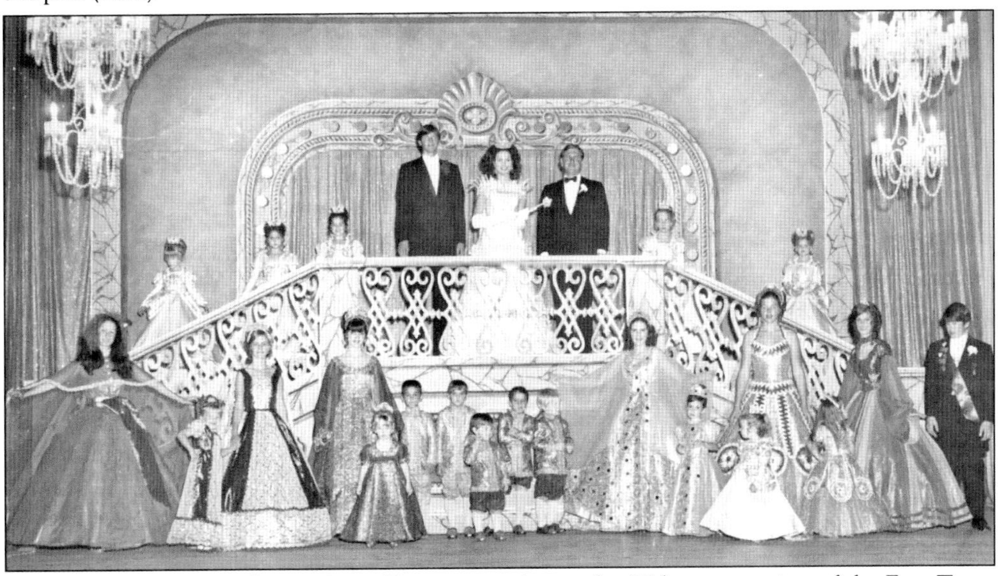

Queen Laura Potter and Pres. Steve Dean reigned over the 35th presentation of the East Texas Yamboree. Joining them on stage were, from left to right, (first row) Lady Angela Clark, Laura Lukas, Lady Sandra Hill, Lady Sally Greene, Brittani Youngblood, Darrell Seahorn, Michael Maines, John Dean, Brett Mitchell, Paul Taylor, Lady Lesa Jones, Linda Wilson, Lady Ann Stembridge, Amy Dean, Michelle Garrison, Lady Debbie Chandler, and Tom Proctor; (second row) Kimberly Long, Rebecca Nelson, Dana Blasingame, O. W. Loyd II (escort), Queen Laura, Steve Dean, Lea Pickitt, and Pamela Stegall. (GM.)

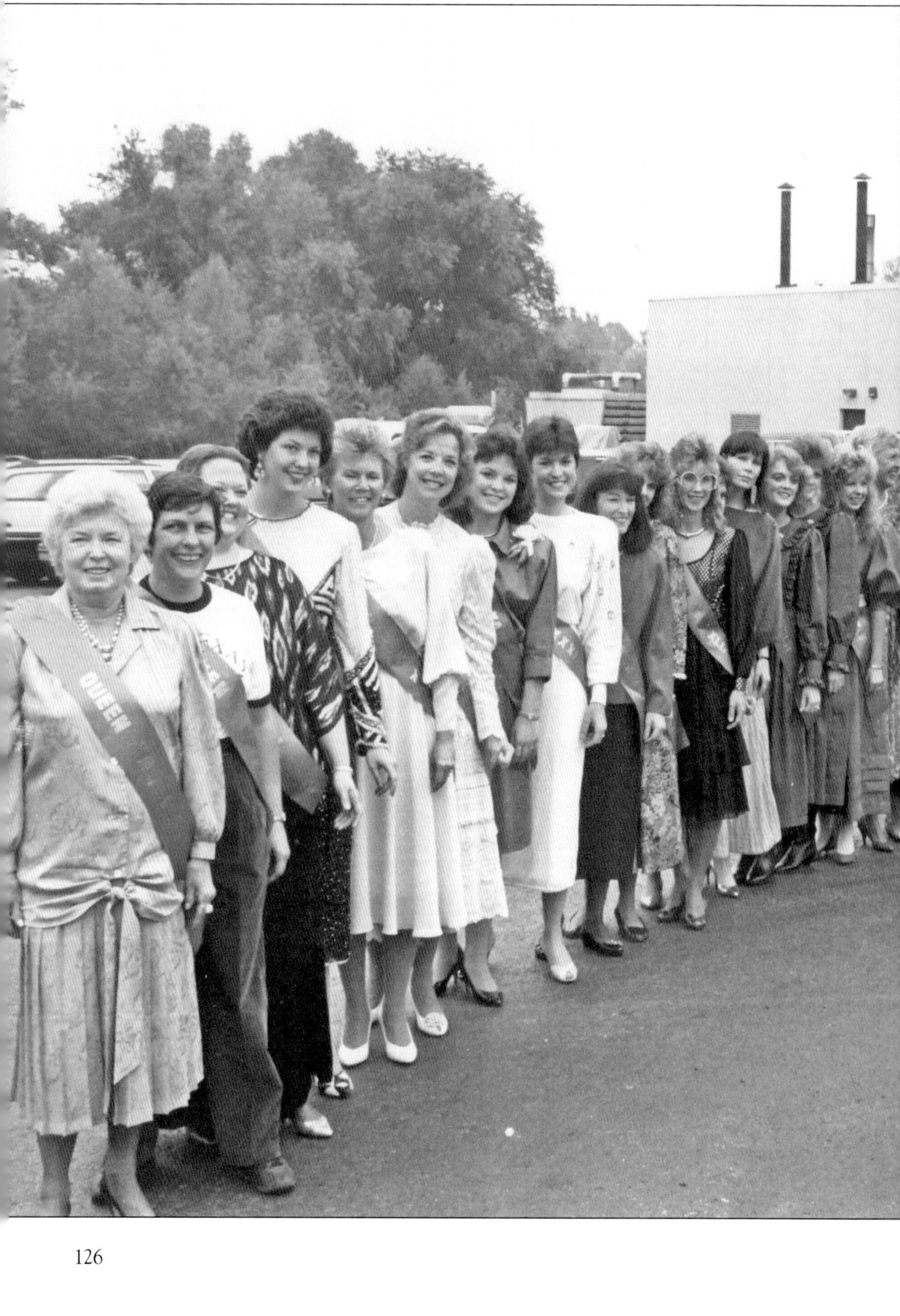
QUEEN

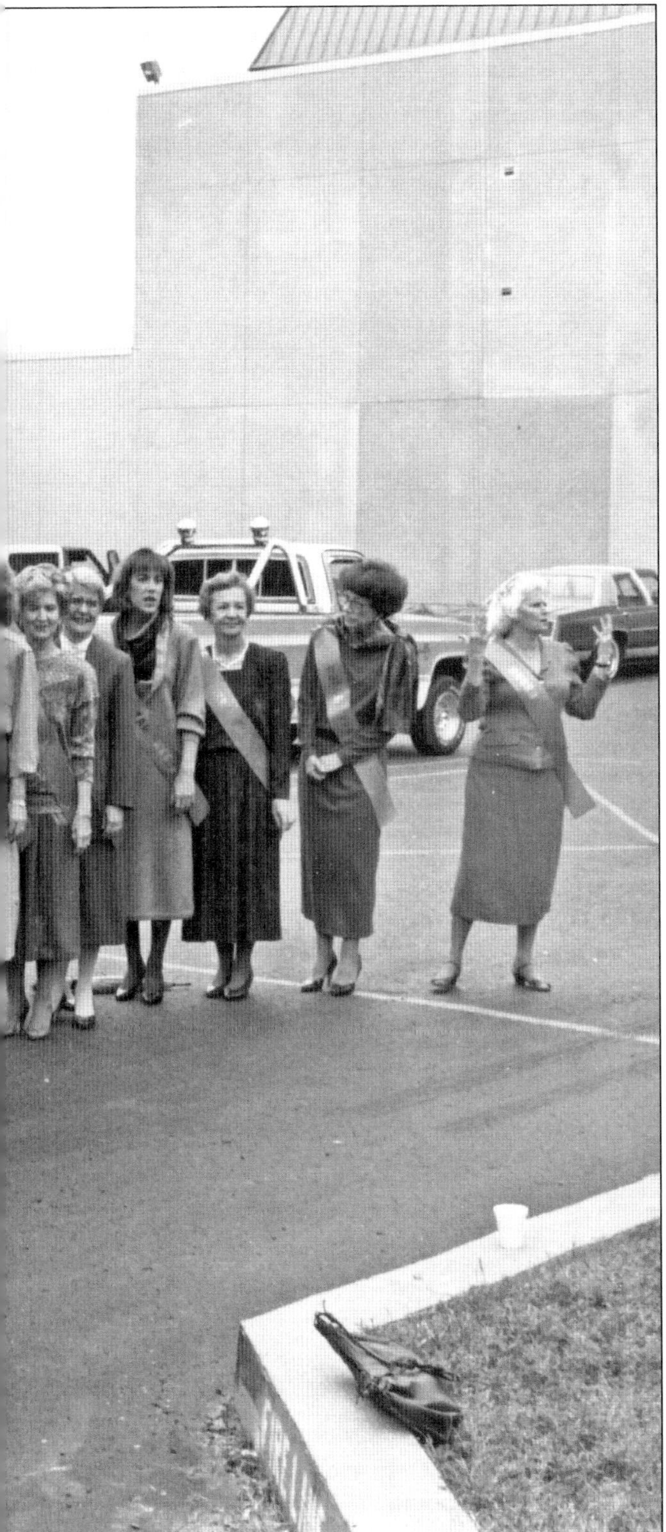

At the 50th East Texas Yamboree, before the parade, 25 former queens gathered for a group portrait while Queen Amy Dean and her court went to their float for the Queen's Parade. In a continuity that continues in Gilmer to this day, the group begins with Queen I Jane Tuttle Jones and continues, from left to right, with Mary Laschinger Kirby, Laine Potter, Laura Potter Parsons, Kay Floyd Meadows, Nancy Williams Davis, Victoria Mitchell Frazier, Mary Jo Proctor Holloway, Cindy Clark Gabehart, Fran Traywick Walker, Pam Yocom Smith, Phebe Phillips Hargrove, Nan Poole Fowler, Ann Poole Mask, Kim Listenbee Willeford, Diane Dupree Dill, Mary Lou Ragland Davidson, Stephanie Mayfield Hall, Ernestine Dedman Wolfe, Nell Brison Pursifal, Susan Stracener Johnson, Donna Stracener Worsham, Betty Ann Quin Tillery, Joyce Isbell Phillips, and Angela Hogg Castloo. Thirty of the 44 living queens took part in one event or another. (MLK.)

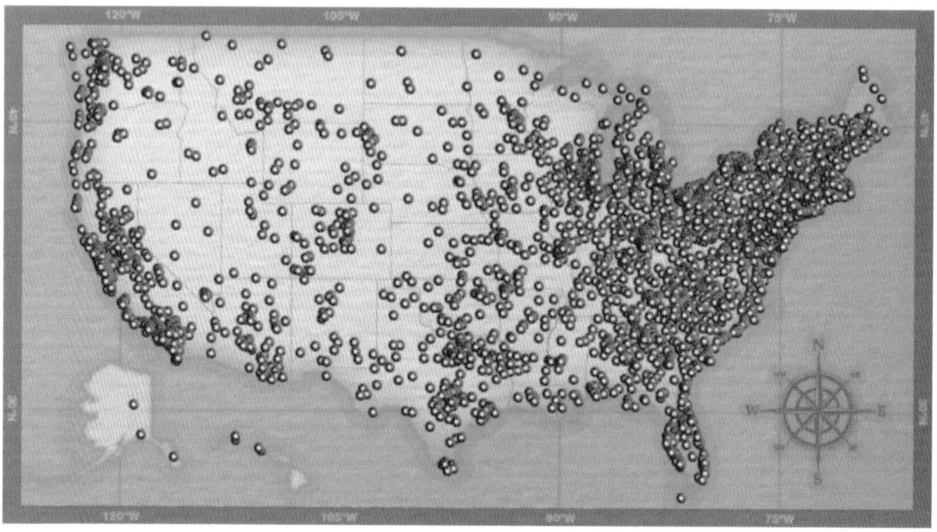